GOETHE'S POETRY FOR OCCASIONS

ERNST M. OPPENHEIMER

Goethe's Poetry for Occasions

UNIVERSITY OF TORONTO PRESS

© University of Toronto Press 1974
Toronto and Buffalo
Printed in Canada
Reprinted in 2018
ISBN 0-8020-5293-2
ISBN 978-1-4875-7876-3 (paper)
LC 73-81761

To Bettina Oppenheimer and Northrop Frye

Contents

ACKNOWLEDGEMENTS ix

ABBREVIATIONS xi

1 Introduction: *Gelegenheitsdichtung* 1

2 Frankfurt and Leipzig 1756–67 5

3 From Strassburg to Frankfurt 1770–5 25

4 Weimar 1775–80 41

5 'Schule geselliger Empfindung' 1780–3 73

6 The Limits of Sociability 97

7 The Poet and His Public 107

8 Weimar Skirmishes and Imperial Battles 133

9 A Midwinter Night's Dream 161

10 Once More into the Breach 189

APPENDICES 215

NOTES 221

INDEX 235

Acknowledgements

This small book is carrying a heavy load of indebtedness. It is not the alphabet that places Professor Stuart Atkins (Santa Barbara, California) at the head of the list. His profound scholarship, encouragement, and kindness have kept this project alive. Other scholars who have helped are Professors W. Emrich (Berlin) and I.S. Stamm (Rutgers, Newark), as well as my former departmental colleagues Katharina and Momme Mommsen; the latter has scrutinized the manuscript thoroughly.

Thanks are also due to my parents, who saw to it that I should not be without a very serviceable Goethe edition at a time when one had to travel light and who have furthered my work in other ways; and to Carleton University, for encouragement of every kind – Davidson Dunton, David Farr, and Trevor Tolley were the principal agents.

My principal creditors have kindly agreed to share the dedication of this book. The contributions of my wife Bettina are beyond reckoning. Not the least of them was that before the world at large could have done so she told me about a very great teacher at a time when I needed one most: Northrop Frye.

This book has been published with the help of grants from the Humanities Research Council of Canada, using funds provided by the Canada Council, and from the University of Toronto Press, using funds provided by the Andrew W. Mellon Foundation.

EMO

Abbreviations

Goethe quotations prior to 1775

DjG   *Der junge Goethe*, ed. Hanna Fischer-Lamberg (Berlin 1963–74)

DjG(M)   *Der junge Goethe*, ed. Max Morris (Leipzig 1909–12)

After 1775

WA   *Goethes Werke* Hg. im Auftrage der Großherzogin Sophie von Sachsen (Weimar 1887–1919)

Other Goethe editions referred to

JA   *Goethes Sämtliche Werke* Jubiläums-Ausgabe, ed. Eduard von der Hellen (Stuttgart 1902–12)

HA   *Goethes Werke* Hamburger Ausgabe, ed. Erich Trunz (Hamburg 1948–55)

GES   *Goethes Gespräche*, Eine Sammlung zeitgenössischer Berichte aus seinem Umgang. Auf Grund der Ausgabe und des Nachlasses von Flodoard Freiherrn von Biedermann ergänzt und herausgegeben von Wolfgang Herwig (Zürich & Stuttgart 1965–) Eckermann references are given by date only.

Gräf   *Goethe über seine Dichtungen*, ed. Hans Gerhard Gräf (Frankfurt 1902–14). Consecutive volume numbers of the entire work are referred to, i.e., Epos, vols I–II; Drama, vols III–VI; Lyrik, vols VII–IX.

Düntzer   H. Düntzer, *Goethes Maskenzüge* (Leipzig 1886)

JVT   *Das Journal von Tiefurt*, ed. Eduard von der Hellen. Schriften der Goethe-Gesellschaft 7 (Weimar 1892)

G-L   *Goethe und Lavater. Briefe und Tagebücher*, ed. Heinrich Funck. Schriften der Goethe-Gesellschaft 16 (Weimar 1901)

GOETHE'S POETRY FOR OCCASIONS

·1·
Introduction
Gelegenheitsdichtung

THE DESIGNATION OF Goethe as *Gelegenheitsdichter* has long been among the means used in attempts at defining his genius. The principal text upon which this characterization is based is the paraphrase of one of many of the poet's attempts to explain himself and his work to the man he was training to be his literary executor. According to Eckermann, Goethe said on 17 September 1823: 'Die Welt ist so gross und reich und das Leben so mannigfaltig, dass es an Anlässen zu Gedichten nie fehlen wird. Aber es müssen alles Gelegenheitsgedichte sein, das heisst, die Wirklichkeit muss die Veranlassung und den Stoff dazu hergeben. ... Alle meine Gedichte sind Gelegenheitsgedichte, sie sind durch die Wirklichkeit angeregt und haben darin Grund und Boden.'

Strictly speaking, posterity should have drawn encouragement from this statement to assume the habit of referring to the poet as *Wirklichkeitsdichter*, but instead, the designation of *Gelegenheitsdichter* as one means of containing the ocean in a cup came into frequent use.[1] In the same year and month, Friedrich von Müller recorded a related conversational fragment: 'Dabei verglich er sich einem Gärtner, der eine Menge schöner Blumen besitze, ihrer aber erst dann recht gewahr und froh werde, wenn jemand einen Strauss von ihm fordere. So mache ihm die Poesie erst wieder Vergnügen, wenn er eine Nötigung zu einem Gelegenheitsgedicht erhalte' (GES III(1) 588).

It requires no systematic survey of the poetics of the period to prove that the term *Gelegenheitsdichter* had acquired a highly pejorative flavour in Goethe's lifetime. E.J. Koch's *Compendium der deutschen Literaturgeschichte* of 1795 refers to 'Gelegenheitsgedichte' as 'Auswüchse der deutschen Dichtkunst.'[2] Lessing contrasted the 'miserable occasional poet' with the 'true poet' as a matter of course: 'Nur ein elender Gelegenheitsdichter gibt in seinen Versen die eigentlichen Umstände an, die ein Zusammenschreiber nötig hat, einen Character einmal daraus zu entwerfen.'³ Wieland found a reference to an occasional poem in Lucian to be a suitable place for speaking his mind on the subject. In *Das Gastmahl oder die neuen Lapithen* there occurs this passage: 'Vermutlich eine Lobrede auf die Braut, oder ein Hochzeit-Carmen, dergleichen jetzt bei solchen Gelegenheiten Mode werden?' and Wieland adds the following footnote: 'Diese Mode ist also schon über 1600 Jahre alt, und wäre nicht zu früh, sie abgehen zu lassen.'⁴ Herder speaks of the 'Canzleipoesie' of the court poets (Besser, König, Neukirch, etc.) and its doom 'auf eben diesem plattgetretenen Hofwege.'⁵ These casual observations by three eminent emancipators are recorded merely as indications of a consensus on a literary phenomenon that probably had at best symptomatic significance for them; else, a more systematic critical treatment might have issued from the pen of any one of them. If pressed to enlarge on the reasons for their expressed contempt for court or family occasional poetry, each one would presumable have stressed a different facet of its shortcomings according to his own convictions on the sources and prerequisites of good poetry. And indeed, even a cursory glance at the output of occasional verse to be found in collections and periodicals throughout the century before these observations were made shows it to be as convenient a mirror as one might wish to find of the social and cultural inadequacies which these three critics were attempting to reveal and alleviate: dilettantism, literary and social obsequiousness, mechanization of sentiment and the violation of dignity and decorum through the disproportion of occasion and utterance.

In 1823, then, Goethe was inclined to define his poetic identity by recourse to a term which had fallen into disrepute for quite some time. The attempted rehabilitation and extension of the semantic area of a term usually serves polemical ends, and the sweeping and emphatic statements quoted above were made at a time when Goethe had reason to feel isolated and misunderstood as a poet and was perhaps anxious to explain himself at least to those close to him; such assertions were likely to linger in the minds of those charged with the task of being his executors. And, regardless of the full implications of these declarations of adherence to an apparently outmoded and problematic code of poetic behaviour, there remains the fact that in looking back on his work late in life Goethe was bound to take into consideration the large number of works he had written for occasions, institutional and personal anniversaries and such. Dedicatory poems of an occasional nature may be found in the

Introduction: *Gelegenheitsdichtung* 3

collections or posthumous gleanings of any poet of any age,[6] but few, if any, of Goethe's contemporaries were writing court masques.

Concentration on the last decade of Goethe's life, however, involves the risk of distortion. We come a step closer to the true proportions of the question when we turn to a remark made a decade earlier by Zelter, who possessed a good ear for controversy: 'der Verfasser [i.e., Tieck] äusserte sich letzthin sehr laut und bestimmt gegen den Schutz, welchen Du dem Gelegenheits-Gedicht angedeihen lassen, und dass der Gehalt für die Poesie, in souverainen Staaten, von Oben her komme...' (to Goethe, 12 February 1813).[7]

Tieck's complaints were not the vague grumbles of a disaffected citizen of the republic of letters, but objections to emphatic assertions he had found in the second part of *Dichtung und Wahrheit*, published in 1812. In Book VII: 'In allen souveränen Staaten kommt der Gehalt für die Dichtung von oben herunter;' and in Book X: 'Das Gelegenheitsgedicht, die erste und echteste aller Dichtarten, ward verächtlich auf einen Grad, dass die Nation noch jetzt nicht auf einem Begriff des hohen Werthes desselben gelangen kann...' (WA I XXVII 82, 295, resp.).

The involvement of a leader of the Romantic movement in this debate may be taken as a signal that I am probably conducting our business of inquiry on top of an iceberg and that a further pursuit of its contours could not but lead us into deep and chilling waters. Cautious by nature, I therefore came to the conclusion that a relatively narrow and dry approach would offer greater promise of survival. I resolved to set out by the slow chronological road and examine a number of Goethe's works that have 'occasions' in the plain and traditional meaning of the term – most of them overt and revealed in the title, some concealed. There will be one substantial deviation from this plan; an appropriate explanation will be offered when it occurs. In each instance, the treatment of the work, or group of works, will have to justify its inclusion in this inquiry. With regard to *Maskenzug ... 1818* I confess to an additional motive: for reasons that cannot possibly be good, posterity has heaped neglect upon this work. The emptiness of the scholarly larder intensified the desire to examine this peerless work with especial affectionate care.

It will now be apparent that the reader is being asked to undertake this journey without a detailed conceptual map.[8] The direction of the route will in any case be determined by the powerful magnetic pole of Goethean uniqueness. Yet I trust that – unlike Captain Hatteras – I shall know when to stop, nor need the reader harbour apprehensions of being asked to join a hymn-singing procession towards a Holy Grail in the Castle of Genius. The very fact that much of the work to be examined is related in one way or other to events, political, courtly, theatrical, situated in the imperfect sphere of social and practical exigencies, will forestall that risk. I hope that at the end of the enterprise a cumulative process of observation will have occurred revealing typical ways in which Goethe reacted to and was reacted upon by occasions.

This latter duality of occasional poetry points in the abstract to the extreme positions in which a poet may find himself: absolute submission to external exigencies on the one side, and absolute creative initiative on the other. Some guidance may be derived from expressing these poles in Goethean terms. It has been pointed out[9] that Goethe liked to use a biblical reference to describe the situation of finding himself under some compulsion, including, sometimes, the kind of social poetic obligation that will concern us: the apocryphal Habakuk whom the angel 'took by the crown and bare by the hair of his head.' On the other hand, the poet's assertion of power, his control of a situation, has traditionally been expressed through the figure of Occasio: 'Calvus comosa fronte, unde occipitio ... occasionem rerum significat brevem.'[10] Goethe's adoption and transformation of this bald allegory in one of the Roman elegies sums up the goal of preservation and renewal implied in his declaration of adherence to the discredited guild of the practitioners of *Gelegenheitsdichtung*:

> Diese Göttin, sie heisst *Gelegenheit*, lernet sie kennen!
> Sie erscheinet euch oft, immer in andrer Gestalt.
> Einst erschien sie auch mir, ein bräunliches Mädchen, die Haare
> Fielen ihr dunkel und reich über die Stirne herab,
> Und ich verkannte sie nicht, ergriff die Eilende ... [WA i 1 237]

This inquiry, then, will largely consist of attempts at finding out who is tugging whose lock in a number of Goethe's poetic works. No graphs, percentage tables, least of all, summary formulas will be supplied. But I hope that the tangle of 'Vorsatz, Drang und Muss' (see below, p 166) will be seen more clearly as the intricate system of conduits of poetic energy that continues to flow through these works, ready to be tapped.

·2·

Frankfurt and Leipzig 1756-67

IS IT PROPER to set out with a consideration of Goethe's earliest surviving poem, 'Bei dem erfreulichen Anbruche Des 1757. Jahres wolte Seinen Hochgeehrtesten und Hertzlichgeliebten Gros Eltern ... Folgende Segens Wünsche zu erkennen geben ...' (DJG I 70)? Or should the twenty-four alexandrines with their florid title be left to the obscurity to which Goethe assigned them at a hardly less tender age? For by the time of his long letter to Cornelia of May 1767, he had forgotten or disowned this poem: 'Ich habe von meinem zehenten Jahre, angefangen Verse zu schreiben ... (DJG I 126). But regardless even of whether this poem is altogether Goethe's own – both Morris (DJG I 449) and von der Hellen (JA III 303) doubt it because of a polish superior to that of the New Year's poem of 1762 – it does have a place here because of its mixture of formality and familiarity. In this respect it reflects the spirit of the New Year's celebrations of the Goethe-Textor families – and probably of any number of well-situated family groups of the time. This mixture remains a conspicuous ingredient in most of Goethe's occasional poetry. The description of New Year's Day in *Dichtung und Wahrheit* (Pt I Bk III) seems reliable enough as a source of information. Public life moved into the private house; the Textor residence became, as it were, the ceremonial headquarters of the city.

Erst erschienen die Vertrauten und Verwandten, dann die untern Staatsbeamten; die Herren vom Rathe selbst verfehlten nicht ihren Schultheiss zu begrüssen, und eine auserwählte Anzahl wurde Abends in Zimmern bewirthet, welche das ganze Jahr über kaum sich öffneten. Die Torten, Biskuitkuchen, Marzipane, der süsse Wein übte den grössten Reiz auf die Kinder aus ... genug, es fehlte diesem Feste im Kleinen an nichts was die grössten zu verherrlichen pflegt. [WA i XXVI 129–30]

Another side of such events is revealed in Goethe's letter of 2 January 1774 to Johanna Fahlmer:

6 Goethe's Poetry for Occasions

Wir haben gestern gessen Wildprettsbraten und Geleepastete und viel Wein getruncken und zwischen Houries gesessen ... Vom zeitigen abermaligen Hern Burgemeister Reus, wo ich scharlach mit Gold, das Neue Jahr verkündigt hatte. [DJG IV 3]

The poem and the following one are both appropriate to a civic reception *cum* Christmas Eve occasion of this kind. With a nice sense of balance the poet merges respect with affection, public and family feelings, when he wishes the 'erhabene' ancestor many more years in which to guide 'Moeniens Ruder' and simultaneously places his offering before the 'Grosspapa.' The reiteration of the plainness or inadequacy of his gift may in itself be entirely conventional, but the promise of better things to come – 'Die Feder wird hinfort mehr Fertigkeit erlangen' – suggests also the unworried assurance of continued recognition and standing in the family.

In the second New Year's poem of 1762 ('Bey diesem neuen Jahres Wechsel überreichet ... dieses Opfer aus kindlicher Hochachtung,' DJG I 71), these family tones are heard more strongly. They could, of course, serve as a reason for believing that in the earlier opus the boy's pen was guided by a respectful tutor or other outsider. But there is also the possibility that the older boy himself was more concerned with telling his grandparents what was actually on his mind, or even that the image of the grandfather had assumed more definite shape as against that of the *Schultheiss*. In the mind's eye of a growing boy adults are likely to assume more human proportions as time goes on. This is a simpler poem as far as the rhyme scheme of the alexandrines is concerned, since couplets replace the alternating rhymes of the earlier poem. The source of inspiration, too, seems now closer to immediate experience. Such a passage as

... Glück und Heyl von Gottes Hand und Güte
Sein guter Engel sey bey Euch in aller Zeit.
Er geb Euch das Geleit in Wiederwärtigkeit,
Sowohl als in dem Glück, und lass Euch lang noch leben ... [DJG I 71]

is more likely to be an echo of the church service than of literary models. There is an amusing break in the voice and sensibility of the grandson who presents his proofs of literary progress in the past year – 'Was er diss Jahr hindurch im Schreiben hat gethan' – and who promises even more impressive deeds (a poem in Latin or French, no doubt) 'Wenn mich biss ubers Jahr die Parcen schonen thäten.'

Frankfurt and Leipzig 7

In turning to the genuinely 'professional' poems of Goethe's Frankfurt days, those that in the most commonplace sense of the term could be called occasional, there is a handicap that is rather more serious than the question of the independent composition of the New Year's poems. We not only do not possess them but we are also obliged to wonder whether they existed at all. Yet the pages of *Dichtung und Wahrheit* in which Goethe recounts the episode of the Frankfurt Gretchen are too relevant to the matter on hand to be passed over on the ground of lacking documentation.

The story in *Dichtung und Wahrheit* (Pt 1 Bk v) contains several distinct phases. First, the challenge to the boy's talent as a maker of verse, raised by an expression of skepticism, leads to the composition of a poem on a set theme (a girl declaring herself to a bashful young man) and is followed by the use of this poem in an elaborate practical joke. Next, we see this talent, now verified, commercialized. What had been a contribution to sociability becomes a means of acquiring standing in a circle of semi-respectable companions and of gaining money for their social gatherings.

One of the turning points of this episode is the exchange between Goethe and Gretchen when the former is trying to put together yet another of the series of poems with which to dupe the youth who had been made the butt of the 'Mystifikation.' The work is progressing with difficulty because Goethe's feelings for the girl caused her presence to play havoc with an undertaking that had been so easy heretofore:

Ich hatte eine Zeitlang verschiedenes geschrieben und wieder ausgelöscht, als ich ungeduldig ausrief: es will nicht gehen! ... Desto besser! sagte das liebe Mädchen, mit einem gesetzten Tone: ich wünschte, es ginge gar nicht!

and then:

Das ist recht hübsch, sagte sie ... nur Schade, dass es nicht zu einem bessern, zu einem wahren Gebrauch bestimmt ist! [WA I XXVI 269, 271]

There is irony in these last words because it turns out that Gretchen's intervention puts an end to the prank, but instead of supplying a setting for Gretchen's hoped-for feelings, the ore of the poetic vein is worked for purely commercial purposes:

Wir ... machten die Betrachtung, dass wir so ganz umsonst, andern zum Verdruss und uns zur Gefahr, aus blosser leidiger Schadenfreude, euer

Talent missbrauchen, da wir es doch zu unser aller Vortheil benutzen könnten. Seht, ich habe hier eine Bestellung auf ein Hochzeitgedicht, so wie auf ein Leichencarmen ... ich hatte schon von Jugend auf die Gelegenheitsgedichte ... mit einem gewissen Neid betrachtet, weil ich solche Dinge eben so gut, ja noch besser zu machen glaubte. Nun ward mir die Gelegenheit angeboten, mich zu zeigen, und besonders mich gedruckt zu sehen. [WA i xxvi 273–4]

When the whole story is told – which is done contrapuntally with the description of a truly formidable occasion, the coronation of Emperor Joseph II – the boy's facility with words has brought him close to the seamy side of life most remote from the exalted spectacle of the coronation and to the very edge of the law. The Gretchen idyll, which turns out to be an illusion, takes place on the thin ice of poetic activity that is altogether dedicated to the articulation of feelings not felt and of qualities inflated beyond human proportion. The finale, the psychosomatic crisis, plunges the confident scion of the local patriciate into the throes of self-tortured imaginings (intensified, as the draft of *Dichtung and Wahrheit* [WA i xxvi 374ff] shows, by appropriate reading matter, *Manon Lescaut*).

Regardless of accuracy of detail and chronology,[1] the Gretchen episode casts a most revealing light on the tribulations and dilemmas in Goethe's earliest moral crisis, which was to a large extent one centring on the ethics of the poetic vocation. The surrounding circumstances reported by Goethe with meticulous care have been too often overlooked in the readers' determination to place this episode in line with later affairs of the heart and to see Gretchen as a shadowy anticipation of the more verifiable events in Leipzig and Sesenheim. To be sure, we here watch for the first time the aristocratic Leander brave the Bosphorus of social distinctions and of his own passion, but the specific situation encountered is that of the young man who is enabled not merely by birth, but – and this is more important – by his facility with words, to come closer to the mastery of the outside world of which his young friends can only daydream and which Gretchen must achieve imperfectly by becoming a seamstress. We see the accomplished professional who is kind enough to let one of his circle in on the tricks of the trade:

Ich ... munterte ihn auf, selbst eine Disposition zu machen, ein Sylbenmass nach dem Charakter des Gegenstandes zu wählen, und was etwa sonst noch nöthig scheinen mochte, [WA i xxvi 386]

and now the self-assured holder of these skills and powers comes face to face with a twofold risk involved in their possession. Gretchen protects him from the first by pointing out to him the real grief that can grow out of their careless and unscrupulous application, but *he* is unable to extricate her from the difficult position into which he thinks he has helped to place her, however indirectly and innocently, by the exercise of his verbal powers. The name of the girl suggests the potentially Faustian proportions of the predicament. In this instance, the destructive magic powers at the hero's disposal consist of the mastery of a verbal craft that gets him what he thinks he wants and needs in blissful unawareness of the price eventually to be exacted. Whatever measure of autobiographical accuracy this episode may possess, its core must surely be made of the stuff of a real crisis in Goethe's poetic development.

This crisis of earliest 'professionalism' during the Frankfurt-Leipzig period is alluded to in two further statements. One is contained in a letter to Cornelia from Leipzig and is quoted further on (see p 13); the other is even later than *Dichtung und Wahrheit* but written on an occasion when the autobiographical tone was more spontaneous and less burdened with ulterior artistic motives. It is to be found in a review which Goethe wrote in 1827, in *Kunst und Altertum*, of a new instalment of Varnhagen von Ense's *Biographien* containing the lives of Fleming, Canitz, and Besser. Confirming the information of *Dichtung und Wahrheit*, Goethe tells us that deluxe editions of these poets were constantly before him from his earliest youth and were the models of his earliest efforts, and he goes on to say that they had a nightmarish effect on him:

Ich lernte darin lesen, mehr als dass ich sie las ... das Charakteristische freilich ihrer Verdienste ... blieb mir, ich gestehe es gern, mein Leben lang verborgen; doch erinnere ich mich, dass sie sämmtlich, mit andern ihrer Zeitgenossen, da ich eine Weile auf ihrem Wege fort zu dichten begann, mir als Knaben und Jüngling wie ein Alp beschwerlich auflagen. Diese Wirkung begreife ich erst jetzt, da sie beim Lesen obengenannten Bandes als das wiederaufsteigende Gespenst einer uralten Zeit auf dieselbe Weise lasteten ... hatte ... auch mich in jenen Tagen zu vergegenwärtigen, wo ich mich weder mit solcherlei Lieb- und Hofschaften noch mit derlei gestaltlosem doch blumenreichem Inhalt mit dem halb gewandten und meist gehaltleeren Ausdruck, mit der unerquicklichen Dogmatik des protestantischen Kirchenliedes in keinem Sinne befreunden konnte, wenn dasjenige, was sich in mir zu entwickeln strebte, nicht unterdrückt oder missgeleitet werden sollte. Und missgeleitet wurde es doch meistens... [WA I XLI (2) 267-8]

the term 'Alp' is a strong expression from the pen of a man who is looking back over sixty years. And it is indeed a *danse macabre* of faceless spectres that is being evoked here. The absence of recognizable individuality, of 'das Charakteristische,' in the writings of this group must have been disturbing and nightmarish to one endowed with Goethe's passion for observation. The denial of all poetic merit to the poets in question in the mellowness of age and the context of a review written in the friendliest spirit towards the author of the book reviewed is sufficient evidence that the crisis described was a genuine and violent one. When Goethe's Leipzig letters are read with this crisis in mind, there emerges a consistent impression that he is disturbed by the displacement of his earlier assumptions about his professional standing and proficiency and that the matter of occasional poetry plays a substantial part in the process of self-examination. Goethe's first letter to Cornelia, of 12 October 1765 (DJG I 81), written slightly over a week after his arrival in Leipzig, is in the self-consciously and jocularly didactic vein that is characteristic of most of its successors, but it contains the significant phrase and affirmation 'Wir Poeten.' It is not a timid freshman who has come to Leipzig, but a young man of accomplishments. The first occasional poem about which we read in this phase is the 'Neujahrsgedicht an den Grospapa,' presumably, as suggested above, a fixed annual obligation. It has been inferred above from those extant that these poems took on a more familiar and relaxed tone over the years. Now, in the first year of Goethe's absence from Frankfurt, the project seems to have blossomed out into an elaborate joke, perhaps on the assumption that distance made for safety. This assumption would explain Goethe's insistence on secrecy before the proper date:

Steck ihn am Neujahrstage zu dir, und des abends wenn sie alle beysammen sind; so überreich ihn, aber nicht eher und mache wenn du kannst dass ihn Herr Ohme Textor laut liesst. bemercke dann der ganzen Gesellschaft Gemühtsbewegungen und schreibe mir sie treulich. Dass sich aber ja niemand gelusten lässet den Brief vorher etwa zu eröffnen. [12 December 1765 DJG I 94)

Some hint of the nature of the poem and its reception is given in the letter of 17 January 1766. I assume here that Goethe is still speaking of the New Year's poem, Gräf's misgivings[2] notwithstanding:

je n'ai eu que la nature et les fautes universelles devant les yeux, en peignant ces portraits, et non pas, comme on pourroit penser, quelques personnes en particulier. [DJG I 96]

Goethe must have worried a little about the boldness of the enterprise, or possibly there had been a suggestion of paternal disapproval in Cornelia's reply. One should not erect a weighty tower of interpretation upon the light foundation of this group of New Year's poems, but there is a perceptible shift from a stage of naïve utterance when the author is securely locked in the embrace of the social structure into which he was born (the municipal family bosom, so to speak in this case) to an attitude of relative detachment conducive to type satire and parody behind which lurks the quest for individuality, for the discovery of poetic truth, and the apparent emancipation from convention. This progression is further illustrated by the circumstances attending another occasional poem referred to in the same letter to Cornelia:

J'ai tremble de pied en cap en lisant la fin de la lettre de mon pere. Juste ciel qui auroit cru, que la voix du public seroit la voix de la verite. Cependant je ne puis dire ni mon sentiment, ni du mal, ni du bien de ce mariage. J'attens avec impatiençe meme les plus petites circonstances de cette affaire, en me preparant pour faire valoir mes talens poetiques dans une occasion si favorable. (DJG 196)

The marriage was that of his maternal uncle Johann Jost Textor to Maria Magdalena Möller (cf. DJG I 457). 'La voix du public' was presumably gossip that had linked the groom to the fifteen-year-old bride. It is obvious that the match was regarded either as unsuitable or absurd by the family poet, who was clearly enjoined by his father to contribute to the festivity. Goethe's reaction is a mixture of irony and a renewed affirmation of his professionalism. Because he cannot hope to be aided by the desire to express his own feelings, he will have to muster up all his skills; at the same time he feels confident that these suffice for a creditable performance. It might be added that a *Hochzeitscarmen* for this wedding by another hand is available. It is truly antipodal in language and spirit to what we can guess about Goethe's offering. It is written in *Judendeutsch* and was recited by a representative of the Jews of Frankfurt, Wolff Maas: 'Ein schön Schir/hübsch und bescheidentlich/Rauffe Textor/Sing ich Dir.'[3] While undoubtedly not devoid of 'political' motivation, it does betray a measure of that genuinely congratulatory spirit that Goethe as a nephew could not muster.

The effects of Goethe's *carmen* seem to have been more far-reaching on the maker than on the recipients. In *Dichtung und Wahrheit* we are told (Pt II, Bk VII WA I XXVII 137ff) that when the poem was submitted to C.A. Clodius, professor of philosophy and belles-lettres, in the poetry 'seminar,' it was objected to because of its excessive mythological apparatus, by which, as Goethe suggests, personal feeling was to be camouflaged. Yet it is to be wondered whether Clodius failed to see the parodistic element, as Goethe claims. It seems more likely that the man who was the official poet of the university in fact, if not by appointment, and thus perhaps embodied institutional authority though a mere eleven years older than Goethe and who was imbued with the spirit of reform and sincerity as a follower of Ramler and lieutenant of Gellert, sensed a touch of frivolity in the poem. The Olympian council described in *Dichtung und Wahrheit* may have carried the satirical overtones of the mock epic that would sound indecent to one who took his cues from Gellert, if the latter's sample of a wedding poem, 'O Freund, welch angenehm Gesichte / Rührt meinen Geist, indem ich dichte!'[4] is any indication. If this was the true cause of Clodius' criticism it was not and could not be hinted at in Goethe's reference to the incident in his letter to Cornelia quoted below.

Except for the symbolic value of the Goethe-Clodius conflict, a poem we do not possess would hardly be worth lingering over. But the spectacle is an intriguing one. On the one hand, there is Clodius, obviously concerned with infusing authenticity of feeling in the occasional poem by demanding a reduction of the decorative elements to a point where the emotions of a reader of Gellert could be engaged, and on the other side there is the young professional whose detachment from 'official' poetry has brought him beyond the line of assumed seriousness and thus outside the rank of the professionals. As in the Gretchen episode, the ethics of the occasional poet entered into the incident. When, in May 1767, Goethe claims that Clodius' criticism had prevented him from writing for half a year, we need not take him too literally:

Vorm Jahre als ich die scharfe Critick von Clodiusen über mein Hochzeitgedichte lass, entfiel mir aller Muht, und ich brauchte ein halbes Jahr Zeit biss ich mich wieder erholen und auf Befehl meiner Mädgen, einige Lieder verfertigen konnte. [DJG I 126]

But it helps us gauge the strength of his convictions concerning his professional standing and of his mission: 'habe ich Genie; so werde ich Poete werden, und wenn mich kein Mensch verbessert, habe ich keins; so helfen alle Criticken nichts' (DJG I 126). The conditional formulation in this statement does not hide any gnawing doubts about his talents.

Goethe's low opinion of his critic helped him to reach for parody to redress the balance. There is no way to prove that the ode 'An den Kuchenbäcker Händel' (DJG I 166) would not have been written if the earlier clash with Clodius had not taken place. Goethe does not resolve that question fully:

Wir fanden es höchst anstössig, dass er, der uns die heidnischen Götter verkümmert hatte, sich nun eine andere Leiter auf den Parnass aus griechischen und römischen Wortsprossen zusammenzimmern wollte. [WA I XXVII 140]

The suggestion that the Händel poem represents an attack on the critic, as well as a reaction to the object of the criticism, is based on the assumption that a compensatory relationship exists between a number of Goethe's least voluntary occasional works and others containing satirical elements written simultaneously or shortly thereafter. It is unsafe to speculate about the sincerity of a poet, but when lofty sentiments are lavished on occasions towards which he feels obviously indifferent, perhaps even hostile, we may anticipate an aggressive reaction. More striking evidence might be found in the work of Schiller, who found himself expressing 'Empfindungen der Dankbarkeit' on behalf of his fellow students at the academy to the official mistress of his duke,[5] but there are like instances in Goethe's work at Weimar, although of a rather subtle kind.

But another example is at hand. The close vicinity of the two French poems in the letter of 27 September to 18 October 1766 (DJG I 115–23) is a case in point. One is again a commissioned poem: 'A Monsieur le Major General de Hoffmann Au sujet de la mort, de Madame son epouse' (p 121). Goethe was not even sure whether this lady (his great-aunt) had actually died, or whether the poem was demanded by his father as a long-distance home assignment or perhaps for future use. 'J'attens avec impatience, d'entendre, le sucçes de ce petit poeme, et la raison pourquoi my cher pere, m'ordonna de le composer' (DJG I 122). And once more, as in the Händel poem, authority is teased and official mythology demoted in the accompanying 'Vaudeville a. Mr Pfeil' (p 119), addressed to his teacher of French. The parallelism is by no means perfect. It is not a question of a personal attack on Pfeil or on his teaching, but the gesture of cocking a snook at authority, this time in whimsy and good spirits, is discernible.

It can be concluded that soon after leaving the rigidities of home Goethe found himself facing the question of the adequacy of occasions and its relation to the status of a professional poet. In order to indicate the complexion of this problem I shall merely adduce a passage from *Dichtung und Wahrheit* about a work which may well have supplied food for reflection to Goethe. The analysis of König's 'August im Lager' (Pt II, Bk VII WA i XXVII 82ff) amounts to the statement that the main requirement for the successful occasional poet is a proper occasion. The meeting of the rulers and the attendant display of pomp and luxury seem eminently suited for glorification by poetry, yet the poem fails altogether because of the inherent unworthiness of the occasion.

In order to proceed in chronological sequence I will not discuss at this point the much vaster question that arises from these observations, i.e., the search for the modern epic which was of such great concern to poets of the sixteenth to the eighteenth centuries. Inherent in this search is the problem of seizing upon an event or theme of epic proportions. The proper occasion for suitable reflections will arise when Goethe's project for a biography of Bernhard of Weimar comes into view.

We now move from the 'commissioned' occasional poem to the far less neatly bordered territory of 'spontaneous' occasional poetry. In such cases the impulse is no longer external, but the event itself arouses in the poet a sense of obligation to employ his talent. The impulse in the case of the 'Elegie auf den Tod des Bruders meines Freundes' (DJG I 179) is manifestly urgent. His letters to Behrisch reveal a relationship between two friends that made it imperative for the young Goethe to react to the death of the older friend's brother with a well-wrought poem. In a sense, the tribute to the dead brother was also an expression of sympathy for the living friend because the lives of both were affected by an unwillingness to submit to authority. Regierungsrath Behrisch died on 23 March 1767 at the age of thirty-four – 'Nah schon dem Herbste seiner Jahre' – a description in which the perspective of the eighteen-year-old poet and a literary formula merge. He appears to have suffered some interference in his personal life from his master and employer: 'Da riss sein Fürst von ihrer Seite/ Tyrannisch ihn.' The details are unknown but we may be sure that Goethe received a highly dramatic report from his friend. Whether Ernst Wolfgang Behrisch was, for Goethe, a strong influence towards social nonconformity seems somewhat doubtful. It might be more accurate to describe him as a sounding board for notes which would have been struck in any case, and there was no lack of reluctant *Hofmeister* in that era who disliked their social position and vented their feelings in the half-hearted performance of their duties.[6] That he was more of an eighteenth-century man of the world than a Jacobin is amply demonstrated in Goethe's description in *Dichtung und Wahrheit* (WA i XXVII 131ff) and in Eckermann's report of 24 January 1830, which tells of Behrisch's later career. Behrisch was willing to grant his much younger friend an equality based on indulgence and admiration and his rebelliousness was of the smiling, not the fist-clenching, variety. He was involved in the Clodius episode, which was a revolt against academic as much as against literary authority, and he elicited from Goethe words about the prevailing order of things which were probably stronger than any he ventured since: 'Ich möchte nicht Fürst seyn; er muss sich doch manchmal schämen...' (3 November 1967, DJG I 148).

The elegy impresses by its comparative lack of finish and elegance as compared, for instance, with the smoothness of the Hoffmann *carmen*. Goethe stumbles especially in the last stanza, perhaps because he has attempted too ambitiously elaborate a rhyme scheme (ababcddcee), and so the words of the departed become tangled:

> ... es wein bey meinem Grabe
> Jed' zärtlich Herz gerührt von meiner Treu,
> Dann eil' die stolze Tyranney,
> Der ich schon längst vergeben habe,
> Dass sie des Grabes Ursach sey,
> Unwillig fühlend, schnell vorbey. [DJG I 181]

The principal cause of the confusion is the shift of focus first from the poet to the girl and then to the deceased. That there is a degree of confusion is indicated by the fact that the poem could be read by Gundolf as referring to a seduced maiden whose lover had been sent to war and death by his prince.[7] Although this reading is hardly warranted by the text, one can but agree with Gundolf's observation that the grieving girl displaces the object of her laments from the centre of attention. The Goethe of that time, as his letters and the Annette poems show, was indeed perpetually willing to write about a 'Mädgen' weeping or laughing. But death and tyrants could not command so ready a pen, and it is thus not surprising that the spontaneous flow of language should be slowed in the labyrinth of grammar and that archaic awkwardness should appear when these subjects are broached.

It may be rewarding to glance briefly at comparable elegies in order to acquire a clearer idea of another problem that confronts the writer of an occasional poem of this type. One of an author's concerns must be the choice of a setting or the situation out of which the poem is developed. To speak of choice here should not offend even the staunch believer in the spontaneity of lyrical creation. In starting out by addressing an individual or a group, the occasional poet must aim at producing a calculated effect. Hence it is easier to employ terms implying conscious craftsmanship in this field of poetry than in many another. Regardless of the scope of the poem, whether it be limited to a recital of a particular event or whether the event be made the point of departure for treatment of a broader theme, a frame of some kind is necessary. The simplest and, to judge by the example, the least promising approach would appear to be the direct address: 'Du, den ein weiser Gebrauch der Jugend, welche dich schmückte/ Das Ziel der glücklichsten Greise verhiess/ … O Wille! Redliche weinen um dich!' (Gellert, 'Auf Herrn Willens Tod').[8]

Schiller wrote two elegies on the death of young friends[9] when he was little more than two years older than Goethe was when he wrote his Behrisch elegy. But the circumstances of the two cases are sufficiently different to bar a more detailed comparison. Schiller is less direct in his approach and paints a backdrop in heavy colours:

> Mit erstorbnem Scheinen
> Steht der Mond auf totenstillen Hainen,
> Seufzend weicht der Nachtgeist durch die Luft –
> Nebelwolken schauern …
>
> ['Eine Leichenphantasie']

In the other elegy of the same year nature is treated by Schiller as the antagonist of man:

> Prahlt Ihr Fichten die ihr hoch veraltet
> Stürmen stehet und den Donner neckt?
> ['Elegie auf den Tod eines Jünglings']

Goethe, too, introduces a nature background:

> Im düstern Wald auf der gespaltnen Eiche
> Die einst der Donner hingestreckt
> Sing ich um Deines Bruders Leiche ...

It is perhaps possible to discern in these three passages the future poetic personalities of the two men. Whereas Schiller's use of sharp contrast would seem to show a certain stage-consciousness, note that Goethe chooses to place himself into the scene which is in harmony with the elegiac mood and address the living friend, rather than the departed or a remote audience. The beginning of the elegy at least allows us an anticipatory glimpse of the fusion of nature and emotions in later and greater poems. Because this glimpse lasts only a moment — before the entanglement described above sets in — a visual source of inspiration suggests itself, some frontispiece engraving, perhaps. It is well to remember that Goethe saw much of Oeser's work in those days.

The 'Elegie auf den Tod des Bruders meines Freundes' showed signs of awkwardness, the result, aside from lack of craftsmanship, of an unhappy mixture of personal and social-conventional motivation. On the one hand, Goethe challenged himself to write the poem, much as his father had commissioned him in the case of the Hoffmann *carmen*; on the other hand, this self-imposed task was an act of friendship towards Behrisch. But no such complications are likely to have been operative in the writing of the 'Ode an Herrn Professor Zachariae' (DJG I 181). The occasion, the departure of a poet of some renown and, as Goethe undoubtedly felt, a fellow artist, presented an opportunity for a display of his abilities; although here, too, a brother of the person addressed was involved as a member of the Schönkopf dining circle, but the relationship seems in no way comparable with the Behrisch one. Faithful adherence to the model of the rhymed Horatian ode and to the ideal of massive conciseness with the monstrous parenthetical insertion in the second stanza, and the generous use of mythological and allegorical apparatus ('Stymphaliden,' 'Venus,' 'Apollo,' 'Freude ... angekettet fest an deinen Wagen'), all point to a willing suspension of originality in the fulsome Ramler manner, as Morris perceives it (DJG(M) VI 35). The pose of the young adept raising his eyes to the recognized master is pervasive: 'O gäb er mir die Stärke, seine mächt'ge Leyer/ Zu schlagen, die Apoll ihm gab' (l 17); and 'Er liebet mich, dann lieben mich die Musen,/ Weil mich ihr Liebling liebt' (l 31). It is possible that Goethe was not too reluctant to apply glaring colours in the description of the slough of Leipzig that Zachariae was leaving behind; a crisis of feelings about this place was well in the making by May 1767. It is also extremely difficult not to suspect that the writer had his tongue in cheek, yet this is not a necessary hypothesis. Goethe's career as a poet and public figure was such that the Leipzig period was perhaps the only one during which his age and position even remotely necessitated the writing of occasional poetry for the reason that prompted so much of it among his predecessors and contemporaries: for gain pure and simple, be it of wealth or of prestige. The examination of the preceding poems and of later ones shows that compulsion appeared in many guises, but there are no other instances of the plain pursuit of recognition that could be placed beside the Leipzig situation under discussion. Hence the uniqueness of the Zachariae poem and the possibility of taking it at its face value.

General custom and the fact that the young Goethe had long been 'conditioned' to the writing of New Year's poems make further inquiry into the existence of the 'Neujahrslied' ('Wer Kommt! ...') that Goethe wrote for 1769 unnecessary (DJG I 290). But we must note the very personal content that he gave to it, thus obtaining a measure of the distance between abstract convention and the use made of it. Here Goethe found an opportunity to let his Leipzig friends and acquaintances know that the young bon vivant and man of the world had not succumbed to physical and spiritual weakness nor gone to sleep in Frankfurt provincialism. He had the 'Neujahrslied' printed with the dedication: 'Seinen Freunden, zum Zeugnis dass er noch *lebt* beym neuen Jahre der kranke Goethe.' His misgivings about the rôle he had played in Leipzig and about the manner of his leaving, which can be felt so strongly in the 'Briefgedicht' to Friederike Oeser of 6 November 1768 (DJG I 251–5) are not hinted at here. One need not go on to conclude that Goethe takes refuge behind the mask of the *Bänkelsänger* to hide his true state of mind. It is instead more likely that he employed this convention to speak openly to an audience which was heterogeneous in itself, as well as in the relationships of its members to the poet. And the sentiments expressed, especially the attack on possessive jealousy, did probably require a fictional intermediary:

> Du junger Mann, du junge Frau,
> Lebt nicht zu treu, nicht zu genau
> In enger Ehe.
> Die Eifersucht quält manches Haus,
> Und trägt am Ende doch nichts aus,
> Als doppelt Wehe. [DJG I 291]

Just as one of the functions of pastoral poetry, be it of the seventeenth-century French or the eighteenth-century German variety, consisted in supplying a Utopian landscape for erotic freedom, so the *Salonbänkelgesang* associated with Gleim, Loewen, and Schiebeler enables the poet to assess or attack his surroundings with a lesser regard for the restrictions of prevailing mores. The ancient stigma of dishonourableness attached to actors and other itinerant professions allowed the *Bänkelsänger* a certain detachment which thus could be carried into the drawing room. Cronegk and Hagedorn's social satires may be considered as belonging more or less to this genre, as may Uz' 'Neujahrswunsch des Nachtwächters zu Ternate.'[10] Brüggemann quotes Mendelssohn's characterization of the *Bänkelsängergesang* as representing a spirit of 'possierliche Traurigkeit.'[11] A glance at the Uz poem just mentioned reveals the mock distress and diluted emotion involved, and indicates that Goethe's 'Neujahrslied' is by no means cut from the same cloth:

> Denn unsre Weibchen kosten viel
> Wenn sie uns lieben sollen:
> Wie viel erfordert Putz und Spiel
> Und wenn wir schmausen wollen.

Goethe's poem, furthermore, lacks that feature which gives to so many of the products of *Anakreontik* as well a faint aura of obscenity: the confidential wink from the poet to the reader or listener. Instead, there is a measure of urgency and involvement which can be detected even by the reader who does not know that the poem was written at a time of crisis:

> Die ihr schon Amors Wege kennt,
> Und schon ein wenig lichter brennt,
> Ihr macht mir bange.
> Zum Ernst, ihr Kinder von dem Spass!
> Das Jahr! zur höchsten Noth nur das!
> Sonst währts zu lange. [DJG I 291]

When Goethe wrote to Käthchen Schönkopf that he had written the poem 'in einem Anfall von groser Narrheit' 30 December 1768, DJG I 262), he was possibly spreading yet another protective veil over the seriousness of the 'Neujahrslied.' The strange counter pull of the flippancy of the salon and of the sense of personal urgency becomes apparent especially in the last stanza: 'Mir Jüngling, jetzt des Mädchens Spott,/ Mir helfe doch der liebe Gott/ Zu meinen Waden.' One may generalize from this that the pietistic influences, often emphasized by biographers, that were coming Goethe's way in these months were being refracted in a most peculiar way. In any case, 'der liebe Gott' had to make room for 'Cytherens Sohn' in the next version, and the entire stanza appears in greatly changed form in the *Neue Lieder*; personal health and attractiveness are no longer solicited but instead 'Der Himmel geb zur Frühlingszeit,/ Mir manches Lied voll Munterkeit ... (DJG I 293).

One cannot argue, however, that the 'Neujahrslied' is an occasional poem sailing under a false flag. The common denominator of all such poems, from the most mechanical to the most unorthodox, is likely to be the concern with the passage of time. And this is most emphatically the case here, as is demonstrated by the iterated use of such phrases as 'Nur noch dieses Jahr,' 'Das Jahr, zur höchsten Noth nur das,' 'gar manche Nacht im Jahr,' and 'in künftgen Jahren.' The feeling of urgency about the passing of time connects with the writer's principal concern: his own physical collapse and the realization that he has reached a crossroads. The poem comes very close to the commonplace *carpe diem* utterance which presented the poet with a convenient means of communication with his friends in Leipzig, but it becomes interesting because it bears the stamp of heavy-heartedness, if not despair. It presents the spectacle of an altogether ordinary mould being subjected to a change of shape in Goethe's hands – without, it must be added, the loss of control that occurred in the 'Elegie auf den Tod des Bruders meines Freundes.' It was this process, perhaps, that caused Goethe to describe his mood during the composition of the 'Neujahrslied' as one of 'groser Narrheit.'

One of his utterances shows us directly that he was aware of the danger of an occasional poem getting the better of the author. The 'Neujahrslied,' it was seen, could be changed or disguised sufficiently to make it fit for publication in the *Neue Lieder* collection. A 'Hochzeitscarmen' for Käthchen had to remain undisclosed. 'Kein Hochzeitgedicht kann ich Ihnen schicken, ich habe etliche für Sie gemacht, aber entweder, druckten Sie meine Empfindungen zu viel oder zu wenig aus' (12 December 1769, DJG I 284). Here, then, is an instance where an occasional poem remained undispatched, though probably not unwritten. One can take at face value the reason Goethe gives for his failure: that he lacked the necessary detachment for writing a poem which would presumably be recited or distributed on the occasion. This is a situation where Goethe's later utterances about the *Gelegenheitsgedicht* leave us stranded. And the famous passage in *Dichtung und Wahrheit* about the 'Bruchstücke einer grossen Konfession' (WA I XXVII 110) ceases to be helpful when we are faced with a poem that is engendered by this or that event, or befits a particular occasion. Yet the question of a poem's fitness must rate as the principal criterion in any consideration of this aspect of Goethe's work. But it is not easy to recover or reconstruct the sense of social fitness of a past era. Much that has been condemned in the social poetry of the period from 1650 to 1750 as bombastic and out of proportion, as insincere or suggestive, must have been eminently satisfying and proper to makers and customers alike. Many social poems of that period now strain our responsive capabilities intolerably, but we are likely to be more empathetic when we observe the lingering uneasiness pervading the occasional work of Günther, and when we see the foundations of earlier practices questioned in the controversies about the nature of poetry in the 1740s. The social interpretation comes to our aid with what are perhaps suspiciously satisfying results. G. Lukács aptly characterizes this aspect of the 'Misere' of the eighteenth century:

Ideologie und Kunst des französichen Grand Siècle erscheinen in den deutschen Versailleskarikaturen der kleinen Höfe bereits in einer entstellten und entwürdigten Form. Werden sie nun ins Bürgerliche übersetzt, so muss ein philiströser Gegenpol zu der adlighöfischen Armseligkeit entstehen.[12]

Lack of dignity and lack of proportion are not easily separated. The aesthetic problem with which Goethe had been confronted in the Clodius episode and which is hinted at in the passage to Käthchen merges with the ethical one of the content's authenticity. In this sense, it is perhaps permissible to state that Goethe's failure to dispatch a wedding poem at the time is a relevant episode in his career as an occasional poet.

The subject of marriage poetry prompts a consideration of 'Brautnacht,' which Goethe had sent to Behrisch in his letter of 7 or 9 October 1767, under the title of 'Hochzeitlied, an meinen Freund (DjG I 134). Strack has attempted to find an occasion for what is normally the occasional poem par excellence, the epithalamion: '[Behrisch] selbst muss damals die Absicht gehabt haben, sich mit ihr zu verheiraten, und der Freund sendet ihm, etwas frühzeitig, das Hochzeitsgedicht...'[13] But the remarks Goethe added to the poem in the above-mentioned letter to Behrisch seem to indicate that there was no specific occasion:

Ich schicke dir dieses kleine Gedicht, dessen Verfasser, du an der Denckungsart, und an der Versifikation gar leichte erkennen wirst, um deine Meinung darüber zu hören. Mir kommt es noch so ganz artig vor. [DjG I 135]

One would not have to enter into this question at all if the poem were not so successful. There is unanimity on that point among readers of the most diverse provenience and persuasion. Strack of the Scherer school calls it 'die Krone des Leipziger Liederbuchs und die schönste Blüte jener Gattung.'[14] Gundolf includes it, along with five others, among the number where the true Goethean voice is heard for the first time, expressing the 'Urerlebnis' of love successfully.[15] Fuchs singles it out as well:

Et une fois, l'amour de deux jeunes êtres mariés, don total des âmes et des corps, et célébré avec ferveur, au delà de toute inquiétude, de toute frivolité, de tout jeu, dans un 'Hochzeitslied' où vibre par endroits comme une action de grâces et un hymne à la vie.[16]

There are hardly any components of this poem which have not, in some form or other, appeared in previous wedding poems: The setting, the bridal chamber as the sacred precinct guarded by Amor, the contrast between the noisy crowd of guests milling about outside and the silence of the place of consummation, and the traditional more or less playful attempts at 'desecreation' or frustration on the part of family and guests – all this can be assembled, piecemeal, from the large number of seventeenth- and eighteenth-century wedding poems (as Strack has done). How much of this Goethe knew is difficult to tell. Morris, for instance, thinks that he was familiar with Günther's poem where occur the lines: 'Hymen adest lustratque torum myrtoque coronat.../Extremum matri jam dedit ante Vale' (DJG I 500). In 1770 Goethe made an entry into his Strassburg notebook which refers to Ramler's 'An Hymen' and to the father of all epithalamia, Catullus: 'Rammlers [sic] Ode an Hymen ist eine offenbare Nachahmung des Catullischen Epithalamii' (DJG I 432). Assuming from the phrasing that this observation was made on first acquaintance with one of the poems mentioned (which is by no means certain), it probably can be concluded that the Ramler ode was the new poem being related to the other one already known to him. Ramler published his volume of odes in 1767, although 'An Hymen' had already been printed separately in 1760 and 1763. But these questions of literary ancestry are of secondary importance in the present context. All that needs to be acknowledged here is that there exists a long tradition, from Catullus onward, of wedding poems which embraced all of the constituent elements found in the poem under consideration. It is also again possible that the chief model of the poem may have been pictorial.

But what is distinctive about 'Brautnacht'/'Hochzeitlied' and qualifies it for the place assigned by the writers quoted above? What accounts for its seriousness, its delicacy of feeling? I suggest that it was Goethe's ability, first, to trim away those parts of the traditional apparatus which had ceased to be viable, and secondly, to lend it a note of personal involvement. We are reminded of 'Bänkelsängerlied,' but with the difference that in the present case the result is a rehabilitation of a recognized branch of poetry, while the former represents the absorption of a lesser one. If I read Catullus LXI correctly, it is essentially a serious work, a devout invocation of a god for the sake of social stability and fertility. The light touches are altogether subordinated to this religious élan, which suggests distinctly the basis of primitive rite. As this ritualistic dimension disappears, as it necessarily must in the eighteenth century, a dissociation takes place. What I called earlier the anacreontic 'wink' becomes more visible. Descriptive elements displace the hymnic ones. The poet comes to present the spectacle of maidenly blushes and raucous guests to his public. It is relevant that Goethe, who from the beginning had held the revelling crowd at a distance and focussed altogether on the sanctuary, makes changes in the *Neue Lieder* version (as against the original one in the letter to Behrisch) which move the poem even further away from the tendencies noted above. Instead of the folksy and a little conspiratorial 'Dass nicht die List muhtwill'ger Gäste,/das Brautbett dir unsicher macht,' we now read the rather arch and formal 'Des Brautbetts Frieden untergräbt,' which throws quite a different light on the crude traditional pranks. Secondly, the line 'Du gehst, und wünschend geht die Menge,' which also established a somewhat equivocal bond between reader and poet, is dropped in the final version. Yet another change, rightly deplored by Morris, the sacrificing of 'Wollust,' an anacreontic *terminus technicus*, betrays the same intention. And it is this general purification of the poem that clears the way for the cordiality of it and for the gentleness that impressed Fuchs. Perhaps because it was not written for an occasion, but addressed 'an meinen Freund,' because it needed not be printed and distributed or read to the throng, the poet became free to accompany the groom into the 'sanctuary' and point to him the delights of the occasion. The poet turns his back on the guests, as it were – note the accumulation of personal pronouns 'du,' 'dich,' etc. – and guides and protects the protagonist.

Thus 'Brautnacht' occupies a crucial position in that phase of Goethe's growth as a poet during which the question of professionalism was a prominent one. Regardless of whether or not the poet solved the problem in this poem by beating 'the withered old poetasters at their own game,'[17] the competitive posture repeatedly observed so far is absent in the period to follow. Hence, new criteria arise in the definition of Goethe's occasional poetry.

3

From Strassburg to Frankfurt 1770-5

THE STRASSBURG-WETZLAR-FRANKFURT PHASE of Goethe's career as a poet appears at first glance to lack almost completely occasional poems like those examined heretofore. It seems unnecessary to recount step by step the biographical details of the years 1770-5 to show that the circumstances in which Goethe lived imposed few, if any, obligations on him to produce occasional poems in the manner of earlier years. It has been noted that the two principal sources of compulsion for Goethe at that time had been paternal authority and the desire to take a place among the established professional poets of the day. To trace the waning of the former might be a rewarding task for the post-Freudian biographer. As for the latter impulse, it will surely suffice to suggest that it must have receded considerably by the time Goethe found himself referred to as the author of *Götz*, and even more, of *Werther*.

The reader should feel quite free to regard this as an aspect of the emergence of a Storm-and-Stress Goethe, but I shall merely attempt to gather together symptoms of Goethe's new attitude towards occasions and the occasional poem, and then venture some conclusions.

Shortly after Goethe arrived in Strassburg there occurred a state occasion — Marie Antoinette's formal entry into the city on her progress from Vienna to Versailles as the betrothed of the dauphin. This event must have been important enough and have created enough of a stir in the city that any reaction to it, including the absence of one, deserves our attention. There is no reason to distrust the delayed testimony in *Dichtung und Wahrheit* on how Goethe took note of the occasion:

Vor Ankunft der Königin hatte man die ganz vernünftige Anordnung gemacht, dass sich keine missgestalteten Personen, keine Krüppel und ekelhaften Kranken auf ihrem Wege zeigen sollten. Man scherzte hierüber, und ich machte ein kleines französisches Gedicht, worin ich die Ankunft

Christi, welcher besonders der Kranken und Lahmen wegen auf der Welt zu wandeln schien, und die Ankunft der Königin, welche diese Unglücklichen verscheuchte, in Vergleichung brachte. [WA I XXVII 241-2]

Here are the satirical tendencies variously observed in the Leipzig phase carried a step beyond the limits of that time. Then, it will be recalled, poems in which absurdities were pointed up seemed to act as counterweights to commissioned poems. This juxtaposition had been found applicable to the Kuchenbäcker Händel poem, and a similar connection was tentatively suggested as existing between the Hoffmann and the Pfeil poems. Now we seem to be dealing with the parody of an occasional poem without the prior necessity for a 'serious' one. The admittedly tenuous quality of this suggestion may be somewhat relieved by the consideration that the poem was written in French and that a poetic celebration of the event would presumably have been composed in that language. Other motives involved here are the persistence of religious impressions from Frankfurt which would put the display of secular splendour into a questionable light, as well as the manifestations of linguistic and cultural patriotism discernible during the Strassburg days. I would not fasten upon this small and somewhat hypothetical matter if it were not a conveniently located segment of the entire structure that makes up Goethe's social and poetical view of the world in the half decade now under examination. The phenomenon as a whole is too pervasive and too well known to permit or require detailed exposition. Suffice it to refer to it in the terms of the distinction between 'Die Grosse Welt' and 'Die Kleine Welt' with all its attendant convictions of the superior worthiness, specific gravity, indeed, reality, of the latter compared with the former. Of the uncounted expressions of this view of the world present in everything Goethe wrote from his first Strassburg letters through *Werther* and onwards I want to single out but two at this point. In the first, the hierarchical pyramid of the established order is turned into a toy-like tiny merry-go-round:

Jeder hat doch seine Reihe in der Welt, wie im Schönerraritätenkasten. Ist der Kayser, mit der Armee vorüber gezogen. Schau sie, Guck sie, da kommt sich die Pabst mit seine Klerisey. Nun hab ich meine Rolle in der Kapitelstube auch ausgespielt. [to M.J. Engelbach, 30 September 1770, DJG II 15]

The qualitative difference between the two worlds is made explicit in the court scene of *Götz*: 'Es ist ein fürtrefflicher Mann, hat wenig seines gleich. Und wenn er nie an Hof gekommen wäre, könnte er unvergleichlich geworden seyn' (DJG II 116).

But this aspect of Goethe's thinking or, rather, feeling during these years cannot be reduced to a simple formula, which might be characterized by the expressions anti-political or anti-monarchical. I am simply dealing with one side of the style of life which makes something of a unit out of the half decade before Weimar. One need not arrive at the picture of a semi-pathological state, suggested by Barker Fairley,[1] when one observes in Goethe's poetic work as well as in the more strictly biographical evidence a restlessness, a search for new sensations in a widening circle of acquaintances, a refusal to be pinned down, geographically as well as emotionally. Reasons for all this have been sought for and found in so many directions, in Goethe's personality as well as in the tenor of the times, that it would be futile to summarize all and impertinent to elevate any one of them to the rank of sole validity here.

The passages note above pointed to a negative position. Is there a complementary, positive one to fill the vacuum? *Dichtung und Wahrheit* once more helps to supply an answer, with a passage appearing, to be sure, towards the end of the work and referring to the last months in Frankfurt, but having a wider range of applicability. Speaking of the 'didactic realism' he found in Hans Sachs and the use he made of it, Goethe writes: 'Es schien diese Art so bequem zur Poesie des Tages und deren bedurften wir jede Stunde' (WA I XXIX 83). This is a truly happy definition of the situation that prevailed during the entire period under discussion. The phrase 'Poesie des Tages' would seem to suggest something like 'week-day' poetry, poetry as a daily fare. And in the choice of the verb 'bedürfen' one senses the idea of the need for poetry as daily bread is needed. A related passage in *Dichtung und Wahrheit* makes a similar point, though not quite so clearly, but it is quoted here because it refers specifically to the Strassburg period. Speaking of his excursions into the upper Alsace, Goethe observes:

Die vielen kleinen Verse, die uns bei jeder Gelegenheit entquollen, und die wohl eine muntere Reisebeschreibung ausstatten könnten, sind verloren gegangen. [WA I XXVII 339]

Clearly, Strassburg had its share of 'Poesie des Tages,' a phrase which is particularly welcome in its usefulness as a substitute for the shimmering term 'Erlebnis,' which has come to mean everything and nothing in the course of time.

Poetry that is needed at any hour is, in a sense, the opposite of poetry for a particular occasion, the exceptional and memorable hour above the daily routine. But it is obvious that this bursting forth of poetry cannot be continuous. There are mounds and valleys even in a life lived at as high a level of tension as Goethe's. But if these do not coincide with those of his contemporaries, the occasions for poetry are not reached with the progress of the calendar. It must be recalled here and everywhere that generalizations of this kind are only meant to apply to that part of Goethe's production which can in any way be designated as occasional. The situation as described leads, then, to the phenomenon of occasions being created, chosen, occasions rising to the words instead of words rising to the occasion.

The *Schäkespears-Tag* address is one example of how an occasion is sought out rather than encountered. Eulogistic speeches are a traditional institution, not far removed from birthday, wedding, or funeral poems. But the situation is reversed in the manner indicated when we learn that Goethe had suggested a commemorative meeting of the *Deutsche Gesellschaft* in Strassburg and arranged for a ceremony in Frankfurt – which cost his father over nine guilders (DJG II 328). This event was precariously attached to the existing order, as it were, by being made to take place on Wilhelm's day (14 October, according to the Protestant Calendar). It seems rather doubtful whether anyone had ever instituted a 'Schäkespears-Tag' before in this manner, although groups like the 'Hainbund' were quite capable of doing so. In this connection it is proper to draw attention to the commemorative Shakespeare celebration of 1769 proposed, planned, and financed by David Garrick. The fact that Garrick used the dedication of the new Town Hall in Stratford-on-Avon as a 'pretext' for his true purpose, the rehabilitation of Shakespeare, makes the jubilee a remarkably parallel instance of a 'chosen' occasion.[2]

The second such instance leads us into the rather labyrinthian world – as regards personalities and emotions – of the Darmstadt circle in which Goethe moved in 1772 and 1773. The dedication of the rock which is celebrated in 'Fels-Weihegesang' occupies a position somewhere between an authentic occasion, such as a wedding, and a device to which a poem is being conveniently attached. The physical setting of all three poems in the group, 'Elisium an Uranien,' 'Pilgers Morgenlied an Lila,' and 'Fels-Weihegesang an Psyche' (DJG II 259–63) is an ideal landscape, and the reader can dispense with a knowledge of the location and the individuals behind it – indeed, that is one of the poet's principal aims. Yet, especially taken as a group, they suggest the existence of the flexible social framework into which they fit and which the *Gemeinschaft der Heiligen*[3] in fact was. It is hardly possible to determine the extent to which the content of the series of poems – 'Der Wandrer' and 'Wanderers Sturmlied' belong here, too – is governed by the specific composition of the Darmstadt group; how, in other words, they would have read if Merck had been a different person, or if no links had existed with the absent Herder through Caroline Flachsland. It seems, in any case, that these poems of Goethe's are to a greater extent creations of the community for which they were destined than any others before. More than in other situations does Goethe seem here to waver between identification with, and aloofness from, a group. This wavering was perhaps at the root of the frequent complaints about himself that pervade the entire seventies. One is reminded of the chameleon image which, to be sure, also occurs in Goethe's Leipzig writings and which Barker Fairley finds so significant.[4] In relation to Goethe's concept of occasional poetry the environmental aspect of this notion comes to the fore because it is the colour of the surroundings that sets off and determines the changes of colour of the chameleon; they are not spontaneous. It is not easy to measure the degree of Goethe's awareness of this factor in the use of the image.

We step on firmer ground when we consider the poetic and personal qualities necessary to hold this type of sentimental association and its social and artistic manifestations within the bounds of propriety, where the overstepping of the line leads directly from the acceptable to the ridiculous. To be a driving force and *laureatus* in a group so heterogeneous in temperament and social standing, and so dedicated to the practice of the difficult art of sensibility must require an impressive endowment of social tact and a sense of the fitness of spoken and written utterance. Such a position calls for an instinctive maintenance of balance between spontaneity or 'natural' behaviour on the one hand, and pretence or the use of the mask on the other. The Court of Love and the pastoral groups of the sixteenth and seventeenth centuries may be more illustrious examples of such phenomena, but the problems and rules in Darmstadt cannot have been very different in principle. How precarious the whole situation was, how easily the make-believe might have exploded, how quickly the scales could be tipped in the direction of the

30 Goethe's Poetry for Occasions

'real world' – in this case the 'grosse Welt,' the reality of which was a doubtful matter to Goethe at that time – can be seen from Caroline Flachsland's letter to Herder of 8 May 1772:

> O wenn Sie das Mädchen kennten [i.e., Luise von Ziegler], sie ist ein Engel von Empfindung und tausendmal besser als ich! Sie gab mir Blümchen aus ihrem Garten, und ich legte sie in Yoriks empfindsame Reisen. Wenn Goethe von Adel wäre, so wollte ich, dass er sie von Hofe wegnähme, wo sie auf die unverantwortlichste Art verkannt wird – aber so gehts nicht.[5]

It was surely fortunate that the patron saint of this Arcadia was the shrewd Sterne, rather than Klopstock, who held sway over the Hain in Göttingen at almost the same time.

More strikingly even than Caroline's sigh does Herder's reaction to 'Fels-Weihegesang' illustrate the delicate balance of personalities and feeling required in the situation. In brief, he, too, confused *Schein* with *Sein*, Arcadia with Darmstadt. He became jealous and expressed his feelings in 'Antwort auf die Felsweihe an Psyche,' a little poem which is actually neither very angry nor vicious:

> Nicht 'des verlebten Tages Zier
> 'o Psyche! keine welke Rose
> 'sei Traueropfer dir
> 'auf todtem Moose!'
> Welch Opfer! Welch' Altar! Und düster
> die Gegend! und ein irrer Götzenpriester
> der diesen Fels erstieg und ungeweiht ihn sang,
> und frecher Hand ihm ein den Namen zwang
> und traurig Opfer dir befahl!
>
> O Psyche, sieh von Fels und Oed' Einmal
> gen Himmel! Wie er weit
> und blau und schön sich wölbt, und ohne Maas und Zahl
> umher die Stralen Gottes streut ...[6]

Goethe's anger, as his reply to Herder from Wetzlar shows (10 July 1772), was caused not so much by the poem itself as by Herder's failure to enter into the spirit of the occasion, his insistence 'eurem Mädgen melankolisch Stunden zu machen' (DJG II 256).

This incident strikes one as an anticipation, on a small scale, of a situation that was to arise later at the Weimar court. Herder's failure to strike the right note became a growing cause of unpleasantness. Merck's tongue may have been sharper but he seems to have had a much surer instinct for drawing the line indicated above. The most conspicuous example of failure – an artistic as well as a social one, it must be emphasized – is offered in the person of Lenz. This point will be discussed further in connection with Goethe's first Weimar period (below, p 47), but one shudders to think what sort of a figure Lenz would have cut among the *Empfindsamen*.

The Darmstadt episode must not be viewed in isolation, however. Indeed, one might venture to say that Goethe, the *précieux*, only fails to become a *précieux ridicule* because the Ariel-like airiness of the circle and the utterances emerging from it are founded on a solid basis of not too elevated sociability which also made for the creation of occasions in the sense defined before. Most obviously relevant here are two poems written in Frankfurt in the summer of 1770, which bear the names of parlour games: 'Blinde Kuh' and 'Stirbt der Fuchs, so gilt der Balg' (DJG I 308). The latter poem especially, with its prominent anacreontic features, allows us to connect their themes with the tendencies observed in the Darmstadt poetry. For the parlour games, too, may be regarded as a device for the shifting of 'serious' social impulses into an area of make-believe where actions and words, however important they may be at the moment, do not really count. They run, it is true, in much deeper grooves of tradition than the improvised rites of Darmstadt, but in their own way they require the striking of the proper tone and the exercise of tact. This would apply particularly to the marriage game,[7] which has become best known because of its connection with the composition of *Clavigo*. I have not found any doubts expressed concerning the reliability of Goethe's description of this incident in Book xv of *Dichtung und Wahrheit*. Nor do I think it possible to account for aspects of the drama by means of the challenge that led to the writing of it. One might observe at best that the choice of the source, Beaumarchais' 'Mémoire,' was consonant with the circle in the first place, and further, that the drama might have remained unwritten but for the interest his friends showed in that source. But such considerations take us far beyond the concept of occasion, even in the loose sense in which it is being employed.

There is, however, an indirect reference to the marriage game in the *Concerto dramatico*, a work of some interest in the present inquiry. It originated during the period 1772 to 1773, and in its apostrophe to 'Langeweile' ('Allegretto 3/8') we read:

> Machst Jungfrau zur Frauen
> Gesellen zum Mann
> Und wärs nur im Scherze
> Wer anders nicht kann. [DJG III 63]

Of all works written by Goethe before his move to Weimar that can qualify as dramatic, this one most directly anticipates those later entertainments of his which are processional rather than stationary in character. These would include primarily the 'Maskenzüge,' but the definition has been kept purposely loose because the *Concerto dramatico* lacks important elements essential to the latter category. The connection between the papier mâché doll alluded to in the 'Arioso' ('gekaut Papier! Sollts Junos Bildung sein ...') and the rag doll in *Der Triumph der Empfindsamkeit* is probably purely coincidental. The more significant parallels are found in the structure of the piece, in the grouping of types in single stanzaic units, in the alternation of moods expressed here by musical speed indications. *Concerto dramatico* is dedicated to the *Gemeinschaft der Heiligen* and fits readily into the context of the 'chosen' occasions which was outlined above. Its vigorous tone, which contrasts sharply with the Klopstockian ethereality of the three poems ('Felsweihe-Gesang,' etc., cf. above, p 28) discussed earlier, tells us something of the range of conviviality possible in the Darmstadt circle (although it could be argued that Goethe's overwhelming personality imposed its earthier aspects upon it). As a footnote to the question of the place of the *Concerto dramatico* in relation to the marriage game and court entertainments, it should be added that the game played a rôle in the evolution of court entertainment in the late seventeenth and early eighteenth centuries, as Moser[8] has shown – it was used, for example, during the festivities at the Brandenburg court when the Electress Sophie Charlotte and Besser were their moving spirits.

Equally popular and by no means confined to that court were other kinds of festivities: *Bauernwirtschaft* and *Jahrmarktsfest*. By conjuring up inferior social settings, they, too, charmed by their remoteness from daily routine and ceremonial. This does not mean, however, that we must look for the direct ancestors of the *Jahrmarktsfest zu Plundersweilern* (DJG III 134) in them. There is no reason not to follow the clue offered by the subtitle *ein Schönbartspiel* and its associations with Hans Sachs. Herrmann's study[9] of Goethe's *Jahrmarktsfest* has shown that this is a rather involved problem, but we need not pursue it here. For the considerations to follow, it is only necessary to allow that the *Jahrmarktsfest zu Plundersweilern* was associable with court entertainment. The Darmstadt circle was a peculiar growth as far as its relationship to the 'real' court in Darmstadt is concerned – a tentative and loose structure on the periphery of an established institution. One of the basic impulses behind its establishment was a feeling of antagonism towards the court itself – hence Caroline Flachsland's complaints about the lack of recognition extended at the court to Luise von Ziegler. Accordingly, one might think of it as a 'court-away-from-court,' a place of refuge from and of passive resistance to the established order. One of the forces, incidentally, that drew these rather passive malcontents together was Pietism, which contains strong non-conformist tendencies.[10] Goethe's choice now of the 'Jahrmarktsfest' convention may be called significant because the same form had been used at 'real' courts at a time when the staid and grandiose apotheosizing court spectacles of the latter sixteenth and seventeenth centuries had come to lose their justification in the eyes of their sponsors and participants. At a time, that is, when absolutism had ceased to take itself fully seriously, when its metaphysical foundation had somewhat softened, when the desire to lay aside the solemn rites of state on occasion had begun to get the better of the urge to glorify the function of the court in the magnifying mirror of myth by means of music and ballet, by the theatrical machinery of pomp and circumstance. Thus the *Jahrmarktsfest zu Plundersweilern* criticizes the pseudo-court of Darmstadt, laughs at it, but it is a criticism from within which is the decisive point. Granted, the barbs of ridicule aim outside the circle as well, but that does not destroy the argument. The fact that the *Jahrmarktsfest zu Plundersweilern* lent itself to revision and amplification at the Weimar court (or a section of it) is in part due to the breadth of the satire, but also, to the 'courtly' origin of the piece, however faint that may have been.

The *Jahrmarktsfest zu Plundersweilern* was suitable for inclusion in the luggage that Goethe took to Weimar; it must be assumed that *Hanswursts Hochzeit* (DJG v 183) was too drastic for that. Since the latter, furthermore, was not written for an occasion, one might ignore it at that. And yet to do so would be to leave a gap in the picture of Goethe's activities that interest us here. It is true that the few pages of text and the lengthy lists of dramatis personae which make up the fragment constitute an insubstantial basis for any elaborate theories. But it will not do merely to mention the piece in order to dismiss it for its 'lack of wit.'[11] Goethe intended to use the rogues' gallery dramatically, at least in part, as the relevant passage in *Dichtung und Wahrheit* (Pt IV xviii WA i, XXIX 84ff) indicates, although the characters mentioned there do not appear in the original lists. The distinct note of regret at his failure to have carried the project further which pervades the passage in *Dichtung und Wahrheit* seems to indicate that we are not dealing with a whim but with a full-fledged component of his way of looking at the world. The dialogue between Kilian Brustfleck and Hans Wurst, i.e., between disproportionate reverence and utter indifference towards marriage, adds up to a denial of the value of that institution:

> K.B.   Es ist ein groses wichtigs Werck,
> Der ganzen Welt ein Augenmerck
> Dass Hanswurst seine Hochzeit hält ...

and

> H.W.   Ich mögt wohl meine Pritsche schmieren
> Und sie zur Thür hinaus formiren
> Indess was hab ich mit den Flegeln
> Sie mögen fressen und ich will vögeln.
> [DJG V 184, 186]

The laughter is surely at the expense of both when Wurst says:

> Euer fahles Wesen, schwanckende Positur
> Euer Trippeln und Krabeln und Schneider Natur
> Aber seht meine Figur
> Wie harmonirt sie mit meiner Natur
> Meine Kleider mit meinen sitten
> Ich bin aus dem Ganzen zugeschnitten. [DJG V 193]

We must not take this sketch too seriously, too literally, and underestimate the literary model behind it (i.e., the Christian Reuter version of *Harlekins Hochzeit*). And yet, are we not dealing here with a dramatic *Hochzeitscarmen* in reverse, with a declaration of war, so to speak, on the occasion for commissioned poetry par excellence? And we must assume that the piece was written for its own sake, for what is known about social diversions with a literary slant – through *Dichtung und Wahrheit*, for example, and the Crespel[12] correspondence – would hardly lead us to believe that *Hanswursts Hochzeit* had any place there. It was noted in the discussion of the Kuchenbäcker Händel poem that Goethe directed his satire in two directions, at the critic as well as at himself. The same phenomenon appears in *Hanswursts Hochzeit* much more clearly, in the juxtaposition of Kilian and Hans. This observation suggests that the various manifestations of hostility to the traditional occasional poem represent only one side of the works in which they are displayed. Inseparable from them is the criticism of the critic. This point will become clearer shortly.

The uncertainty of the date of origin of *Hanswursts Hochzeit* offers the advantage that we need not attach it too closely to the episode of Goethe and Lili Schönemann, can, but need not, take it as a sardonic outburst of Goethe as fiancé, as Morris suggests (DJG(M) VI 471), and are able to contemplate it alongside *Clavigo*, *Stella*, and even *Götz* – an entire battery of misgivings aimed at the universal feasibility of a permanent attachment. We are not dealing here with attacks on the institution of marriage itself from one who would overturn it, nor, of course, with condemnation of those who would not accept it for themselves. But such formulations are inappropriate to poetry – we also are not dealing with a sociologist or a reformer. It is better to think of marriage here as a symbol of a rigid and irksome bond between human beings, imposed and perpetuated by external forces and considerations to the detriment of their substance. What could better serve as a symbol of a relationship like this one than the traditional, thoroughly conventionalized, and commonplace *Hochzeitscarmen*?

All the more interest must therefore belong to the wedding poem which Goethe wrote at a moment when the tendencies sketched above reached their climax, biographically speaking, a few days before the decisive break with Lili Schönemann and Frankfurt:

Lieb Gustgen – da ist ein junges Paar in der Stube das erst seit acht Tagen verheurathet ist! eine iunge Frau liegt auf dem Bette die der angenehmsten Hoffnung eines lieben Kindes entgegenschmerzet.
[To Auguste v. Stolberg, 14–19 September 1775; WA iv ii 292]

The young couple were J.L. Ewald and his bride, for whose wedding on 10 September Goethe had written 'Bundeslied – einem iungen Paar gesungen von Vieren' (DJG v 266). A measure of the distance by which this poem is removed from what was still the 'normal' wedding poem is given by the ease with which the original version, 'Den künftgen Tag und Stunden' (so published in the *Teutsche Merkur*, February 1776), lent itself to later revision as 'In allen guten Stunden' (for the 1789 edition [WA i 1 117–18]). A *Hochzeitscarmen* that can become a song in praise of sociability without much change obviously cannot be too deeply anchored in the occasion on hand nor in the social institution to which it was dedicated. No mythological apparatus required removal; only modification of tense, person, and number were necessary:

1776	1789
Den künftgen Tag und Stunden,	In allen guten Stunden
Nicht heut dem Tag allein	
Euch bracht ein Gott zusammen	Uns hält der Gott zusammen
Der uns zusammen bracht.	
Nicht lang in unserm Kreise	Wer lebt in unserm Kreise,
Bist nicht mehr neu darinn;	und lebt nicht selig drin?

The one major excision of a passage that had tied the poem to the occasion affected a reference not to the groom or bride, but to the singer:

> Ach! dass von einer Wange
> Hier eine Thräne fällt!
> Doch ihr sollt nichts verlieren
> Die ihr verbunden bleibt,
> Wenn einen einst von Vieren
> Das Schicksaal von euch treibt:
> Ists doch als wenn er bliebe!

The biographical knowledge that Goethe and Lili Schönemann were two of the four is hardly required of the reader, who senses that the person who places himself so conspicuously at the end of the poem finds himself in a position or mood unsuitable to the glorification of the marriage feast. Quite apart from the tearful ending, we are transported here into the sphere of rather self-conscious wistfulness, of controlled abandon, that is associated with the products of Gellert's pen. There is also a layer of determined Rousseauism ('Durch Zieren nicht geenget, schlägt freier unsre Brust') that suggests at once the enfant terrible outlook of Lenz and the attitude of open-shirted defiance that was destined to linger so persistently in German life and letters.

This has perhaps been an excessively biographical reading of 'Bundeslied.' It is quite possible that much of what it is can be ascribed to the fact that it was a labour of co-operation with André, the composer, whose talents seem to have run in such channels.[13] Indeed, the fact that it is in the first place a song must be taken into account. But the 'Bundeslied' nevertheless holds a definite and curious place in the history of Goethe's occasional poetry. It is the product of a state of mind suspended halfway between two extreme attitudes. On one end of the scale we have the attractions of idyllic passivity, the blissful submission to biological and social rhythms faintly expressed in the passage of the letter to Auguste von Stolberg quoted above, and more fully formulated in the idyll, 'Der Wandrer,' and in the domestic scenes of *Götz*. At the other end of the scale we find the spirit of *Hanswursts Hochzeit*, or of some of the even less bridled outbursts from among the 'Einfälle und Notizen' (DJG V 378–92).

By contrast, the earlier wedding poem of the latter Frankfurt days, 'Dem Passavant und Schüblerischen Brautpaare, die Geschwister des Bräutigams' (DJG IV 227), written for 25 July 1774, is devoid of the ambiguous feelings with which we have been dealing. It was written at a distance – geographical and human – from the protagonists. Even distance in time enters into its history, since it did not reach the recipients on their wedding day proper and was not presented to them formally until their golden wedding anniversary. In this instance, the return to older models impresses as having been made quite deliberately. Hyperbole abounds, especially in the first stanza:

> *Er fliegt* hinweg *Dich* zu umfangen,
> Und unsre Seele *iauchzt* ihm *laut*;
> Mit *innig heiserem* Verlangen
> Flog *nie* der Bräutigam zur Braut.
> ...
> Auf, bring uns *doppelt Ihn* zurück!
> Wir wollen *alles* mit *Dir* theilen ...

The poet appears in the rôle of commissioned troubadour stoking the well-controlled fires of celebration. For once, the drabness of daily living is being veiled by the superlative. The lines that follow, with their naïve calculus of happiness, seem to belong to the fourth and fifth decades of the century:

> Die besten Eltern zu verlassen,
> Die Freunde, denen *Du* verschwindst,
> Ist Traurig. Doch um *Dich* zu fassen
> Bedencke was *Du* wiederfindst.
> *Dein* Glück, o Freundinn, wird nicht minder,
> Und unsers wird durch dich vermehrt.

Thus navigating the conventional waters of a tradition still fully acceptable to his audience, the poet can achieve what he was unable to do a year later in the 'Bundeslied.' He can keep his mind on the business at hand and close by addressing the couple on a note of serenity:

> Und war das Band das *Euch* verbunden
> Gefühlvoll warm und heilig rein,
> So lasst die letzte eurer Stunden
> Wie *Eure* erste heiter seyn.

Goethe must have felt that this poem was sure to please the man who had commissioned his earliest *carmina*: 'und meinem Vater doch auch einige Exemplare dieses Carmens' (letter of 20 July 1774, DjG IV 221).

If the criteria that were applied have contributed to the understanding of the occasional (and 'anti-occasional') works of the years surveyed, they may help to account for an instance of conspicuous silence (where external obstacles cannot be counted as decisive). It has been suggested [14] that Goethe's failure to commemorate his sister's wedding, 1 November 1773, was an after-effect of the rejection of his *carmen* in Leipzig. An immeasurably more far-reaching answer to this question is implied in the whole of Eissler's psychoanalytic study of Goethe [15] in which the sister necessarily plays a crucial part and where her marriage inevitably must assume the proportions of a vast cataclysm in the poet's life. It is inherent in the nature of this work that no part of it can be appropriated and utilized without acceptance of the fundamental principles upon which the entire structure is erected. However that may be, Eissler's monumental study, so replete with shrewd observations of detail and pervaded by genuine appreciation of Goethe's poetry, and the present modest inquiry share an interest in occasions in the broad sense of the term. Goethe's silence can perhaps be put in relief by reading an epithalamium which actually did adorn the festive occasion. (Appendix A) [16] It may be regarded as representative in form and tenor of domestic occasional poetry of the period. It is not necessary to pass judgement on it to recognize the epithalamium as being symptomatic of a civil order and of a way of life which the author of *Werther* viewed with misgivings. A court may be a prominent symbol of this order; it can also represent a different world altogether. Such considerations render necessary a closer examination of the court to which Goethe proceeded with considerable eagerness in November 1775.

·4·
Weimar 1775–80

IT IS ONLY NATURAL that Goethe's move to Weimar should, for the time being, reduce the vaguely defined expanse of occasional poetry under survey to its more manageable subdivision of literary territory called court poetry. The fact is, after all, that for years to come Goethe's life and work unfolded at the courts of Anna Amalia and Carl August: the majority of persons with whom he dealt were closely linked with one member or the other of the ducal family, all of whom in turn were more or less active participants in the interests and activities of court life. When this has been said, it becomes necessary to add the emphatic reminder that Goethe did not go to Weimar with the expectation or inclination to place his literary gifts at the disposal of the duke personally or of the court in any way. It is not easy to say exactly what rôle he envisaged for himself as the guest of the duke, nor what exactly the duke's expectations were, whether friendship, support against entrenched forces at home, or the pleasure of attracting a remarkable and famous man to his entourage. Some brief observations are therefore in order about the situation at the Weimar court at the time of Goethe's arrival.[1] It would be inaccurate to speak of a conflict between two generations that was decided by time in favour of the younger when Duke Carl August reached the legal age for receiving the reins of government from his mother, but the rapid succession of three decisive events, or rather, the addition of a third (Goethe's arrival on 7 November 1775) to two (Carl August's assumption of rule on 3 September and his marriage on 3 October) which had been anticipated and planned for beforehand, indicates a consciousness of passing into a new era.

The older era, Anna Amalia's regency, had been characterized by the presence of a court poet, to the extent, at least, that such a figure could be conceived of at a minor Protestant court in the eighth decade of the century. A princess of Anna Amalia's convictions would not think of hiring a *Hofpoet* à la Canitz, a professional singer of praises, a glee-man in Robert Graves' terminology, whose functions included some of those of *maître de plaisir* and court jester. But there was a demand for professional dispensers of wisdom. One might say that the expectations formerly attached to the court alchemist and court astrologer were not shifted to the shoulders of the *philosophes*, who were expected to work miraculous enrichment of the mind and to do so entertainingly. If a Voltaire was suitable for mighty rulers like Frederick the Great and Catherine of Russia, then a minor prince could be more than satisfied with a Wieland,[2] even though the financial sacrifice of retaining him was formidable. Wieland, on the other hand, regarded Weimar as a proving ground for, and stepping stone to, higher spheres, viz, the court of Vienna. His bonds were not irksome, his obligations loose and informal. The duchess was strongly motivated by a genuine admiration for the man and the writer, as well as by the sincere and urgent solicitude of the enlightened ruler for the intellectual welfare of her sons, and hence, for the welfare of her subjects. Nevertheless, the character of the relationship was that of a formal appointment contractually binding and subordinating – exactly the kind that Goethe was unable to face in the pre-Weimar years, as implied in his 'negative' occasional poetry.

Goethe's wrathful satire *Götter Helden und Wieland* (DJG III 344) on Wieland's conception of heroic figures and passions of antiquity in *Alceste* and *Die Wahl des Hercules*[3] emanates from the totality of his views and attitudes towards the subject. But it seems likely that an itch to his fingers was added by the knowledge that Wieland had written for a court audience as the servant of a court. After the first mention of Wieland's name the Literator identifies him for Merkurius:

M. Wer ist der Wieland?
L. Hofrath und Prinzenhofmeister zu Weimar.
M. Und wenn er Ganimeds Hofmeister wäre sollt er mir her. [DJG III 347]

And a moment later his shade appears 'in der Nachtmütze.' One of the most burlesque moments of the skit occurs when Wieland, in rapture or distress, interrupts Alceste with 'Meine Fürstin,' echoing, as W. Kayser (HA IV 539) reminds us, the address at the head of Wieland's dedicatory letters to Duchess Anna Amalia. There are other remarks scattered through the play which indicate that Goethe was thinking of Wieland's works not merely in their printed form but as spectacles for the court.

These considerations apply equally to Hercules' rôle, Wieland's *Die Wahl des Hercules* being the second butt of satire in *Götter Helden und Wieland*. It had been published in the August 1773 issue of *Der Teutsche Merkur*, and Goethe wrote his skit sometime that fall. Wieland's *Hercules* was a straightforward occasional court piece which had as its immediate predecessor Metastasio's treatment of the same theme on the occasion of the wedding of Joseph II.[4] When Hercules and Wieland debate the concept of *Tugent*, when Goethe finds Wieland's *arete* wanting, we are not over-stepping the borders of likelihood in assigning to Goethe certain misgivings about the probable effect of Wieland's activity as a prince's tutor upon the object of his pedagogy. This belief is strengthened by another passage in *Götter Helden und Wieland* which, although it refers to Admetus, can easily be read as the portrait of a prince who was not educated by a *Hofmeister*:

Ein iunger, ganz glücklicher, wohlbehaglicher Fürst, der von seinem Vater Reich und Erbe und Heerde und Güter empfangen hatte, und drinne sass mit Genüglichkeit und genoss und ganz war, und nichts bedurfte als Leute die mit ihm genossen, und sie wie natürlich fand, und des Hergebens nicht satt wurde, und alle liebte dass sie ihn lieben sollten, und sich Götter und Menschen so zu Freunden gemacht hatte ... [DJG III 353]

A young prince who only lacks friends with whom to share as equals what birth had granted him – this vision of 1773 cannot have been very submerged when Goethe met Carl August for the first time at Frankfurt in December 1774, when the highly uncourtly views of Justus Möser became the first meeting-ground of their minds. The seeming collapse of this vision must have enhanced the mortification that kept Goethe indoors while the hope for a message from the duke faded from day to day. The last mention of Goethe's father in *Dichtung und Wahrheit* (Pt IV Bk XX) tells of his taunts, the I-told-you-so's, when the ducal invitation seemed to prove him right: that an absolute prince was playing his little game or a practical joke on his inferior; in other words, that Carl August was not a Euripidean but a Wielandian Hercules for whom *arete* 'ist ein zweideutiges Ding.' The associations attached to the name of Wieland – including his rôle as *Hofrat* and court poet – merge with the world of Frankfurt as a state of mind, of which Goethe's father may have been the outstanding symbol to his son. It is not too difficult to think of *Hanswursts Hochzeit* and *Götter Helden und Wieland* as fairly close neighbours on the spectrum of motivating emotions.

The belief that the latter work does not exclusively belong to the sphere of literary controversy, but that it touches on the sociopolitical notions of its author as well, is clearly expressed in the following passage from Goethe's conversation in June 1774, recorded by Johanna Fahlmer, in which he speaks of Wieland's generous criticism of *Götz*:

Da, Da! ... Das ists just, was mich an W. so ärgerte und mich reitzte, mich gegen ihn auszulassen. Da, der Ton ... 'Mit der Zeit! Mit der Zeit!' Ja, das ists! just, just so spricht mein Vater; die nehmliche Händel, die ich mit diesem in Politischen Sachen habe, hab' ich mit W. in diesen Punkten. Der Vater-Ton! der ists just, der mich aufgebracht hat. [DJG IV 331–2]

The Wieland incident has been dealt with at some length because, aside from its own relevance, it helps to enlighten Goethe's probable notions and prejudices concerning the question of the place of the poet at a court. Only one more pre-Weimarian utterance will be added, one which seems to suggest that his mind occasionally came back to the cluster of associations suggested by the words *Prinzen-Hofmeister, philosophe*, wise counsellor. It is written in the spirit of ironic self-deprecation and would be much more valuable if we knew about which of his poems he was writing. (The guesses in this direction – 'Grenzen der Menschheit,' 'Das Göttliche,' and 'Königlich Gebet' – are not satisfactory.)[5]

anbey die Ode. Wie gefall ich Ihnen auf dünnen Prophetenstelzen, Fürsten und Herren ihre Pflicht einredend? [April 1775, DJG V 20]

The situation which prevailed during the early part of Goethe's stay in Weimar fits the irony of this utterance. Rejection of and compliance with the traditional and courtly style of living intermingle curiously. On the one side, the stay at court subjected Goethe to restrictions more severe than any he could have experienced in Frankfurt as a member of a leading family. The most marked example in this respect is his being seated at the *Marschallstafel* along with the younger court nobles, and not with his host at the *Fürstentafel*. Mention of this circumstance is not made to suggest in any way humiliation or degradation. There is nothing that would indicate a failure on Goethe's part to accept this arrangement as altogether proper.

If all this points to a measure of stability in the conditions at court at the beginning of Goethe's stay there, it can be no more than the necessary corrective of the customary view of the state of affairs at that time, which tends to over-emphasize the changes caused by, or coinciding with Goethe's arrival in Weimar.[6] But even in so judiciously balanced and detailed a presentation as Willy Andreas' *Carl August von Weimar*,[7] the impression of flux and upheaval must certainly dominate. A court such as this need not be touched by the ideas of *Sturm und Drang* to be profoundly affected by such fundamental changes as took place in Weimar between September and November 1775: the end of the regency, the transition from female to male ruler, from one generation to another, the introduction of a new leading personality (the Duchess Luise), and the consequent establishment of a second court, that of the dowager duchess' household. All this would have sufficed to create an unsettled situation, with only a gradual solidification to be anticipated. When the factors of the strong personality of Carl August, of the background and character of the new duchess, the inevitable turn of the wheel of fortune for established office holders, such as Counts von Görtz and von Fritsch, are included in the picture, we begin to understand a development that amounts to more than a changing of the guard. Some aspects of the situation in Weimar may have reminded Goethe of the one he had encountered and found congenial in Darmstadt: a border zone between stability and chaos, between respectability and indifference to the opinions of the respectable, between social discipline and surrender to spontaneous impulses.

The first Weimar poem to claim our attention is one addressed to the Duke: 'Durchlauchtigster! Es nahet sich' (WA I IV 205). No definite date of its origin is known, and the chronological question has some bearing on my argument. It is generally placed in the early months of the Weimar period. Düntzer argued for a later date;[8] he felt that Sebastian Simpel's plea that the duke think of the peasants as his most loyal subjects, and hence show greater interest in them, did not fit the early Weimar months either as regards the spirit of those days or the relationship of the poet with the addressee of the poem. But Düntzer's argument leaves unaccounted for a passage in Gleim's letter to Bertuch of 14 February 1776, in which Gleim reports: 'dass er [Goethe] dem Herzog in einen Bauer sich verstellt und ihn in Knittelversen regieren gelehrt hat' (Gräf VII 40), nor does it really justify Düntzer's much later date of October 1780. But the latter's objections do point up the connection between the interpretation of the spirit of the poem and the chronological matter. If it is a plea of this kind, it does describe an attitude which Trunz defines as, 'Goethe's Auffassung des Bauerntums, sozial, voll Achtung, patriarchalisch ... ' (HA I 465). One may doubt the validity of this interpretation. For one thing, Goethe's other written attempts – the great majority were oral ones – to teach the duke how to govern strike more solemn and insistent notes. 'Ilmenau,' and Goethe's admonitions to the duke concerning the effects of his boar hunts on the economy of the country in his letter of 26 December 1784 (WA IV VI 415), are cases in point. Furthermore, the choice of a Sebastian Simpel, who surely belongs in the family of bumpkins employed in *Singspiel*, would hardly make for an effective conveyance of 'message' or a 'lesson' in the art of government. These difficulties – and Düntzer's chronological misgivings – are removed if Simpel's message is read as a mocking echo of some of the criticisms directed at the duke and his guest by members of the court. The alienation and concern that had spread among those who liked to consider themselves entitled to being thought of as the duke's 'bestes Gut' (although hardly 'Bäurisch treues Blut') are now given an ironic twist. The expressed desire for a 'gnädger Blick' which in itself creates 'Untertanenglück' could as easily be an oblique reference to the slighted malcontents at the court as an expression of genuine concern for the neglected peasantry. Andreas has given us large samples of such critical utterances [9] by those interested in letting the duke know that they constituted the duke's 'bestes Gut' (Seckendorff, the Görtz couple, and the Hofmeisterin Countess Gianini). There is a poem by Einsiedel of January 1776, written in a similar spirit, 'Schreiben eines Politikers an die gelehrte Gesellschaft,' which is quoted by Andreas [10] (who nevertheless regards 'Durchlauchtigster ...' as a serious admonition).

There is general agreement on the probability that 'Durchlauchtigster ...' was actually recited to the duke by Goethe disguised as a peasant. This is stated as a fact by Eckermann and Riemer in their Goethe edition of 1836, but it must necessarily be based on hearsay. One can thus justifiably speak once more of a 'chosen' occasion in the sense that the occasions for the Shakespeare speech and the 'Fels-Weihegesang' had been manufactured. But a new factor enters. In that poem the poet had set the tone, had spoken spontaneously with his own undisguised voice, assuming – wrongly in the case of Herder – that by doing so he was giving emphatic expression to feelings which were already shared by his audience. Now, however, the element of diplomacy seems to enter into the situation. That is to say, the message – regardless of its exact meaning – is being conveyed in a coded form with the aid of a mask, since a direct statement could have caused embarrassment to the originator, to the recipient, or to bystanders.

But strictly speaking, all these considerations apply only to the first half of the poem. It is the existence of two distinct sections within this short work that makes it so suitable a point of departure for the examination of the earlier occasional poetry of the Weimar years.

> Zieht ein und nehmet Speis und Kraft
> Im Zauberschloss in der Nachbarschaft,
> Wo die gute Fee regiert,
> Die einen goldnen Szepter führt
> Und um sich eine kleine Welt
> Mit holdem Blick beisammenhält.

Biographical detail becomes unimportant here. The Eckermann-Riemer note suggests that these lines refer to a visit to the Stein estate in Kochberg. The important thing is the break within the poem. Everything that has been said so far is brushed aside abruptly at this point. Whatever ironic or magisterial overtones the *Knittelverse* may have carried, this verse is now employed as the vehicle of the simple and straightforward evocation of a fairy kingdom. Its identification with the *kleine Welt* will reveal a greater degree of significance when it is recalled that this concept has already been found to designate a world embodying a greater measure of reality than its opposite. This observation was made in connection with the Strassburg period (see above, p 26). In the period now being surveyed the use of the fairy world becomes crucially important.

It has been observed that Goethe's position as a poet at the court was altogether undefined from the time of his arrival. 'Durchlauchtigster ...' gives us a clue as to how he solved the problem of his peculiar status. Yet, in order to gain a fuller view, it may be advisable to glance at Lenz' attempts in this direction.

Lenz' failure and disgrace in Weimar can be easily described in pathological terms or the jargon of psychology. But since we are here concerned with the exploration of another poet's writings, we can safely ignore Lenz' behaviour, his personal relationships, and the mysterious gaffe that terminated his stay at Weimar. The relevant poems by Lenz are: 'Auf einem einsamen Spaziergang,' addressed to the Duchess Luise, and 'Als jüngst Amalie zu ihrem Prinzen reiste' and 'Auf die Musik zu Erwin and Elmire,' both for Anna Amalia. A more distant relative of this series is 'Aus einem Neujahrswunsch aus dem Stegreif aufs Jahr 1776.'[11] The first poem is a reminder of the noteworthy fact that during the first years in Weimar Goethe hardly ever addressed the Duchess Luise in a poem, the one exception being the dedicatory lines to Lila, 'Was wir vermögen' (WA i XII 342). The more general tribute, 'Wie alle dich verehren müssen' (WA i IV 364), which is closer in spirit to the Lenz poem, has not been authenticated. This failure must have puzzled Morris,[12] too, when he proceeded to relate to the duchess a vast portion of Goethe's works from *Proserpina* to *Märchen*. We are left wondering whether Goethe did not consider the occasional poem a suitable means of communication with the duchess, or whether he felt unable or unwilling to adopt the attitudes demanded by convention. The Lenz poem and Herder's series of 1783[13] might suggest the latter answer, as would the duchess' well-known views of her position and of the proprieties involved. No definite answer can be expected, but it is possible to derive from this juxtaposition an intimation of the sense of discrimination that controlled Goethe's activity as an occasional poet.

Lenz' two poems to Anna Amalia, too, tell us something by indirection. Lines like 'Als jüngst Amalia zu ihrem Prinzen reiste/ Und Zeus vernahm, dass sie die Nacht dort speiste' lead us into territory that Goethe consistently avoided. It does not seem too surprising in retrospect that the author of 'Prometheus' would not indulge in mock-mythological exercises (except for satirical purposes, as in *Götter Helden und Wieland*) in order to vindicate the superhuman proportions of the Olympians. The only other possible instance, Askalaphus' monologue in *Der Triumph der Empfindsamkeit* merits separate treatment in a different context. It is not too difficult to sense the embarrassing, even humiliating overtones of

> Nun stelle man Vater Zeus sich vor,
> Dem dies zum zweiten Mal arrivierte,
> Dass solch ein Geck ihn kompromittierte ...

in our own myth-conscious age. And yet, this was a most convenient device to pay tribute to a ruler at a time when it was no longer possible to present the equation of Zeus and ruler in earnest.

Furthermore, the mock-mythological method, the scaling down

of mythological personalities and incidents to all-too-human proportions, the prettification of the gods – this device was employed to suggest a mild sort of social revolt and to provide a bridge across the traditional barriers of propriety. This may be an element in Lenz' poems, but it is particularly discernible in Wieland (*Komische Erzählungen* [*Das Urteil des Paris*], the Lucian translation). It would seem that Goethe passed through this phase of occasional poetry early and fast. We may properly recall here the wedding *carmen* for his uncle and the ensuing Clodius crisis, and the decisive rôle that incident had played in Goethe's development as an occasional poet. Similar considerations apply to the other poem by Lenz, 'Auf die Musik zu Erwin und Elmire':

> Ich setzte meinem lieben Schwärmer
> Ein klein Spinettchen in sein Tal
> Und spielt ihm auf dem kleinen Lärmer
> Der Herzogin Musik einmal.
> Wenn dann mein Erwin aus seinen letzten Zügen
> Nicht aufsprang ...

Such devious praise for the duchess' achievements would seem to point to a sense of unsureness about the true proportions of the social setting in which Lenz found himself. Taken together, these tributes produce an impression of oldfashionedness. They seem to be closer to the world of Wieland, even of Günther, than to that of Goethe; yet there could be little doubt in anyone's mind that the Wieland era had reached its end.

Another sample of mock-mythological poetry brings us to another personality who was unsure about his proper position at the court. Seckendorff's *Minervas Geburt* (1780)[14] is a *Schattenspiel*, a parlour game, and hence it is not to be measured with the yardstick applied above. Nevertheless it illustrates a prevailing manner of occasional poetry on which Goethe turned his back. A small sample of this work will illustrate my point:

> Im 3 Act lässt Jupiter
> Nachdem ihm Ganimed vorher
> Die Schokolade überreicht
> (Die er heraus vor andern streicht)
> Minerven hohlen vor dem Thron;
> Der kleine Page eilt davon,
> Nachdeme, wie man sehen wird,
> Er mitt dem Adler sich brouilliert ...

The avoidance of conventional manners and means of expression encountered above ought to be regarded as part of Goethe's notions about occasional poetry. Consciously or otherwise, he was avoiding pitfalls by addressing only a few poems to individual members of the ruling family during the first years of his stay in Weimar. Instead, he let the court community speak for him and to itself from the amateur stage.

Lila[15] is hidden from our view today under several layers. The first may be said to be found in the deprecatory note of the lines with which the original version of the play was presumably introduced and dedicated to the Duchess Luise on her birthday on 30 January 1777:

> Du fühlst, dass bei dem Unvermögen,
> Und unter der Zaubermummerey,
> Doch guter Wille und Wahrheit sey. [WA I XII 342]

Goethe persisted in this estimate of production in his correspondence with Count Brühl in 1818–19, when the latter planned a revival of the play with a new score which later proved disappointing. At that point (1 October 1818) Goethe regretted the lack of an opportunity to bring the piece closer to the 'Singspiel' proper and raise it, he implies, above the level of a staged trick or joke, namely the 'psychische Cur,' which had been more or less improvised by a group of jolly amateurs.[16] The second obstacle to a proper evaluation of *Lila* in the present context is raised by the loss of the complete original version. There is some knowledge of the changes which Goethe apparently began to make almost immediately after the first performance in time for the second on 26 February 1777, and we do know that in the following year the shift from male to female protagonist was made; while we possess the arias in their earliest form, not enough of the dialogue of the versions preceding that of 1788 has survived to permit us to draw conclusions from the changes in the successive designations of *Lila* as 'Feenspiel' (February-March 1777), then as 'Schauspiel' (spring 1778), and finally as 'Festspiel' (later the same year). (Cf. Gräf v 309.) But these terminological changes help to indicate that Goethe had undertaken a project which had no real antecedents in his own work. *Lila*, Goethe's first work written for a festive court occasion, possesses some characteristics which have not been encountered thus far, but are destined to recur in many of the subsequent contributions.

Three works of Goethe appear on the list of performances[17] by the court amateur group in 1776: *Die Geschwister*, *Die Mitschuldigen*, and *Erwin und Elmire*. Only the first of these had been written in Weimar and it bears little resemblance to *Lila*. The spectacular components – music, song, and dance – are totally absent. *Lila* displays them in abundance in the later versions, and there is no reason to think that they were much less conspicuous at the beginning. One can only guess that the original version differed from the later ones in the amount of comic exchanges and incidents. The 1788 version does not fit very well the description of the play in the 1816–18 correspondence mentioned above, of the gay, informal pastime of a small private circle. In fact, unless the humour escapes me completely, it is the solemnity of the whole that attracts attention, a solemnity that is systematically intensified as the play progresses, once the flippant two sisters have shot their arrows of satire in the direction of the medical profession in the first act. The comic aspects of the situation in which the protagonist is hoaxed into health were perhaps more fully exploited when that was a male rôle; the play would then have undergone a process of refinement when the change was made. Perhaps, too, Goethe's recollection of the original was dimmed after forty years; certainly, *Der Triumph der Empfindsamkeit*, *Lila's* pendant piece, fits such a description much better. But unless the early *Lila* differed more substantially from the final version than we need to assume, we are dealing with an essentially solemn, operatic work in which the magic that had been invoked as a conscious and rational device becomes, as it were, dominant and real by its own momentum.

And since we are interested here in the fact that this is Goethe's first venture in large-scale occasional poetry in Weimar, it may not be inappropriate to recall the abrupt change of tone in the small occasional poem found in a similar strategic position. In 'Durchlauchtigster …' we had observed a passing from the tongue-in-cheek attitude to the naïve acceptance of, and entrance into, the fairy world. This must remain a loose parallelism, but it tells us something about Goethe's *modus operandi* in these years. In the form known to us, *Lila* seems to pull, not necessarily with the poet's consent, participants and spectators alike into the realm of opera. Dr Verazio 'plays' the Magus, and in doing so he becomes a figure nearly as commanding and lofty as Sarastro of *The Magic Flute* in his possession of a magic power which is identical with moral power. But it required two decades – and possibly contact with Mozart's opera – and a new insight into the nature of opera before Goethe was ready to grant himself the freedom of roaming in this realm without self-consciousness and equivocation. We must not underrate the obvious limitations of the amateur theatre of the early Weimar period, which offered no hope of gradual advance towards greater achievement by the systematic training which their professional successors were made to undergo. Nevertheless, one can perhaps account in the main for what *Lila* is now (and probably had been even more so at the beginning) by the fact that this was a task of a new kind for Goethe. One might say that he was actually writing his first Weimar play, his first play for the court. The completion of *Die Geschwister*, which he had written a few weeks before, was announced to family and friends in Frankfurt (6 November 1776). But about *Lila* he maintained silence.

It is not quite clear whether *Der Triumph der Empfindsamkeit* was expressly intended for the duchess' birthday in 1778, when it had its première. When Goethe first reported on the work in progress, he called it a 'komische Oper' and anticipated its performance 'this winter,' and so one can assume that he had the birthdate in mind as a deadline. The subsequent pace of preparation, completion of the sixth act at the end of December (WA iv III 203), and the rehearsals of January, as well as the subtitle of the second MS of the 1777 version, 'Ein Festspiel mit Gesängen und Tänzen,' permit the assumption that once more we are dealing with a work at least as genuinely occasional as *Lila*. The expense of staging this play is comparable to that of *Lila* (398 thaler for the former and 516 for the latter).[18] It should be added that January 1778, was a most busy month as far as court entertainments were concerned.[19] Amateur theatricals received the impetus of Ekhof's participation in the performance of Cumberland's *West-Indier* with the duke, Prince Constantin, Goethe, and Musaeus all in the cast. And in the middle of the month there occurred outdoor festivities, among them possibly one of the skating carnivals which were always remarkable for their elaborateness and length.

Der Triumph der Empfindsamkeit itself would not require especial attention for the present purpose if it did not contain *Proserpina*. Without this interlude, it could be characterized as a reversion to pre-Weimarian ways, although it cannot be definitely claimed that a 'Weimar style' had emerged by this time. The version of 1778 in some ways recalls *Satyros*, *Götter Helden und Wieland*, and *Claudine von Villa Bella*. There is nothing particularly 'courtly' about it. It could have been written for any small group of congenial persons, as may be readily seen from a comparison of the first words of Andrason in the first act which, to be sure, was later more thoroughly changed than the rest of the work. In the 1786-7 version of the Göschen edition, we read:

Ich umarme dich, meine Schwester! Ich grüsse euch, meine Kinder! Eure Freude macht mich glücklich, eure Liebe tröstet mich. [WA I XVII 5]

The audience of 1778 had heard:

Gott lohns ihr Kinder! Schwestergen, Gott lohns! dass ihr euch freuen mögt mich wieder zu sehen, ich had auch eine rechte Freude. Gebt mir immer einen Kuss ihr Puppen, wer weiss wenn ich wieder was gutes geniesse. (:er küsst sie:) [WA I XVII 324]

On the other hand, it should not be thought that the revision drained all comedy from the play. One of the more amusing exchanges, which is especially effective because it combines topicality with a more general applicability, did not occur in 1778:

Lato   Wie soll man euch denn nennen?
Andrason   Ihr wisst dass ihr keine Umstände mit mir machen sollt.
Mana (für sich)   Nur damit er auch keine mit uns zu machen braucht. [WA I XVII 5]

Aside from details, however, the earlier version with its good-natured gruffness, especially in the parts referring to women, the explosiveness of the dialogue, and the concentration on literary controversy recalls Goethe's pre-Weimar satire. This similarity could be accounted for by the realization that *Lila* had strayed too far from the path of entertainment without attaining its desirable measure of stateliness and magic, as was suggested above. The numerous parallels in source (Crébillon, Marmontel, etc.) and plot (the 'trick') pointed out by Feise[20] tend to suggest that the two works are related experiments, with the later utilizing the lessons learned from the earlier one. Nor should another factor which dominates so many interpretations of *Lila* and *Der Triumph der Empfindsamkeit* be altogether ignored. The earlier work especially was aimed with perhaps excessive accuracy at the matrimonial difficulties of the ducal couple, and so *Der Triumph der*

Empfindsamkeit may have been intended to act as a counterweight to it. Thus it might be said that the proportions of ingredients, which according to Petsch constitute in *Lila* the 'eigentümliche Mischung von derbem Spass, feinsinniger Seelendeutung und liebenswürdiger Mahnung,'[21] have been changed so that, in a manner of speaking, *Der Triumph der Empfindsamkeit* becomes the caricature of *Lila*. The title itself might point to this, for allegorical Triumph (*trionfo*), the most orthodox form of serious courtly entertainment and of glorification of prince and princeliness, has now become a triumph of wrong-headedness.

When one is speculating about the choice of the plot of *Der Triumph der Empfindsamkeit*, it is necessary to consider the opportunities for the display of stage machinery and local technical skills which it afforded. The original stage directions for the transformation of the Chinese Room into the forest in Act Two are more specific and technical than the later ones, and point to the enthusiasm with which such theatrical effects were attempted and no doubt received. At this point in Goethe's poetic development, at least, the attractive power of stage 'business' ought not to be underestimated. We are perhaps too inclined to think of the literary satire as the poet's primary motivating force when we take for granted that the attack on excessive sensibility necessitates the stage apparatus for the transformation of a hall into an artificial forest. The argument that moves in the opposite direction – the availability of stage machinery suggests the possibility of utilizing it in a given manner – should be allowed to make its claims. 'Des Dichters Welt entstand auf sein Geheiss' (WA I XVI 136) may be read in two ways, supporting either argument with some strength. In the light of our knowledge of the respectful and affectionate use of the title of 'Direktor der Natur' in 'Auf Miedings Tod,' the ambivalence of the satire in connection with the 'directeur de la nature' who is mentioned by Merkulo as the chief abettor of the prince's derangement, takes us beyond *Der Triumph der Empfindsamkeit*, which does contain within itself a much more striking instance of ambivalence – the Proserpina monologue or 'monodrama.'

The widespread notion that we are dealing here with a lapse of good taste was probably engendered by Goethe's own 'confession' in the *Tag- und Jahres-Hefte* that it had been 'Freventlich eingeschoben' (WA I XXXV 6). This view fits neatly into the pedestrian critical pattern which presents us with a 'serious' and a 'frivolous' Goethe. Nor would 'Variety of entertainment, and the provision of a good part for the best actress'[22] seem to be adequate criteria. Vordtriede[23] reminds us that there is a third element to be accounted for, namely, Askalaphus' prologue to *Proserpina*. It is of course true that the Proserpina monologue is capable of a separate existence. It was printed and performed separately in 1815 when Goethe himself supervised the composition of Eberwein's new musical score as well as the details of the staging. But in order to do the problem justice we must concentrate on the situation as it prevailed in January 1778. It is not conceivable that *Proserpina*, with its special music by Seckendorff and the strong hints pointing to it in the earlier acts, impressed the audience as an inconspicuous interlude. So long as we do not definitely know that *Proserpina* was written altogether independently of *Der Triumph der Empfindsamkeit* – be it for its own sake, or as a vehicle for Corona Schröter, or as a commemorative work[24] – we ought not to rely on the assumption that the insertion was a casual afterthought. But even if it were so, the integration of *Proserpina* into the play would change its character. For the pomegranate seeds eaten by Proserpina with such catastrophic results do not appear out of nothing. In the original myth[25] they were placed in her way by Askalaphus, but for different reasons. Whereas the myth regards Askalaphus' action as a ruse on the part of Pluto to hold Proserpina in his realm, the Weimar Askalaphus seems to be without malice, to be eager to please the unhappy queen and reap his rewards when his artist's skill is revealed:

> Dass meine Königin vermeine,
> Es wüchse alles aus dem Steine,
> Und wenn sie den Betrug verspürt,
> Den Künstler lobe, wie sich's gebührt. [WA I XVII 39]

Aside from the suggestion of the tempted Eve (Askalaphus had raised the fruit with the aid of 'unterirdischem Feuer' and Proserpina asks later on: 'Warum den Apfel?/ O verflucht die Früchte!/ Warum sind Früchte schön,/ Wenn sie verdammen?' [WA I XVII 48]), one finds here a juxtaposition of rock and vegetation, stone and wood, wilderness and valley, 'natural' nature and nature interfered with. Askalaphus tells us at length of the attempts at transforming the nether world into a park, not in order to make Hades more like Elysium, but to falsify the character of both regions. Earth, necessary for vegetation, is carried from Elysium to Hades and rock in the opposite direction. The key word is 'Kommunikation' and the project meant to bring it about is that of connecting Elysium and Erebus by means of a wooden bridge. Stone is despised for aesthetic reasons, and failure ensued because the fiery border rivers will not tolerate such a structure. 'Andrasons Schloss, eine rauhe und felsige Gegend, Höhle im Grunde,' the setting of the fourth act of *Der Triumph der Empfindsamkeit*, is a proper one for the despair of a young woman who mourns 'blumenreiche Täler.' She would, no doubt, feel more at home in the 'Wald, die Laube im Grund' of the third act, where we meet the prince for the first time, the prince who will later perform a 'Monodrama zu zwei Personen' (flying in the face of the axiom of identity that one equals one) with the puppet Mandadane-Proserpina of whom he is so fond because she does not have a heart of stone but of chaff (a vegetable matter, akin to the wood of the bridge in Hades).

Sketchy as these considerations are, they will suffice to suggest the structure of the play which Goethe offered to the court for 30 January 1778. It differs from its predecessor *Lila* not only in the increased vigour of its tone but also in its dramatic character. In *Lila* the entire apparatus of disguises, stage devices, music, dance, and plot complications had been placed at the service of the dramatic goal, the cure. But the relationship of the parts to the whole are different in *Der Triumph der Empfindsamkeit*. That there are close connections between the 'interlude' and the play proper has been demonstrated. But the play within the play does not change the progress of events. Mandadane is not 'cured' through her recitation of the monodrama and the prince is not cured at all. All the change that occurs through Andrason's manipulations is one of the relative position of the various static participants.

It would seem then that we are dealing with a problem of dramatic genre. One can derive some assistance here from the generic theory of Northrop Frye.[26] It is not practicable to set forth the entire scheme, but a reference to the terminology employed by him, with some clarifying quotations, ought to be helpful. Comedy, we learn, may display a greater or lesser degree of irony, depending on the degree of predominance exerted by folly or ridiculousness. If these undesirable features are represented as being in conflict with, and overcome by characters whose outlook engenders the sympathy of the audience, then the ironic quality of the play is lessened. In the case of such a conflict the ridiculous figures tend to appear as 'humours,' as victims of a ruling passion or 'spleen' (in eighteenth-century German usage), whose compulsive behaviour hinders the fulfilment of the ideal or proper state of affairs.

The further comedy moves from irony, and the more it rejoices in the free movement of its happy society, the more readily it takes to music and dancing. As music and scenery increase in importance, the ideal comedy crosses the boundary line of spectacular drama and becomes the form of the masque. ... The further comedy moves from irony, the less social power is allowed to the humors. In the masque, where the ideal society is still more in the ascendant, the humors become degraded into the uncouth figures of the ... antimasque.[27]

If these criteria are applied to *Lila* and *Der Triumph der Empfindsamkeit*, the following observations suggest themselves. In both cases, we are dealing with a 'humour,' an obsession which separates its victim from the world which the audience accepts as normal or desirable and which is (in both plays) strongly represented on the stage. The intensity of conflict is further diminished by the fact that, entirely in *Lila*, and as far as Mandadane is concerned in *Der Triumph der Empfindsamkeit*, the victim of the humour is identical with a partner of the couple in the interests of whose happiness the desirable balance is to be recovered. That is to say, the conflict can be resolved by the gentlest possible means; there is a cure rather than a struggle. In this way, the mellowing influences of music and dance, which can only operate when there is no profound gap between the audience and those on the stage, who are in control of things, can be brought into action from the first. Everthing is assured from the beginning, and even 'der Oger' of *Lila* is only a friend in disguise.

If, as was first suggested and then confirmed in the light of Frye's analysis of genres, *Lila* hovered in a region between genres too much committed still to the comedy of humour to permit complete surrender to the lure of courtly masque and opera, then *Der Triumph der Empfindsamkeit* represents a compensatory move in two directions at once. On the one hand, the poet pulls us back onto the more solid ground of ironic-satirical comedy. The figure of the prince is important here. He is left in the end without pity, one might say, in the shadow of his obsession; the only concession to a happy ending that is made is the circumstance that his is a relatively free choice. It is conceivable that this 'mercilessness' of the poet is suggested by his interest at that time in Aristophanes, an interest which appears directly in the play in the paraphrase of a passage from the beginning of *Ecclesiazusae* in Merkulo's song to the moon in Act Two, 'Du gedrechselte Laterne.'[28] On the other hand, *Der Triumph der Empfindsamkeit* moved more resolutely into the realm of the spectacular with its greater freedom from the need for a logically developed plot. In manner of speaking the oracle acts as a device which tells the story from the beginning. It requires decoding, to be sure, but the audience can, from the start, surrender to the guiding hand of the poet to be enlightened gradually, rather than involved in intrigue. It is more of a game, a verbal charade, than the dramatic pursuit of a solution. And within this frame, of course, there is room for changes of mood, of locale, such as the Proserpina melodrama represents. *Der Triumph der Empfindsamkeit* is then at the same time more relaxed than *Lila* in that the difficulty which must be overcome is never given the rank of a genuine crisis, and more taut in the sense that the satire is sharper and the castigation of folly more merciless and less tempered with pity and pathos.

The presence of *Proserpina* in *Der Triumph der Empfindsamkeit* calls forth another consideration with respect to the development of Goethe's occasional poetry in Weimar. Alongside the poetry which is lyrical, i.e., musical, evocative, and personal to the highest degree (essentially the *Lida* poems), there develops quite steadily another kind which, by contrast, could be called visual, pictorial, statuesque, and – in a general sense – allegorical. This group uses, often as its culmination, a figure or a group of figures, and ends, so to speak, in silent contemplation. The mind's eye is to be left with a definitive impression, and the poet's descriptive arts are subordinated to it. Clearly, such a method is most useful for purposes of occasional poetry, but is not exclusively dedicated to it. It is significant that in the first poem of this type the visual dominates the word and the idea even in its title: 'Erklärung eines alten Holzschnitts vorstellend Hans Sachens poetische Sendung' (1776, WA I XVI 121–9). That the woodcut is an imaginary one, i.e., that the poetic scheme rendered necessary the visual *pendant*, confirms the point. In the next one – decidedly occasional – 'Gellerts Monument von Oeser' (WA I II 148), which Goethe sent to the Duchess Anna Amalia with the drawing of the monument (24 October 1777), the written tributes to the poet are actually unfavourably compared with Oeser's silent one of stone: 'Und sammelte mit Geistesflug/ Im

Marmor alles Lobes Stammeln.' On a larger scale, *Proserpina* has a function within *Der Triumph der Empfindsamkeit* analogous to Oeser's monument. The recollection of the spectator will have been that of a lone, static figure surrounded by the hustle and bustle, the folly and the confusion of the characters of the play proper. And again, seen in this light, the offering of 30 January 1778 reveals itself as anticipating the processional and spectacular entertainments which Goethe gave the court from the early eighties onwards.

It is difficult to resist the impression that the tendency sketched above is related to the presence of Corona Schröter at the court. To suggest that *Proserpina* was written as a vehicle[29] for her may not be accurate, but it seems permissible to speculate that the amalgamation of *Der Triumph der Empfindsamkeit* and *Proserpina* might not have taken place in her absence. And while it may not be possible or necessary to make the same claim for her participation in the jocular miniature masque *Epiphaniasfest* (WA i I 149–50; 6 January 1781), the rôle assigned to her in *Auf Miedings Tod* (WA i XVI 133–40) must engage our attention. This remarkable occasional poem is deliberately made to culminate in the vision of the muse paying tribute to her faithful servant:

> Zum Muster wuchs das schöne Bild empor
> Vollendet nun, sie ists und stellt es vor.

If the text of *Proserpina* itself should not suggest sufficiently that the final, the dominating impression was to be a static one, Goethe's instructions for the staging of it, published in the *Morgenblatt* of 8 June 1815, make it amply clear:

Indem nämlich Proserpina in der wiederholten Huldigung der Parzen ihr unwiderrufliches Schicksal erkennt ... eröffnet sich der Hintergrund, wo man das Schattenreich erblickt, erstarrt zum Gemählde, und auch sie die Königen zugleich erstarrend als Theil des Bildes. [WA i XL 113]

The essay contains many other instructions and explanations which serve to support the point under discussion, but because of its date it can only be used sparingly for this purpose. The import of gesture and costume is so strongly emphasized in the same essay that it must at least be mentioned. The *tableau vivant* of 'Auf Miedings Tod' is reached via the maze of chaotic activity backstage

('Gärung'). 'Getümmel' is the initial note, and then the reader is led through the imperfect universe of mixed motives and the harassments of convention and contrivance, through moral and physical ills. Although *Der Triumph der Empfindsamkeit* is more subtly constructed, the principle governing 'Auf Miedings Tod' is the same. It contains a memorable and valid moment of stasis against a background of confusion and error. In this connection, one is also led to think of the conclusion of *Iphigenie auf Tauris*, where the handclasp ('und reiche mir zum Pfand der alten Freundschaft deine Rechte') (WA I X 95) in the presence of all the other stage characters is undoubtedly a *tableau vivant* over which the curtain lingers before its final descent, and above all, of the much-criticized finale of *Egmont*, the crowning of the sleeping Egmont by the genius of freedom. The instructions (WA I VIII 303–4) in the latter work are at least as elaborate as those for *Proserpina*, and as in 'Auf Miedings Tod,' the affinity with the monodrama at the climactic point is obvious. I cast but a passing glance at *Torquato Tasso*, which cannot be related to a single event or occasion. Here the sequence seems to be reversed. A *tableau vivant*, the coronation of the *hermae* of Virgil and Ariosto, stands at the beginning and seems to cast its shadow over the coronation of the living poet in the third scene and on the final tableau at the end of the play.

The mention of these dramas provides an opportunity for a reappraisal of the nature of the 'occasional' elements in Goethe's work at this stage in his artistic development. Much of what has been observed in *Der Triumph der Empfindsamkeit* had been based on the assumption that it was an occasional work in the straightforward sense of the term, a work conceived, written, and prepared for the performance on the duchess' birthday in 1778. The actual evidence for this had, of course, been exceedingly slim, and besides, in contrast to *Lila*, there is really nothing in the play itself which would tell the reader unacquainted with conditions at the Weimar court that such a purpose was involved.

There are two circumstances which must be kept in mind in connection with the distribution of occasional works. In the first place the calendar decreed that the duchess' birthday took place at the height of the social season (30 January), that is to say, between the New Year and Lent. It is tempting to wonder what the effect on Goethe's work would have been if the duchess' and the duke's birthdays had exchanged places on the calendar, since the latter occurred on 3 September, in the spa and hunting season. 'Ilmenau' would necessarily have been a different poem. A similar question concerning the 'Maskenzüge' of the early eighties can be raised more profitably when they have been examined more closely. These formed part of an institution which existed quite independently of birthdays, the 'Redoute.' This fact alone illustrates the rather complicated and decisive interrelationship of entertainment and art, of pastime and politics in a general sense of the word, of the large spheres of nature, poetry, and society which must be explored. The second circumstance, one actually inseparable from the first, is summed up by the term *Liebhabertheater*. Some general considerations have been presented on this subject earlier, in connection with the situation in Darmstadt. They must now be complemented by reference to some simple and factual matters.[30] Whatever the symbolic significance of the event may have been, it is a plain and verifiable fact that the locale of professional theatrical performances in Weimar disappeared in the conflagration of the castle (6 May 1774), after which event the Seyler company was forced to go to Gotha. This happened as the regency of Anna Amalia drew to an end, at a time when considerable changes in the style of living were being anticipated. And the first phase of the new era was amateurish in the fullest range of the term. The resistance of Fritsch to Goethe's membership in the privy council was the careerman's aversion to the amateur, and the obstacles raised by the local clergy against Herder's appointment were of the same order.

It should be possible to look at the entire *Sturm und Drang* movement from that angle. The new writers and poets set themselves not only against the dying guild of professional, 'learned' poets on the one hand, and the elegant amateurs on the other, but also against the newer type of professional à la Wieland and Klopstock. They wanted their products to be taken seriously, but they wanted to leave themselves room to preserve their independence as men who influence the affairs of the world through means other than their pen. The plans of military reforms with which Lenz attempted to influence Carl August are a case in point, and so is Schiller's rather involuntary move into the life of a professional writer. There is no question, too, that Goethe's 'crisis' prior to the move to Weimar lends itself to description in these terms. In Frankfurt he was never faced with the threat of having to sacrifice his career as an author, but rather it was the prospect of becoming a professional writer, permanently tied to his home city, that turned the journey to Weimar into an escape.

Another most tangible cause of the amateurism of the first Weimar years is to be sought in the fiscal department. The first four years of Goethe's stay in Weimar were lean ones indeed for the duchy. One reason for this may be found in the need for two court establishments, the duke's and that of the dowager duchess, and a state that, according to Andreas,[31] had to bail itself out of threatening insolvency by a Swiss loan of 50,000 thalers was not likely to be able to afford a professional troupe of actors, even if they had been strongly desired – unless the ruler resorted to the sale of his subjects or some other device of unenlightened despotism never even remotely considered in the realm of Anna Amalia and Carl August. Be it cause or effect, the professional troupe of Bellomo was in fact brought to Weimar only after the fiscal position of the duchy had been improved noticeably by Goethe's competent direction of the *Kammer* after 1782. It must be added, however, that the origin of the theatrical building, Hauptmann's *Redouten-und Kommödienhaus* goes back to the fiscally difficult years, 1779–80, but public funds were involved only to a limited extent, in the form of a loan.[32] But we should end with a distorted impression if we were to deduce the forms of entertainment of the court of Weimar from the figures appearing in the ledger alone. In order to bridge the gap between the *Lila-Der Triumph der Empfindsamkeit* phase (1777–8) and the winter of 1782, when we find the remarkably heavy concentration of 'Maskenzüge' (*Aufzug der Vier Weltalter*, *Der Geist der Jugend*, *Die Weiblichen Tugenden*), we must necessarily encounter an interlocking set of circumstances which makes the change plausible. With inevitable simplification, this development is that outlined in the following paragraph.

After the experiment of *Der Triumph der Empfindsamkeit-Proserpina*, which was artistically daring and not at all conclusive and which would have tested a public of considerably greater sophistication than the one available, Goethe's remaining contributions of 1778 turned out to be far less exacting. They are the performances of the *Luisenfest* on 9 July 1778, and of the *Jahrmarktsfest zu Plundersweilern* on 20 October. Without discounting chance, these two events reveal something of one of the lingering conflicts in Weimar which we must take into account. The *Luisenfest* was arranged and written for the benefit of the Duchess Luise. According to Goethe's own description, 'Das Luisenfest' (in *Biographische Einzelnheiten*, WA I XXXVI 233–42), it was a gentle, pastoral affair. Seckendorff's little 'Dramolet' was an altogether innocuous and unsubstantial piece of dialogue, more of an excuse for dressing up in monks' robes than anything else. The 'plot,' too, was genteel and courtly. The seeming slight to the court in the monastic simplicity of the table set in the rustic cabin served as a prelude to revelation of the 'wohlgeschmückte fürstliche Tafel' in the clearing of the park – a glorification of rank and propriety, if a serious interpretation is needed, surely fitted exactly to the tastes and the character of Luise. Whether Anna Amalia's absence from Weimar at the time affected the nature of this festivity is no longer ascertainable.

But the performance of the *Jahrmarktsfest* in October under the aegis of the older duchess may be regarded as something diametrically opposed to the *Luisenfest*. This expansion of the pre-Weimarian farce of 1774 was neither genteel nor gentle. The satire was pointed, and at the centre of a mad and bawdy feast was the respectable court of Ahasverus with its senile king and silly queen. The music was composed by Anna Amalia herself. In practice, of course, the separation of the two courts was far from neat, but the juxtaposition of the two events reveals one aspect of the position of Goethe as a social poet at that time: indulgence in a rather tepid and insignificant activity as *maître de plaisir*, and a return to tendencies of some years before which had found their strongest expression in *Hanswursts Hochzeit*. When we now find during the next several months evidence of restlessness, dissatisfaction, and of an attempted redefinition on Goethe's part of his position in Weimar, we have no difficulty in accounting for this state by various circumstances, but we may also include the divergence of interests just described as a contributing cause. A relevant expression of this labour of appraisal, which can be traced in diary and correspondence from late in 1778, and which continued with varying intensity well into the Swiss journey, occurs in Goethe's diary under date of 13 July 1779, when the presence of Merck, the perspicacious outsider, stimulated the process:

Aber auch ausser dem Herzog ist niemand im Werden, die andern sind fertig wie Dresselpuppen, wo höchstens noch der Anstrich fehlt.
[WA iii 1 88]

Goethe wrote this in connection with the clarification of his own and the duke's relationship with Corona Schröter, a matter about which we know very little. But Goethe made enough of a generalization to fit the situation suggested above. The two festivities examined above were indeed appropriate to static personalities, each in its own way. Goethe's urge to guide, to further growth, which had found rather didactic expression in *Lila* and a more sublte form in *Der Triumph der Empfindsamkeit-Proserpina*, and which was the undisguised purpose of the projected journey to Switzerland, had reached an impasse. This is not to say that an unwelcome preceptor had been told to keep quiet. The braking force was exerted as much by the artisitic development of Goethe as by the intractability of his audience.

The dissonance of official work and of poetic labours during the composition of *Iphigenie* between February and April 1779 was well expressed in the phrase about the King of Tauris and the hungry weavers of Apolda (6 March 1779): 'es ist verflucht, der König von Tauris soll reden als wenn kein Strumpfwürcker in Apolde hungerte' (WA iv iv 18). The remark was made during Goethe's travels in connection with his new responsibilities as head of the War and Roads Commission, direction of which became his in January 1779. As Andreas points out,[33] this change took place under the shadow of events in which the safety of the duchy was threatened by the Prusso-Austrian crisis (War of Succession) and Prussia's accompanying demands for recruiting privileges in Saxe-Weimar. If Goethe found anything in his new position to please him, assuming that the acceptance of the burden itself resulted from a sense of responsibility towards the duke, it must have been the prospect of improving upon the work of his predecessor, the younger von Kalb, in whom he appears to have sensed the corruption which brought about Kalb's disgrace three years later. Read by itself, the diary for December 1778 would lead an innocent reader to believe that the court was a den of iniquity:

[8 Dec.] Nach Tiefurt wo mich alles an den Menschen ärgerte... [9 Dec.] Conseil leidig Gefühl der Adiaphorie so vieler wichtig seyn sollender Sachen... [14 Dec.] Indem man unverbesserliche Übel an Menschen und Umständen verbessern will verliert man die Zeit und verdirbt noch mehr... (15 Dec.] Mit Knebeln über die Schiefheiten der Sozietät ... Hundsfüttisches Votum von K[alb] in der Bergw. Sache. ... Ich bin nicht zu dieser Welt gemacht, wie man aus seinem Haus tritt geht man auf lauter Koth. [WA iii 1 72, 73, 74]

This mood, one would think, would lead to a version of *Hanswursts Hochzeit* adapted to conditions at the Weimar court, or to a project such as Goethe sketched almost exactly a year later (3 January 1780) during the anti-climactic end of the journey to Switzerland, when he was visiting the small courts of southern Germany with the duke.

So ziehen wir an den Höfen herum, frieren und langeweilen ... Sie sind schlecht eingerichtet und haben meist Schöpse und Lumpen um sich...
    Den sogenannten Weltleuten such ich nun abzupassen worinn es ihnen denn eigentlich sizt? ... Wenn ich sie einmal in der Tasche habe werd ich auch dieses als Drama verkehren. Interessante *Personae dramatis* wären Ein Erbprinz: Ein abgedanckter Minister; Eine Hofdame... [to Charlotte von Stein, WA iv IV 159–60]

Instead of a drama such as that here suggested, during the following three months Goethe wrote *Iphigenie auf Tauris*. The 'occasional,' courtly nature of *Iphigenie* has often been pointed out. Heinrich Meyer has put it succinctly (and with his usual inflection of impatience):

Es sollte ein würdiges Festspiel werden, eine von wenigen Darstellern auf der Liebhaberbühne aufführbare Dichtung, weder tragisch, noch komisch, sondern höfisch, wie Goethe es idealisierte, also edel, vornehm, gelassen, überlegen. Die Leidenschaften ... sollten also den edlen Frauen, besonders der Herzogin Luise, erfreulich und rührend sein; an sie dachte der Dichter.[34]

This is one side of the matter, but for all that, we might be dealing with a wordier and lengthier *Luisenfest*, which was meant solely to please the duchess. There is some evidence that Goethe's intentions at this point were rather different. In that letter to Charlotte von Stein of 14 February 1779, in which the 'brooding over' *Iphigenie* is announced, we also read:

ob ich gleich zur schönen Vorbereitung lezte Nacht 10 Stunden geschlafen habe. So ganz ohne Sammlung, nur den einen Fus im Steigriemen des Dichter Hippogryphs, wills sehr schweer seyn etwas zu bringen das nicht ganz mit Glanzleinwand Lumpen gekleidet sey. [WA iv IV 11]

If I read correctly the phrase about the 'Glanzleinwand Lumpen,' it expresses the determination not to give the court something merely pleasing and easily digestible. 'Glanz-' or 'Wachsleinwand' seems to have been associated in Goethe's mind with tepid and clumsy occasional poetry. When the count of *Wilhelm Meisters Theatralische Sendung* suggests a plan for a highly conventional mythological tribute to the prince, Wilhelm expresses his opposition to the project by exclaiming: 'Sind wir hier in der Wachsleinwandfabrik? ...' (Bk v ch v, WA i LII 125), Wilhelm refers to the crude homage paid to the owner of such an establishment by his retainers, which he had witnessed with some sympathy and amusement (Bk III ch I, WA i LI 194–5). It is true, of course, that these two incidents of the novel were not composed until 1782 and 1784, but the associations are likely to go back to Goethe's Frankfurt days. The description of an actual 'Wachsleinwandfabrik' in *Dichtung und Wahrheit*, at least, gives rise to some remarks on the connection between art and utility (Pt I Bk IV, WA i XXVI 245–6).

When, during the writing of *Iphigenie auf Tauris*, Goethe urged Knebel to overcome his reluctance to take part in the performance (and in doing so made, a little unfairly, the whole enterprise depend on his decision), he placed the drama in the category of 'andern ernstlicheren Plänen und Hoffnungen,' and described his purpose as 'einigen guten Menschen Freude zu machen und einige Hände Salz ins Publikum zu werfen' (14 March 1779, WA iv IV 22). This description indicates a double purpose, or rather a consciousness that the work would have a divided effect, and it fits in with Goethe's diary notation after the performance: 'Gar gute Würckung davon besonders auf reine Menschen' (6 April 1779, WA III I 84). Looking at *Iphigenie auf Tauris*, then, merely as a creation for domestic consumption, we are dealing with something for which there seems so far to be no precedent in Goethe's Weimar – the deliberate selection of an audience, presumably of two or three individuals, most of whom were not in the audience at all, but on the stage. This is admittedly an overly-pointed way of stating the situation. Yet a reading of Goethe's diary from November 1778 to August 1779, as well as the names of the actors – Carl August, Prince Constantin, Corona Schröter, and Goethe – would hint at the singular involvement of rôles and actors, provided the assumption is granted that Goethe wrote and cast the drama at the same time, and the urgent appeal to Knebel quoted above supports that assumption. Needless to add, it must not be thought that I am speculating about a play within a play, a mousetrap à la *Hamlet*, where the play is intended to affect the course of the events offstage. Rather, it seems to me that Goethe may have had in mind the therapeutic effect upon the persons concerned, the thought that the leveling of decisive conflicts, the diminuendo of motion and emotion towards the tableau of the final handshake would create certain patterns of thought, feeling, and behaviour. The therapy of make-believe had occurred in burlesque form in *Lila*. Now in *Iphigenie auf Tauris* we find a more serious form if it, not least, perhaps, because the author found himself in the double rôle of physician and patient. There may also be a clue here to his choice of a subject so little conducive to the use of spectacular elements. It will be recalled that the masque characteristically tended towards a merging of performers and audience, with the former rendering homage to the qualities of the latter. In the present case, however, the business to be transacted remains on the stage side of the footlights, since actors and audience, in a manner of speaking, are identical from the beginning, and the effect of the play on the total audience was more or less ignored. It is worthy of note that music does not seem to have been used at all in the performance of *Iphigenie auf Tauris*, unless its presence was so taken for granted that the total absence of references to it would carry no weight. In any case it would have been used only in the most incidental manner. In its 'occasional' capacity, *Iphigenie auf Tauris* exalts the power of the word, articulateness, persuasion, and clarification over dark and inarticulate forces. The drawn sword is spirited back into its scabbard by the word, and the incoherent cry of obsession is stilled by calm speech.

In order to explore fully the position of *Iphigenie* in the sequence of Goethe's occasional works, a useful purpose may be served by examining the original version of the play in the light of generic theory, in order to progress, if possible, a step beyond Meyer's definition quoted earlier (p 65), 'weder tragisch, noch komisch, sondern höfisch.' The employment of the concept of comedy in this attempt at clarification should not, however, be regarded as an irritant, as well it may in view of the religious awe that *Iphigenie auf Tauris* has evoked in traditional Goethe criticism.

The designation of the play has remained remarkably vague. In the earliest printed excerpts of 1785, in the *Schwäbische Museum* (Gräf v 157), the readers were referred to an 'ungedrucktes Trauerspiel'; if they paid any attention to this label they were likely to feel a little confused. And the term 'Schauspiel,' which would presumably have to be resorted to, is so vaporous that at best it does not help us, and at worst, becomes misleading, in suggesting the presence of spectacular elements which are not there. The use of the word

'Schauspiel'[35] as a technical term of dramatic classification stems from the last third of the eighteenth century, coined to fill the gap between tragedy and comedy, and reflects the dramaturgical upheavals of the age. One of the first plays to be so designated was Goethe's *Stella* (1776).[36]

The principal merit of Frye's theory of dramatic genres (see above, p 86), consists, to my mind, in its ability to allow for the grouping of transitional forms of dramatic writing around the basic concepts of tragedy and comedy. Thus there is less need to devise new classificatory headings for dramatic phenomena as elusive as *Iphigenie auf Tauris*. Fields (as the term is used in physics) rather than points are thus involved. The following quotations appear to me to be relevant to this 'Drama eines glückhaften Geschehens.'[37]

The further comedy moves from irony, the more it becomes what we here call ideal comedy, the vision not of the way of the world, but of what you will, life as you like it...

In New Comedy the absurd character who blocks the hero's desire is often the father ... Hence comedy often represents the defeat of the older generation by the younger one...[38]

These are fragmentary suggestions, but then we are not engaged in incarcerating *Iphigenie auf Tauris* firmly in a pigeon-hole labeled Comedy. But we are indeed dealing with a defeat of the older generation, is so far as it had affected the lives of the younger. This involves first the cessation of the curse upon the clan of the Tantalides, and second, the blotting out of the deeds of Agamemmon (i.e., the sacrifice of the daughter which is the cause of her confinement in Tauris) and of Clytemnestra (in the sense that she placed Orestes under the necessity of committing matricide). Next, Thoas is defeated in his desire to win Iphigenie, and finally (stretching the term 'older generation' somewhat), so are the gods who preside over the entire unhappy situation and do nothing to disentangle it.

One element in *Iphigenie auf Tauris* in particular may be termed comic without undue strain, and I take it to be an essential part of the play, rather than a convenient plot device. It is the revelation of the true sense of the oracle. In *Der Triumph der Empfindsamkeit* a seemingly undecipherable oracle had spread puzzlement and some confusion, and the final settlement was in part accompanied by, and in part brought about by, the decoding of a piece of apparent gibberish. In *Iphigenie auf Tauris* the situation is not altogether different. Apollo's command to return the sister to her rightful place, a potential source of bloodshed and tragedy, is finally decoded in such a way that those concerned – Thoas and Iphigenie – can acquiesce in it without loss of honour or prestige. The reduction of the divine sister to a human one represents the reduction of the problem to a negotiable one. 'Humanität,' 'reine Menschlichkeit,' which plays such a decisive rôle in the interpretation of *Iphigenie auf Tauris*, is, in its simplest and perhaps simple-minded sense, a determination to transact human affairs in human terms and among human beings. This takes much of the solemnity out of *Iphigenie auf Tauris*, but I would remind the reader in extenuation that we are dealing here with the first, prose version of the play, which even in the reading lacks some of the ethereal music of the final version and shows more of the earthy aspects of the drama. That Goethe was not satisfied with the play at this stage is made obvious by the protracted labour of revision begun so soon afterwards. But in the switch from prose to verse we can sense the resistance which the original version must have engendered. In any case, the latter versions of *Iphigenie auf Tauris* shed the 'occasional' character more and more, and are beyond the boundaries of the present investigation.

Transacting human affairs on human terms is the theme of a poem entitled 'Menschengefühl' which appears to have been written some years before,[39] but which would not be inappropriate as a motto of the first version of the play:

> Ach ihr Götter! grosse Götter
> In dem weiten Himmel droben!
> Gäbet ihr uns auf der Erde
> Festen Sinn und guten Muth;
> O wir liessen euch, ihr Guten,
> Eueren weiten Himmel droben!

The observation made earlier that the word as such, the deliberately expressed argument, functions as a dramatic agent in *Iphigenie auf Tauris* leads to one more glance at Frye's scheme. In the immediate vicinity of Ideal Comedy (which after all encompasses *The Tempest*), at 'the extreme limit of comedy,' he finds the symposium:

the structure of which is ... clearest in Plato ... whose vision moves toward an integration of society in a form like that of the symposium itself, the dialectic festivity which ... is the controlling force that holds society together.[40]

I believe that this characterization can be accepted as reflecting something of the spirit of the original *Iphigenie auf Tauris*.

Nothing that has been said about *Iphigenie auf Tauris* thus far ought to be considered in conflict with the traditional comments on Goethe's emerging classicism or with the 'Charlotte-ism' of the play. The purity of the central figure as the redeeming element, her Stoicism and religious surrender – these are no figments of critics' imagination. Yet the image of *Iphigenie auf Tauris* perhaps has been somewhat blurred by the incense of secular devotion. There is, it seems to me, a little more left of the Euripidean astuteness and rationality than is generally granted. The key word of the *Iphigenie* period, one which occurs often in Goethe's diary, too, is 'rein,' and it seems to me to require a broader interpretation than what is expressed in 'pure' or 'unsoiled' with the association of 'virginal.' When Goethe's use of the work is observed closely it is found also to carry the connotation of 'straightforward, unconfused, orderly, properly proportioned,' etc.; it is the sum of these meanings that made *Iphigenie auf Tauris* a suitable presentation for the court of its time.

It is comparatively insignificant, at this point, that the usual date for a court entertainment, i.e., Duchess Luise's birthday on 30 January 1779, had to and did go unobserved because of her approaching confinement. The nature of *Iphigenie* and the situation that commanded its composition are such that there was slight likelihood of Goethe's offering an elaborate production with particular reference to a birthday or to any one member of the court. His deliberate absence from Weimar on New Year's Day and his deliberately continued absence from that city during the following March bear this out. The concentration on his literary work at a time when his new governmental responsibilities claimed more of him than had been the case so far indicates that, at that point, Goethe regarded writing itself as a therapeutic activity, as a test of his powers and of his integrity. Thus we are dealing here with a 'chosen' occasion in the sense defined earlier. The creation of *Iphigenie auf Tauris* may be regarded as a conscious assumption of leadership on the part of Goethe, and the feeling of responsibility towards his own genius is clearly expressed by him in the letter to the duke in which he also mentions his deliberately chosen absence from a social event in Weimar two days before:

Bey dieser Gelegenheit seh ich doch auch dass ich diese gute Gabe der himmlischen ein wenig zu kavalier behandle und ich habe würcklich Zeit wieder häuslicher mit meinem Talent zu werden wenn ich ie noch was hervorbringen will.
  Nach Weimar wär ich vorgestern gern gekommen, es war mir vor der Zerstreuung bange.[8 March 1779, WA IV IV 21]

·5·
'Schule geselliger Empfindung'
1780–3

UP TO THIS POINT, it has seemed advisable to choose and discuss the works under consideration in chronological order. This procedure suggested itself naturally and is indicative of the relationship of Goethe's occasional poetry to his other writing, the borderlines between which were almost as blurred as in Goethe's much later characterization of his own work as altogether occasional. For the years 1780–6 it is possible to identify clearly distinct groups of works, and in doing so, a statement about these works, as well as about Goethe's productivity as a whole, is implied. The term 'specialization' is barely adequate in this connection, but it will serve as a prop until more substantial notions have taken its place. I shall deal altogether with three groups: the epigrams and related writings; the spectacles and works associable with them; and an uncomfortably miscellaneous category of poems dedicated to sociability as distinct from social ideals.

EPIGRAMS AND RELATED WRITINGS

The epigrams are few in number and more notable for their existence then for their substance. Their treatment at this point is not justified by their eminence, but rather by their proximity to *Iphigenie auf Tauris*. What little had been said and implied previously about Goethe's interest in Greek art and literature must serve here as the point of departure. The poetic method observed in the Hans Sachs poem of 1776 and tentatively described as 'visual,' 'statuesque,' or 'visionary' led, inevitably it seems now from hindsight, to an interest in Greek sculpture in relation to poetry. If the aims of *Iphigenie* were stated correctly above, then there was bound to be less and less room for figures like

> Ein altes Weiblein...
> Sie schleppt mit keichend-wankenden Schritten
> Eine grosse Tafel in Holz geschnitten;

whereas the vision of

> ... ein junges Weib,
> Mit voller Brust und rundem Leib,
> Kräftig sie auf den Füssen steht,
> Grad, edel vor sich hin sie geht, [WA i XVI 125
> and 123–4 resp.]

could easily find its counterpart in Greek art, although in this instance, in 'Hans Sachsens Poetische Sendung', it had had to be placed in an *imaginary* woodcut.

The gist of what has been found in *Iphigenie auf Tauris*, as related to Goethe's poetry for occasions, was that there is a specific conjunction of the power of the word and of the vision (*tableau*) for therapeutic and didactic use which created a public occasion of its own without reference to the 'secular' calendar. All this may find application in the consideration of the epigrams of 1782 and 1783, if it is emphasized from the outset that Goethe treated them literally as such, i.e., that at least some of them were carved on tablets and placed in positions where they were unlikely to overlooked. This applies to 'Geweihter Platz' 'Erwählter Fels,' 'Ländliches Glück,' 'Philomele', and 'Erkanntes Glück' (WA i II 126–8). As for 'Was ich leugnend gestehe' and 'Felsen sollten nicht Felsen' (WA i IV 119–20) of 1784, Goethe expressed the intention of having them carved on tablets (to Ch. von Stein, 23–4 June 1784, WA IV VI 310), although this was not done. How serious the intention actually was at that point is not easily ascertained. But in the cases of epigrams actually displayed in stone Goethe's purpose is made altogether clear by his refusal to allow F.L. von Stolberg to publish them in a *Musenalmanach*: 'Sie sollen noch nicht ins Publicum kommen, um an ihrer Stelle mehr zu wirken.'[1] In passing, it must be mentioned that the display of epigrams is connected with the work on the parks of Weimar and Tiefurt which went on during this period. It is not very helpful to speculate as to whether the tablets would otherwise not have appeared; the fact that they are located in the park, however, bears on their contents and must be taken into consideration.

Before these poems are examined, however, one must be added to their number which, because it stands apart, might help to clarify the characteristics of the group. 'Wandrers Nachtlied' (Ueber allen Gipfeln'; WA i I 98) is not written in the elegiac metre and precedes Goethe's interest in the conventional epigram by some time. And

'Schule geselliger Empfindung' 75

yet, even if we did not know that Goethe recorded it on the wall of the shack on the Gickelhahn (6 September 1780) – not, presumably for the lack of writing paper – we would have to grant a kinship with the classical epigram, indeed with the epitaph which addresses the stranger and establishes a significant relationship, a harmony between the object (there the buried person, here nature) and himself. The epitaph does not merely beg for remembrance as a commemorative sign. It is also a gift of the silent individual to another person for the enrichment of his existence. In 'Wandrers Nachtlied II' the poet performs this function on behalf of silent nature. And each time this mutual giving and taking (i.e., the articulation of nature and the comfort that the wanderer derives from its message) takes place, the poet has created an occasion. If there should be any primitive magic in the original function of the epigram, then a trace of it may be said to have survived into Goethe's time.[2]

A touch of preservative or protective magic presumably adheres to all monuments and a full consideration of those associated with Goethe would linger over the one to $\alpha\gamma\alpha\vartheta\eta\ \tau\upsilon\chi\eta$ erected in front of the Gartenhaus in April 1777 (cf. diary entry for 5 April). Its altogether abstract and non-discursive complexion (cube with sphere) places it at the periphery of the phenomena that interest us here. We are closer to the aspect of Goethe's imagination relevant in the present context when we consider the plan of a commemorative monument which Goethe outlined during the Swiss journey of 1779–80 in a letter to Lavater written towards the end of November 1779. Here the plastic element far outweighs the verbal, but this helps us to recognize the allegorical potentialities inherent in this cluster of conceptions which is to become so important for Goethe's later occasional poetry. The description of the three figures, Fortuna, Genius, and Terminus, is worth quoting in the present context (and for later use in a different one) because their *epitheta* could so easily have been precipitated into an occasional poem. Goethe's explanation of his choice also reads like raw material for such a work. Especially relevant are the expressions of the poet's faith in the possibility of perpetuating a salutary moment (i.e., the journey) by these means:

Von drei Seiten sollte iede eine einzelne bedeutende Figur und die vierte eine Innschrifft haben. Zuförderst sollte das gute heilsame Glük stehen durch das die Schlachten gewonnen und die Schiffe regiret werden, günstigen Wind im Naken, die Launische Freundinn und Belohnerinn keker

76 Goethe's Poetry for Occasions

Unternehmungen mit Steuerruder und Kranz, im Felde zur Rechten hatte ich mir den Genius, den Antreiber, Wegmacher, Wegweiser, Fakelträger mutigen Schrittes gedacht. In dem Felde zur lincken sollte *Terminus* der ruhige Gränzbeschreiber, der bedächtige mäsige Rathgeber stillstehend mit dem Schlangenstabe einen Gränzstein bezeichnen. Jener lebend rührig vordringend, dieser ruhend sanft, in sich gekehrt zwey Söhne einer Mutter der ältere iener der iüngere dieser. Das hinterste Feld hatte die Inschrifft:

>   Fortunae
>   Duci reduci
>   natisque
>   Genio
>   et
>   Termino
>   ex Voto.

Du siehst was ich vor Ideen dadurch zusammenbinden wollte. Es sind keine Geheimnisse noch tiefe Räzel, aber sowohl auf dieser Reise als im ganzen Leben, sind wir diesen Gottheiten sehr zu Schuldnern geworden. Das erstemal dass wir nach einer langen nicht immer fröhligen Zeit aus dem Loche in die freye Welt kommen, zusammen den ersten bedeutenden Schritt wagen, gleich mit dem schönsten Hauche des Glücks fortgetrieben zu werden, in der späten Jahrszeit alles mit günstiger Sonne und Gestirnen. Den ganzen Weeg den wir machen begleitet von einem guten Geiste der überall die Fackel vorträgt hierhin lockt dorthin treibt dass wenn ich zurücksehe wir, zu so manchem das unsre reise ganz macht nicht durch unsern Wiz und Wollen geleitet worden sind...

After appealing for Lavater's aid in turning over the project to Fuessli, who is to be given a completely free hand, Goethe concludes:

Sieh, ob du etwas über ihn vermagst und ob du, der fröhlichen Zeiten, die wir wieder belebt haben, immer gegenwärtiges Siegel dadurch, auf unsere Rechnung druken kannst ... Welchen Preiss er auch auf diese Arbeit sezen möge ist völlig einerlei. Nun ist aber noch ein Hauptpunkt nemlich die Geschwindigkeit. Ich wünsche es diesen Winter fertig zu kriegen und auf das Frühiahr zum ersten Willkomm mit den Blüthen und Blättern aufzustellen. Versuche also, ich bitte dich deine Wunderkräfte um mir zu verschaffen was nicht ein eitler Wunsch ist. Schaff dass er es macht und schnell macht und kröne mir auch dies Jahr und sein Glük mit diesem lezten Zeichen. [WA IV IV 143-4, 146]

'Schule geselliger Empfindung' 77

The tendencies illustrated by 'Wandrers Nachtlied II' and the monument project solidified themselfes in the mould which Goethe found in the epigrams of the Greek Anthology. There are few remarks by Goethe himself on this subject. The placing of the inscriptions would seem to have been done under his personal supervision, and there are no written utterances on his part which would indicate that he considered them at all important. Only the three letters to von Diede (15 July, 8 August, and 12 October 1782, Gräf VII pp 78, 80, 81), which deal with the composition of the epigram 'Was die gute Natur...' and the details of the placing of the tablet, give us an idea of the attention he paid to the visual aspects of these matters. In the correspondence with Knebel, in which court affairs are always treated with a certain ironic detachment, we find a short remark:

... Du sollst auch alle die kleinen Sachen haben mit denen ich mir das Leben würze, ich bin nun auch in den Geschmack der Inschrifften/Epigramms gekommen, und es werden bald die Steine zu reden anfangen. [17 April 1782, WA iv v 313]

But his interest shows clearly nevertheless in the fact that he takes the trouble to copy out a Latin epitaph in the same letter. To be sure, epigrammizing seems to have taken on the character of a fad after a short while ('hier werden Inschriften geheckt und gesetzt')[3] and the presence of B.G. de Villoison, the French academician, antiquarian, and occasional poet who spent over a year at the court in 1782–3, would appear to have been responsible, to some extent, for this pastime. Nevertheless there is some evidence of the genuineness of the epigrammatic impulse as sketched above.

We may assume that Herder's essay on the epigram which appeared in the *Zerstreute Blätter*[4] of 1785 contains ideas shared by Goethe in the early eighties. It accompanied Herder's translations from the Greek Anthology, which had accumulated over considerable time. It is true that closer contact between the two men was not re-established until 1783,[5] but Herder expresses so clearly what has ben found here to have motivated Goethe's interest in the form that his words are not out of place. He speaks thus of the social significance of the publicly-displayed work:

Die schönsten Gegenden Griechenlands bezeichneten Altäre der Götter und Heroen; auf den schönsten Höhen unsrer Länder steht das einzige öffentliche Denkmal, darum sich der Geist unsrer Gesetzgebung bekümmert, Galgen und Räder. [p 215]

After enlarging on the happy articulateness (or garrulousness, 'Geschwätzigkeit') of the Greeks and their possession of the impulse to utilize occasions of any kind, Herder speaks of the suitability of the Greek language and its visual expression, the alphabet:

> Dieser Liebe zu reden, auch auf öffentlichen Denkmälern zu reden, kam nun ihre *Sprache* so sehr zu statten, das Musen und Grazien sie dazu gleichsam ausgedacht zu haben scheinen. Ich schweige der einfachen Buchstaben und der sanften Mischung von Vokalen und Consonanten, die auch auf Denkmälern eine Aufschrift so lesbarer macht, als es die Unsre nie werden kann; ich will hier nur vom poetischen Wohlklange derselben zur Inschrift reden. [p 217]

And finally, Herder enlarges on the 'therapeutic' function of the genre:

> Endlich das sanfte Maass der *Menschlichkeit* ... Die Seele des griechischen Epigramms ist Mitempfindung. Man muss einen Gegenstand geniessen, ihn mit Liebe oder Ruhe anschauen, ihn gleichsam mit und durchempfinden können, damit er in und aus uns rede; auch hierinn, wie in Manchem andern, ist die Poesie eine Schwester der griechischen Kunst. Sowohl zur Hervorbringung als zum Genuss beider ist jene Ruhe, jenes stille Mitgefühl, kurz eine sanftumschriebene heitere Existenz nöthig ... Allem theilt sich dies Gefühl der Humanität mit, allem, was den Menschen umgiebt, was ihn erfreuet oder quält, was ihn lehrt, oder was ihm dienet ... selbst unbelebte Wesen werden mit Liebe belebet. Für den sanftern Menschen sind also diese kleinen Gedichte eine Schule geselliger Empfindung, und wie manches hätten wir auch sonst in den Besten derselben zu lernen! – [p 218]

The expression 'Schule geselliger Empfindung' is an apt heading for more than the rather limited exercises in epigraphy of the time. Organized sociability assumed various shapes in the pre-Italian Weimar years. The anatomical lectures of 1781–2 are one example. The reading group which was formed for the study of Abbé Raynal's *Histoire philosophique des Indes* and met three times a week is another. Goethe mentions this group immediately after referring to park epigrams intended for carving, possibly a significant association of news (to Knebel, 5 May 1782, WA iv v 319–20). But the most conspicuous manifestation of organized sociability during these years is the *Journal von Tiefurt*. Only Goethe's share in this enterprise is of interest here, which actually reduces itself to 'Auf Miedings Tod,' the one genuinely occasional contribution.

The summer of 1781 was the first which Anna Amalia spent in Tiefurt, and this removal to a congenial environment can, with only slight exaggeration, be regarded as a quiet secession, with the *Journal von Tiefurt*, as it were, functioning as a manifesto.[6] We cannot expect to find any direct expression of the reasons for this move, which can only have been motivated by reactions to the younger duchess and her circle. For reasons external and internal, political and personal, Goethe could not identify himself fully with this circle. The style of sociability cultivated by it was one that conveyed to him echoes of earlier pre-Weimarian groupings, the tentative counter-court of Darmstadt on the one hand, the hearty sociability of the Frankfurt period on the other. The prize question, 'Wie ist eine unoccupirte Gesellschaft für die Langeweile zu bewahren?' and the series of answers to it (JVT 2, 9, 26, 31) could as easily have fitted into the Frankfurt milieu. It seems possible that the generous tribute to Goethe on his birthday contained in Seckendorff's 'Schattenspiel,' *Minervens Geburt*, the first dramatic presentation given at Tiefurt, served, consciously or otherwise, the aim of drawing Goethe more closely into the group. It is also reasonable to assume that the publication of Goethe's satirical epigram on Klopstock, 'Er und sein Nahme,' in the eighth issue of the *Journal von Tiefurt* (JVT 72, although probably written in the previous year) was fostered by the existence of a circle willing to smile at Klopstock's name and activities. The non-participation of Duchess Luise, a loyal admirer of Klopstock, may help to characterize the function of the *Journal*. In passing, it is also necessary to refer to Goethe's 'Der Becher' (JVT 75) and the question as to whether it ought to be regarded as an occasional poem, the occasion being the surrender of Charlotte von Stein.[7] Whatever the answer may be, the *Journal von Tiefurt* played a peculiar rôle in connection with this poem because there is some evidence that Goethe allowed it to reach Charlotte's eyes only through the pages of the *Journal*, an unusual procedure for him.

A less elusive problem, and the most important in connection with the *Journal von Tiefurt*, is raised by the appearance in it of 'Auf Miedings Tod.' Put in the simplest terms, the question would be: was this poem written for the *Journal*, of which it took up an entire issue, the twenty-third (at a time, to be sure, when the contributions had shrunk and there was far less variety in a single issue than earlier), and do we therefore owe it to the existence of the *Journal*?

While a negative answer to the question in this form can be offered without quoting chapter and verse, this does not mean that we must or can isolate 'Auf Miedings Tod' from the chronological or social moment in which it appeared. But if these relationships are to be adequately explored, the 'Maskenzüge' of 1781 and 1782 must first claim our attention.

MASQUES AND RELATED WORKS

As if to illustrate the social division of Weimar under its two duchesses, there were performed at the beginning of 1781 two small masques, each of which shows clearly the social tone prevailing around one personality or the other. *Epiphaniasfest* (WA i 1 149–50), which was given at the amateur musicale on the Feast of the Epiphany (6 January) and was followed by a supper to which Anna Amalia invited Wieland, Knebel, and Corona Schröter (WA iii 1 127), is in every way representative of the tastes of the hostess. It is slightly 'subversive' (in the mildest sense of the word) insofar as it thumbs its nose gently at the existing order, and the text is a paraphrase of the traditional text of the boys' *Sternsingen*, which had taken place on the streets of Weimar until it was banned by the police authority, presumably as a public nuisance (cf. JA I 335). *Epiphaniasfest* may also be termed subversive in the sense that the religious sensibilities of persons less detached than Anna Amalia or the poet or Wieland could be offended by the representation of the Three Kings as amiable vagrants. Goethe at least seems to have felt that he owed Lavater an explanation that could be taken as an apology: 'Dass ich den Glauben eines Teils der Welt, sogut als des andern, als Fabelfrazzen im Possenspiel tracktire. Verzeih mir, ich bin nun so' (18 March 1781, WA iv v 88). Appropriate, too, to this environment, as it would have been impossible in the other sphere, is the lighthearted handling of rank:

> Da wir nun hier schöne Herrn und Fraun,
> Aber keine Ochsen und Esel schaun;
> So sind wir nicht am rechten Ort
> Und ziehen unseres Weges weiter fort.

By contrast, Goethe's contribution to the *Geburtstagsredoute* of 2 February 1781, on which the birthday of Duchess Luise was celebrated, was the most formal poetic tribute he had as yet paid to the court since his arrival in Weimar. The exoticism of *Ein Zug Lappländer zum 30. Januar, 1781* (WA i XVI 189–90) is on the one hand in keeping with the style of the masquerade as a whole, during which the duke and others performed a Moorish dance;[8] on the other, it permits the perennial device of symbolizing the high universal prestige of the person addressed. In fact, we find here an elegant variation of the old hyperbole of the ruler outshining the sun, unrelieved, as I read it, by even a small portion of the tongue in cheek:

> Doch jenem hochverehrten Lichte
> Raubt deine Gegenwart die Pracht
> Es glänzt von Deinem Angesichte
> Die Huld, die uns dir eigen macht.

This characterization of the poem is not entirely just, however, since it does not convey the suggestive power of the natural phenomenon described, the aurora borealis. In this respect the present poem anticipates what is most remarkable in some of the later masques (e.g., *Planetentanz*), viz., the fusion of nature and social poetry. Indeed, the second stanza of the poem permits a long glance ahead to the masquerade of the *Divan*:

> Wir preisen jene Lufterscheinung;
> Sie weiht die Nacht zu Freuden ein
> Und muss, nach unsrer aller Meinung,
> Der Abglanz einer Gottheit sein. [ll 5–8]

Aufzug des Winters (WA i XVI 191–4), which followed a fortnight later (16 February 1781), is not dedicated to an individual member of the court, but to the institution as such. It is incomplete insofar as we do not possess the concluding 'Lobgesang,' which Goethe had written and for which music had been composed, because 'die Sänger habens nicht können lernen' (to Ch. von Stein, 15 February 1781, WA iv v 53). This, incidentally, is the first instance of many to come of the vicissitudes of staging a masque, of organizing, dressing, and drilling a group of amateurs whose eagerness and abilities must have varied greatly. Goethe rarely bore his troubles as uncomplainingly as in this case. It seems safe to say that the panegyric referred to the assembly as a whole and the forces that hold it together because this is the subject of the portion we possess. If there is a single 'point' conveyed by the procession, I have been unable to seize it. Whether the joint appearance of Goethe and Charlotte von Stein as Sleep and Night was really so potentially compromising as to make it the cause of Goethe's opposition to any publicity (*if* the letter to Carl August expressing such opposition belongs to this year and refers to this work at all, as Düntzer assumes and Gräf denies[9]), is an exceedingly elusive question. There is no question, however, that in all these specifically courtly entertainments there are topical references, little private allusions and jokes, that can only be placed by guesswork, if at all. For instance, the person alluded to in 'Doch einen, dem ich immer treu geblieben / den find ich nicht,' could refer to an absent member of the court just as easily as to Prince Constantin himself, who spoke the part.

Much as it might contribute to our understanding of the spirit of this and similar works, the exploration of allusive passages needs to be subordinated to a quest for the total effect sought by the poet, which is likely to become apparent from an observation of the relationship of the component parts to the whole of the production. If no other justification for this procedure existed, the intentions of the poet would encourage it. In the letter to the duke mentioned above, which in any case deals with one masque or the other, Goethe stressed the desirability of the retention by the spectators of the work in its entirety. This would of course include the visual and aural impressions, and, at the same time, indirectly discourage detailed analysis of the text. Goethe almost invariably added this caveat in letters accompanying the texts of the much more ambitious products of this sort in the 1800s ('Der grösste Reiz wird bey aller Ueberlieferung das *unaussprechliche* bleiben, die Imagination wird arbeiten...', WA IV V 271).

In *Aufzug des Winters* we encounter three phases: the first includes the speeches of 'Schlaf,' 'Nacht,' and 'Träume'; the second is dominated by 'Winter,' who is escorted by 'Spiel,' 'Wein,' 'Liebe,' 'Tragödie,' and 'Komödie,' the pastimes appropriate to that season; the third phase introduces 'Karneval,' the culmination of winter, accompanied by silent figures representing the humours and followed by four couples in the traditional masks ('Spanier und Spanierin,' 'Scapin und Scapine,' 'Pierrot und Pierotte,' and 'Ein Paar in Tabarros'). 'Studium,' bringing up the rear, does not appear to have a function that could be related to the organization of the procession as given here. To him must be assigned the rôle of an

'Schule geselliger Empfindung' 83

ironic epilogue, the Fool, as it were, who by teasing the audience shakes the authority of the masks established previously: 'Verstündet ihr wohl unsern Witz, / hätt' ichs nicht aufgeschrieben?'[10] The poet would seem to suggest that the rule of the masks, the transformation of society into a disguised, collective entity, brings about an ideal harmonization and an innocent spontaneity of behaviour not otherwise attainable. The first three figures represent forces that are remote from this desirable condition because they exert their effect on the individual in isolation. In this capacity they may be beneficent, as is Sleep ('Ein treuer Freund'), neutral, as is Night ('Der Menschen Freund und Feind'), or arbitrary and potentially hostile, as are Dreams ('Wir können eine ganze Welt ... betrügen'). They are in any case divisive from a social point of view and beyond the control of man; they enslave him in a fashion. This effect applies also to the pleasures marshaled by Winter, which, as the object of celebration, is naturally a beneficent power within the framework of sociability. Winter, a natural force, says:

> Ich nur, ich weiss euch zu verbinden,
> Dess bin ich mir bewusst.
> Vor meinen Stürmen fliehet ihr
> Und suchet eures Gleichen. [ll 17–20]

Yet the pastimes of winter are as divisive as they are unifying. This is true chiefly of games and love, but also to some extent of wine as well (e.g., in the isolating effects of intoxication). There is also a certain parallelism evident among the several elements of the first two groups. Wine resembles sleep in its effect on the state of man's consciousness. Games and love are as capricious as dreams. And games, like night, may act as the friend or enemy of man. All the forces so far mentioned bring either a measure of conflict or a flight from the daylight of reality, and the next figure, Tragedy, embodies this most conspicuously:

> Und euren tiefbewegten Herzen
> Sind Thränen Freude, Schmerzen Lust. [ll 37–8]

This confusion of reality has been expressed up to this point by the liberal use of antithetical figures of speech: 'gefürchtet und geliebt,' 'erschrecken und vergnügen,' 'darin muss der Sommer mir mit seiner Schönheit weichen,' 'manch bekannt Gesicht, doch Einen dem ich immer treu geblieben, den find ich nicht,' 'gerne geben meine Fässer, nehmen gerne wieder ein,' 'so jung ich bin, mich kennen doch die Alten schon lang.' Next, after the crowning paradox of Tragedy, Comedy inaugurates the evocation of the desirable condition of social freedom which Carnival desires to be reflected in 'Fröhliche Gesichter,' 'vergnügtes Herz,' and 'Gunst.' In exhibiting the four humours paired off and forced to form a whole, Carnival exhibits his power:

> Und mit Weinen oder Lachen
> Müssen sie Gesellschaft machen. [ll 53–4]

But this tyranny of the season over human behaviour, the trappings of the celebration ('viele Lichter,' 'Tanz und Scherz,' / 'Pracht und buntes Leben') does not in itself constitute the desired triumph – it merely serves to bring about the transformation of the members of society, their liberation from the caprices of their entertainments and personalities. This is made explicit at least by the first of the masked couples: 'Vor dem bunten Schwarme flieht / Die Melancholei.' But it can be extended, too, I believe, to the qualities displayed by the other masks: the 'List' and 'feinen Künste' of Scapin and Scapine represent the emancipation of society from phlegmatic submission to the arbitrary dictates of dreams and games of chance; the attributes of 'treu und gut' for Pierrot and Pierrotte suggest a disposition that has overcome divisive choler; and the mask of the Tabarro, with its association of nobility, conveys the image of a society that is sufficiently harmonious to be capable of being genuinely represented by two individuals.

> Um noch zuletzt mit Einem Paar
> Die Menge vorzustellen. [ll 69–70]

Furthermore, the transformation of society by and into masks suggests a detachment from the rigidity of caste. The stock characters of the *commedia dell'arte*, rootless and unencumbered by 'face,' draw those who wear their distinguishing dress out of the confinement of their position. The use of these masks could thus be regarded as a variation on and refinement of traditional entertainments such as 'Wirtschaften' and pastoral disguises, in which a make-believe descent on the social ladder takes place (see above, pp 32–4).

'Schule geselliger Empfindung' 85

While the moving forces which prompted the production of *Aufzug des Winters* cannot be clearly traced, there is no lack of evidence pointing to the unique concentration of festive poetry that Goethe supplied during the first two months of the following year, 1782. The calendar reads as follows: 18 January participation in the pantomimic ballet, *Die Entführung*; 30 January Goethe's elaborate 'Pantomimisches Ballett untermischt mit Gesang und Gespräch,' *Der Geist der Jugend*; 1 February *Die weiblichen Tugenden*; 4 February probably participation in a reprise of *Das Neueste von Plundersweilern*; 6 February repeat performance of *Der Geist der Jugend* and possibly of *Aufzug des Winters*; and 12 February, performance of *Aufzug der Vier Weltalter*.

That these were onerous days for Goethe could easily be documented in the letters to Charlotte von Stein if documentation were needed. That this burden was intentionally shouldered and carried is made clear in Goethe's words to Knebel that sum up the festivities:

Unser Carnaval ist zu meinem grossen Vergnügen endlich auch vorbey. Ich habe viel ausgestanden, da ich mich, aus alten und neuen Ursachen, dienstfertig erwiess und verschiedene Aufzüge erfand und besorgte ... So viel von der glänzenden Schaale unsers Daseyns, das Innere ist im Alten, nur dass mit einem immerwährenden Wechsel, sich das eine Capitel verschlimmert, indem sich das andere verbessert. [26 February 1782, WA iv v 272–3]

This sounds considerably more deliberate and 'political,' far less apologetic, than what he had written almost exactly a year before to Lavater about his contributions to that social season:

Die lezten Tage der vorigen Woche hab ich im Dienste der Eitelkeit zugebracht. Man übertäubt mit Maskeraden und glänzenden Erfindungen offt eigne und fremde Noth. Ich tracktire diese Sachen als Künstler und so gehts noch ... Wie du die Feste der Gottseeligkeit ausschmückst so schmück ich die Aufzüge der Thorheit. Es ist billich, dass beyde Damen ihre Hofpoeten haben. [19 February 1781, WA iv v 56]

When due allowance for the different personalities of the recipients is made, it must still be pointed out that the comparative detachment of the words addressed to Knebel continues a mood which can be traced through at least the entire preceding winter. It is one of a not altogether convincing (because so often expressed) adjustment to the exigencies of his position in the life of Weimar. The key word all along is 'einrichten' which, not coincidentally, applies to the general *accommodation* to the situation with its human and administrative imperfections, as well as to the activity of *arranging* these pageants which, in a more literal way, also involves putting the various members of the court in their proper places. That this is at best a temporary agility needs no elaboration. Even while contemplating his situation, Goethe is forced into the paradoxical description of it as 'eng-weit,' as one 'wo die manigfaltigen Fasern meiner Existenz alle durchgebeizt werden können und müssen' (to Knebel, 3 February 1782, WA iv v 257). One must also take into account the circumstance that Goethe was bound to be somewhat sensitive to the reaction of his friends to his rôle as *directeur de plaisir*. Herder's scornful reference[11] to this rôle a few months later, when Goethe took over the financial direction of the duchy, was probably neither the earliest nor the most immoderate one.

Diversification of activity had been highly characteristic of the previous months, what with the addition of anatomical studies to the geological ones, the political missions first to Gotha and later, in 1782, to other courts, as well as work on *Tasso* and *Wilhelm Meisters Theatralische Sendung*, works which were surely not altogether set aside although references to them are meagre. One is almost tempted to believe in a conscious avoidance of Tasso's artistic monomania and perfectionism. (It may be noted here that, in contrast to *Iphigenie*, the project of a performance of *Tasso* at court seems never to have entered Goethe's mind during the writing of it.)

The masque *Die weiblichen Tugenden* (WA i XVI 197) is in most aspects the counterpart of *Ein Zug Lappländer* of the year before. It was also addressed to the Duchess Luise on the 'Redoute' closest to her birthday (1 February 1782). Again, the tribute is quite different from the hearty, yet respectful, familiarity that characterized Goethe's contact with the other members of the ruling family. The recipient here is treated as a remote, tutelary divinity to be approached and revered in whispers. The poem was not spoken at all, but handed on a silk ribbon to the duchess by the most congenial of the Virtues, 'Bescheidenheit.' And the poem itself whispers with its accumulation of sibilants and front vowels and diphthongs: 'Und dein Wille / heisst uns stille / wirkend schweigen.'

The choice of metre in *Die weiblichen Tugenden* also calls for comment. This short, dipodic line, which has been referred to as the operatic line, had been used by Goethe in *Lila* to carry the message of encouragement from a higher, that is, the fairy world ('Feiger Gedanken / bängliches Schwanken,' 'Sei nicht beklommen / Sei uns Willkommen' WA i XII 62, 63). It is particularly suited for use in choral texts because short phrases aid comprehensibility as well as accuracy of phrasing by a group of singers. It is almost indispensable when a continual pianissimo is desired, since short phrases aid the singers in breath control. The best-known use of this device is found in the Faust scene 'Studierzimmer [I],' where the chorus of spirits employs it so successfully in the soporific pianissimo 'Schwindet ihr dunkeln / Wölbungen droben!' that it earns special recognition from Mephistopheles: 'Ihr habt ihn treulich eingesungen! / Für diess Concert bin ich in eurer Schuld.' It is possible that there is some connection, too, between the length of the lines and their intended use on the silk ribbons on which they were presented to the duchess and distributed (cf. WA i XVI 442ff). This may represent an element of convention rather than of necessity, however, because the poem 'Amor,' which was likewise presented to the duchess imprinted on a ribbon at the conclusion of another work of 1782, *Pantomimisches Ballett*, consists of lines of greater length.

Pantomimisches Ballett (which has become known as *Geist der Jugend* – a title not, it seems, of Goethe's making)[12] occupies an exceptional position in the series of court entertainments of 1782, as well as in the canon of Goethe's court productions as a whole. It is distinguished for placing extreme emphasis on the spectacular element rather than on the dramatic, while yet retaining the dialogue. The classification of *comédie-ballet* which occurs in the descriptions of the event to friends abroad[13] is apt only as a technical term. The function of the dialogue of Zaubrer and Zauberin is solely expository and the action itself is developed through dances and music. We are thus dealing with a form that stands halfway between spectacular comedy like *Der Triumph der Empfindsamkeit* and the 'Maskenzüge' proper, in which later works the task of exposition is often given over to a commentator such as the herald. The uniqueness of *Pantomimisches Ballett* must in some way be connected with unusual circumstances that caused Goethe to have contributed so much poetry to the social season of 1782. The exact circumstances are likely to remain obscure, but it does not seem to be an overly bold guess to adduce considerations that lie beyond the range of entertainment or of the expression of personal devotion.

As far as I can tell, the preparations for *Pantomimisches Ballett* go back beyond the time usually given over to the preparations for the birthday season. It was probably outlined as early as the first week of December in a letter to Charlotte von Stein (4 December 1781 [?], WA IV V 231). The rehearsals were numerous and Goethe was present at them more often than was his custom. The expenses were high: over 690 thaler, and 62 hours of ballet rehearsals (Düntzer, p. 17). Considering this expense of money and time in the context of the deliberate attempts to establish closer relations with neighbouring courts (which include Goethe's travels to these courts in December 1781, and again in March and April 1782; the large, if rather unsuccessful hunting party at the end of December; the probable presence at the *Ballett* of Duke Friedrich and Prince August of Saxe-Gotha; and Goethe's repeated assurances that the festivities were necessary evils) I feel justified in stressing the probable political significance of the *Ballett*. What adds to this impression is the observation that, relatively speaking, the *Ballett* is an importation, is less specifically 'Weimarian' in character than previous or later entertainments. There is a ready-made quality about it which would render it more accessible to an audience that was not thoroughly steeped in local tradition of self-glorification tinged with, and relieved by, self-mockery.

Pantomimic ballet is an art form of mixed ancestry. We can clearly discern the strain deriving from *opera seria* with its elaborate stage machinery employed for climatic effects. Goethe's stage direction is explicit:

im Augenblicke verwandelt sich alles, das ganze Theater stellt einen prächtigen Saal vor, der Zauberer und die Zauberin, alle tanzende Personen des Stücks werden verjüngt und verwandelt ... Die Schnelligkeit und Akkuratesse womit dieses alles geschieht, giebt der Entwicklung ihren ganzen Werth. [WA I XVI 451]

But this stiff, courtly material is distinctly tempered by the more popular of the 'Zauberposse' of Viennese extraction which, in turn, proved capable of blending with the Italian and French popular comedy. And, finally, the *Ballett* partakes of the vogue of putting children on the stage. The majority of the participants seem to have been children.[14]

In considering an appeal to an audience of 'outsiders' as an explanation of the unusual features of *Pantomimisches Ballett*, we can still take into account Duchess Luise for the reasons already noted frequently. It is rather touching to read about her reaction to so Weimarian an offering as Goethe's *Die Vögel*. She could simply not discover what people were laughing about so heartily and urged her correspondent not to disclose her bewilderment.[15] Without being able to offer tangible proof, I believe that the 'political' background of the work is an attempt at creating an atmosphere of confidence in the stability of the duchy, and particularly the worthiness of the mining project of Ilmenau, which depended on the good will of the surrounding states as much as on domestic exertions. This possibility is by no means incompatible with a tribute to the ruling lady of the realm. In fact, her personality and the quality of steady devotion which is apostrophized in the final poem were probably the most eloquent antidote to the reputation of irresponsibility which had become attached to Carl August's court in the first years of his rule. The 'argument' of *Pantomimisches Ballett* is, after all, the recovery of a precious jewel ('grosser glänzender Stein'), and its premise is the ability to subject the reluctant guardians of the deep, the gnomes, to the will of the terrestrial majesties at the proper time. The idea of time evolving and maturing and redeeming seems to me to be the principal device in the establishment of confidence. I have stated this aspect of the matter much more bluntly than the text of the work warrants, of course. We are not dealing with a piece of clumsy propaganda, but in order to make visible distinctive features, the 'political' overtones of this work must be put into relief. The attainment of maturity by the quarrelsome pair, Zaubrer and Zauberin, at a moment pre-established by 'der grosse Geist' through the inconspicuously healing action of time, and the subsequent exemption of the protagonists from the workings of time through rejuvenation, constitute the first and most direct expression of what was to become the principal theme of Goethe's occasional poetry during the remaining pre-Italian years. The *Aufzug der Vier Weltalter* of only a few days later is so obviously a case in point that it requires no elaborate treatment at this stage. But the considerably more skilled use of this theme in 'Ilmenau,' of a year and a half later, deserves notice.

'Ilmenau am 3. September 1783' (WA i II 141–7) is an occasional poem in a less direct sense of the word. It celebrates a 'chosen' occasion since the duke's birthday had gone unobserved during all the preceding years. Therefore its links with the *Ballett*, a work of much more conventional occasionality, are of interest. The Ilmenau of the poem is the site of life in nature (the scene of the hunt), unfolding above the elusive presence of subterranean treasure (the mine). Thus it may be thought of as the meeting place of diversion and purposeful activity. Yet, it could be merely a coincidence that in *Pantomimisches Ballett* the treasure is raised with the aid of spirits indigenous to each region: nymphs and gnomes. But the theme of youth that connects the two works is too important to be coincidental.

> O lass mich heut an deinen sachten Höhn
> Ein jugendlich, ein neues Eden sehn! [ll 9–10]

The magic sphere that was unquestioningly accepted in *Ballett* appears now with punctuation appropriate to a different attitude:

> Wo bin ich? ists ein Zaubermärchen-Land?
> ...
> Ist es der Jäger wildes Geisterheer?
> Sinds Gnomen, die hier Zauberkünste treiben? [ll 35, 47–8]

Inevitably, this leads to the rejection of magic. There is no 'magic moment' that will reverse time; instead there is in the end an acceptance of the rhythm of nature:

> ... streue klug wie reich, mit männlich steter Hand,
> Den Segen aus auf ein geackert Land;
> Dann lass es ruhn: die Ernte wird erscheinen
> Und dich beglücken und die Deinen. [ll 188–91]

Without suggesting that the poet of 'Ilmenau' is contradicting or correcting the author of the *Ballett*, I think that the juxtaposition of these two works strengthens the impression that the functional aspects of the latter place it in a position apart from the mainstream of Goethe's other court entertainments. Apart in some ways and at the beginning in others. Wilhelm Emrich has traced the function of the closed container in Goethe's work from the 'Goldkiste' in *Faust* II through works such as *Die Natürliche Tochter, Die Wahlverwandtschaften, Pandora,* and *Der Zauberflöte Zweiter Teil,* demonstrating how the secretness and mysteriousness of the contents and the manner and timing of the opening of these boxes, cases, cabinets, caskets, etc., became a most subtle and meaningful

'Schule geselliger Empfindung' 91

device in Goethe's hands.[16] In this respect, the *Ballett* represents the interesting moment of the introduction of a device which will remain permanently in the poet's collection of devices and situations, although he was probably unaware of the potentialities of his choice at the time it was made. A similar observation is valid in regard to the future use of the subterranean sphere in connection with political symbolism. Again, compared with the extreme refinement of these images in the first act of *Faust* II, their treatment in the *Ballett* strikes one as almost crude. Yet, as far as Goethe's work is concerned – and it should not be forgotten that Goethe was by no means the only one to make use of them – the beginnings are found in one of the most conventional of his works, and one almost totally ignored.

Emrich's observations are all the more valuable inasmuch as they help us to gain a much more comprehensive view of the workings of the poet's imagination than had been possible with a critical attitude of barely concealed boredom or contempt towards what Gundolf called Goethe's 'Amtspflichten.'[17] Thus the scornful evaluation of parts of Goethe's production – one reflected in some remarks by Herder and understandable there in the context of the stresses and strains of contemporary tensions – is being replaced by an unprejudiced appraisal. With the not-too-revolutionary conviction that the same personality and the same technician was at work in all of them, Emrich examined not only these minor works but also those parts of the major ones that had produced chiefly critical cringing or averted eyes, and the results have been most illuminating.

These considerations do not require us to be blind to the very real causes of friction brought about by the performance of official duties. Some of the relevant utterances have been quoted at the beginning of the survey of the works written in 1782. They can be multiplied several times over through the 1790s and almost all of the following three decades. For the present period there is more revealing evidence of the problems involved than impatient exclamations about endless rehearsals and about being a servant of vanity. It will emerge as we consider 'Auf Miedings Tod' (WA I XVI 131–40) in relation to the series of 'Maskenzüge' in the first two months of 1782.

Few poems are as likely as 'Auf Miedings Tod' to raise with such imperiousness the question of the nature of occasional poetry, and none other is so suited to demonstrate why a simple formula that could once and for all silence this insistent voice is not likely to be forthcoming. A commemorative poem, a funeral elegy, is the simplest form of occasional poetry, as conventional as the 'Hochzeitscarmen.' To this extent, then, the words of the poet rise to the occasion. But this elegy to a carpenter also constituted the entire twenty-third issue of the *Journal von Tiefurt*, which was written and copied by and for a small, aristocratic circle. In the latter part of the eighteenth century this procedure is not as unusual as it may sound, but it removes us far from the conventionality noted at first glance. The occasion is now made to rise to the words of the poet, and in a way, an occasion is thus made. A part of the making of the occasion, however, is the fact that the man's death occurred in the service of occasional poetry written for the court. This is amply stated in the entire first half of the poem. From external knowledge we can add that Mieding died during the preparations for *Pantomimisches Ballett*. A deeper perception of the poem is made possible by the acknowledgement of this fact in the light of what has been said about the *Ballett* so far. At least, the irony which pervades the poem is intensified when it is recalled that a man met his drab death working for a spectacle that celebrated the return of eternal youth, and if we remember once more the political overtones of his last labour, we are closer to the reasons for finding him the ally of the politician, 'Du, Staatsmann, tritt herbei! Hier liegt der Mann, / Der so wie du, ein schwer Geschäft begann'; and for the pervasive scepticism about public and court affairs, 'Und, ungleich ihm, denkt mancher Ehrenmann: / Verdien 'ich's nicht, Wenn ich's nur essen kann.' Finally, the rôle of Time in this poem suggests a connection with the festivities of the season. Even the *Aufzug der vier Veltalter*, almost contemporaneous with the *Ballett* (12 February 1782), could be called a second thought on the facile reversal of the workings of time in the latter. Time appears in *Weltalter* as the central figure.

To believe that Goethe consciously chose the subject of *Aufzug der vier Weltalter* as an implied amendment to the *Ballett* would of course be naïve. If there were such a thing as a 'natural' subject for a masque, the Four Ages of Man would have to be called just that, with its all too obvious opportunities for glorification of the present, and its processional possibilities, not to speak of the attraction of general familiarity with the subject because of enforced memorization of the relevant passages of Ovid in childhood.[18] Furthermore, it is quite easy to think of the *Aufzug der vier Weltalter* as a pendant to the masque on the subject of the Four Seasons containing French

'Schule geselliger Empfindung' 93

verses by Count Werthern-Beichlingen (Düntzer, p. 19). Yet the appearance of Time in this context is not so essential as to place its introduction into the masque beyond the will of the poet. On the other hand, the masque in its present form is the outcome of presumably pressing exigencies of the day.

The program of *Aufzug der vier Weltalter* found in Knebel's papers indicates that what became a processional masque had been intended to be a dramatic ballet performed chiefly by children, with the following action:

Die Knaben des goldenen Zeitalters fangen mit einem leichten, angenehmen, sanften Tanz an. Die des silbernen gesellen sich dazu, machen Freundschaft und verleiten sie nach und nach bis zur ausgelassenen Lustbarkeit. Die des ehernen treten gebieterisch auf, stören ihre Freude. Der Ehrgeiz verlangt, dass die ihm folgen sollen. Sie schlagen's ab. Er ruft den Geiz, der seinen Sack bringt. Die vier ersten ergeben sich, nehmen Geld, es werden ihnen goldene Ketten ungehängt; sie tanzen zu Fünfen, den Ehrgeiz verehrend, nachher den Geiz liebkosend. Die des eisernen treten auf; mit Furie zerstreuen sie die andern und überwältigen sie; alle werden ihrer Attribute beraubt. Die Zeit tritt auf, schlichtet den Streit, besänftigt die Wüthenden, gibt jedem das Seinige wieder und heisst sie einen gemeinsamen Tanz aufführen. Dies thun sie; indessen geht sie herum, die Hauptpaare aufzurufen; diese tanzen zuletzt eine Quadrille. [Düntzer, pp 21-2]

One may safely assume that this plan foundered on obstacles of a practical nature. Throughout the entire period of Goethe's participation in such enterprises there is much evidence that the technical resources and the willingness and ability of the designated participants were frequently disproportionate to the projects and required their modification – especially in the execution of ballets. The chief difference between the two versions is, necessarily, the effect of the intervention of Time. In the earlier plan, Time presided over the reconciliation of the warring Ages and restored to each its identity ('gibt jedem das Seinige wieder'); in *Aufzug der vier Weltalter* it merely acts as an organizing force calling the turns of the Ages in their circular procession. Once the Golden Age has been brought back by the gentle power of Time, it will presumably once more be succeeded by the other three. This, then, is an example of how the artistic form can determine the content: a ballet lends itself to – imposes perhaps – solution of a conflict; a processional masque must necessarily convey the impression of inevitable succession.

Through the foregoing considerations there is a degree of blurredness in the relationship of *Ballett* and *Aufzug der vier Weltalter* which does not, however, affect the relation of these two as a group with 'Auf Miedings Tod,' which may be termed antagonistic, with due allowance for the misleading implication of deliberateness that is bound to arise. The juxtaposition is eloquent. On the one hand there is a cluster of fatiguing festivities arranged not altogether for festive motives. (We do not need the ulterior political purposes here, for which accurate documentary proof is not available [see above, pp 88-9]; even the goal of the harmonization of the court, aimed at by the tributes to Duchess Luise, causes these works to become a part of an unedifying situation of long standing and suffices to adulterate the illusion of an 'innocent' joyfulness.) On the other hand, in 'Auf Miedings Tod' we have the apotheosis of an obscure man, palpably involved in the hustle and bustle of everyday existence, tied, as it were, to his stage pulleys and wheels while engaged in the labour of assisting society in its illusory attempts at halting the Wheel of Time:

> Nenn' ihn der Welt, die kriegrisch oder fein
> Dem Schicksal dient und glaubt ihr Herr zu sein,
> Dem Rad der Zeit vergebens widersteht... [ll 53-5]

This elevation of the poor and imperfect craftsman is accomplished by showing that he is entitled to a place in the realm of art, entitled, that is, by the illumination of the true nature of his endeavours through a vision of the Muse. And, as if to confirm emphatically the value that Mieding's springs and nails and scaffoldings assumed through the purity of his impulse, the mutual redemption, as it were, of art and nature, Goethe chose as the object of his vision not a purely allegorical Muse, but an individual who is akin to Mieding in having emerged from among the

> ...Schwestern, die ihr bald auf Thespis Karrn,
> Geschleppt von Eseln und umschrien von Narrn,
> Vor Hunger kaum, vor Schande nie bewahrt,
> Von Dorf zu Dorf, euch feil zu bieten, fahrt. [ll 127-30]

Corona Schröter's speech is accompanied by a gesture which leads us to the full meaning of her homage, and the poet's homage to her. The wreath she throws into Mieding's grave represents the three realms in which Mieding's life, as all human life, moves and must seek its fulfillment: nature, society, art.

I referred earlier (p 54) to the half-ironic, half-serious title 'Direktor der Natur,' which encompasses these three spheres in a not altogether commendatory manner in *Der Triumph der Empfindsamkeit*. But in the visionary climax of 'Auf Miedings Tod' there is reconciliation. The wreath consists of flowers, products of nature. But since these flowers are given human, social *epitheta*, the vision of an ideal society, varied, yet harmoniously organized, is gently evoked:

> Der Rose frohes, volles Angesicht,
> Das treue Veilchen, der Narcisse Licht,
> Vielfält'ger Nelken, eitler Tulpen Pracht. [ll 187–9]

Lastly, these flowers are artificial, 'Von Mädchenhand geschickt hervorgebracht' (l 190). The artificial flower is symbolically capable of breaking the tyranny of time through art, not, as in the *Ballett*, through an arbitrary choice of a moment, or through the acceptance of a perpetual cyclical movement as in the *Weltalter*. One could dismiss as a whim the use of the artificial flower as something slightly discomforting to present-day sensibilities, if it had not been destined by the poet for extended use later, most conspicuously in the 'Mummenschanz' of *Faust*, although in other crucial works as well. With reference to the 'debate' of artificial and natural flowers in *Faust* II (ll 5092–5157) Emrich defines this symbolism as follows:

...Sie zielen auf einen zeitüberwindenden Aufbau von Kunst, 'Künstlicheit,' Mode und Gesellschaft über der Natur, der sich auf längst entwickelte Kunstüberzeugungen Goethes gründet...[19]

And it may be noted, too, that the wreath in the hand of Corona is an early manifestation of the association of artificial flowers with the 'Naturell der Frauen' of the 'Mummenschanz' (ll 5106–7).

On the basis of these considerations it would appear to follow that, for once, we have obtained a glimpse into the motivation of a 'spontaneous' occasional poem. The antagonistic aspect of its relationship with 'non-spontaneous' court works of the same period was the more obvious, but if this had been all, we would have had to anticipate satire or silence. But since the relationship proved to be complementary as well, it has been possible to account more fully than was formerly possible, for some facets of 'Auf Miedings Tod' (and of 'Ilmenau' to a lesser degree). If all these productions are capable of being related in the quest for an understanding of the concept of occasional poetry in Goethe, one can hardly escape the impression that the first few months of 1782 were crucial ones. We found that the entire range of occasional poetry – from the conventional occasion to the unconventional event pressed into service as an occasion, from the use of traditional forms to an altogether personal utterance – is covered here. It is my impression that this is a dialectical process of clarification that was to lead the poet henceforth to a greater freedom in these matters. Emrich claims to see a pattern becoming perceptible in the *Maskenzüge*, beginning with those of 1781 (although he cites works only from 1782 onwards):

Am Anfang steht meist die Unschuld reiner Natur ... dann folgt das, was der Mensch selber erschaffen hat, oder was sich als zweite fremde Welt über die Naturwelt erhebt ... Als drittes erscheint der Ehrgeiz, bzw. Geiz, die lieblos das Geschaffene festhalten wollen und sich am weitesten von der Natur entfernen, worauf zum Schluss die Unschuld, bzw. Sonne, wieder zurückkehrt und der Kreislauf von Neuem anhebt...[20]

Even if this is a rather wide-meshed formula, perhaps too much so, its mere existence singles out the first few months of 1782 as a point of departure, and, looking back, a point of arrival, too.

The exclamation in 'Auf Miedings Tod,' 'O Weimar! dir fiel ein besonder Loos!' has been applied to a great many aspects of Goethe's work. The simultaneous glance at that poem and *Pantomimisches Ballett* has underscored the validity of this sentiment in its immediate context. And even if it has not supplied a formula, it has made more specific the question raised at the beginning of this inquiry as to what was involved in being a court poet during the life-span of Goethe. In the happy conjunction of occasion used and occasion made which was observed at the beginning of 1782, we may find an early explanation and a justification for the boldly comprehensive use of the term 'Gelegenheitsdichtung' by Goethe in his old age.

·6·

The Limits of Sociability

IT HAS ALREADY BEEN ANTICIPATED that a segment of Goethe's occasional poems would require accommodation in a separate miscellaneous category, if a complete picture of his activity as an occasional poet were to be arrived at. The samples are drawn from the crucial half decade before the Italian hiatus, but some considerations derived from them apply to a larger span of time.

'Dich ergriff mit Gewalt...' (WA i II 123), the epitaph for Duke Leopold of Brunswick, attaches itself readily to the series of 'spontaneous' epigrams discussed above. It was written for, and actually affixed to the monument of Duchess Anna Amalia's brother in the Tiefurt park. It is mentioned here to show that a poetic method, begun almost as a fad or a fashionable pastime and used for the creation of occasions, is now (when the vogue has more or less come to an end) a ready form of expression for a genuinely commemorative purpose. There is little doubt that the tragic occasion of the duke's death – the sacrifice of his life in the act of saving the lives of others during a flood – demanded an utterance, in view of Goethe's position. It is difficult to argue that Goethe would have produced a different poem or no poem at all if the earlier epigrammatic group had not existed. One might even suggest that the epigrammatic impulse determined the manner of the tribute. Leopold is apotheosized to equality with the destructive River God, and thus an incantatory situation is created. In the process, the human act is called failure ('was dir als Menschen misslang'). This is far removed from the prevailing assessment of the incident in which this princely sacrifice for others is seen as a supremely humane act – intensified, it would seem, by a trace of astonishment that a prince had proved capable of this extreme manifestation of philanthropy.[1] To have kept the tribute in a totally human frame would presumably have required a more balladesque treatment such as the one accorded to another altruistic victim of the waves twenty-four years later, 'Johanna Sebus' (WA i II 36).

By the same token, it is possible to argue that no readier means of expression than the social song was available to Goethe when the birth of the male heir of the ducal house was at long last to be celebrated in February 1783. This approach leads to an evaluation of the poem which is more just than the one offered by Goedeke, who cites 'Feier der Geburtsstunde des Erbprinzen Carl Friedrich...' (WA i IV 222) as an example of a reluctant offering for an occasion that forbade silence:

Das erste bezeichnende Beispiel dieser Art ist das Gedicht ... das vierzehn Tage auf die Geburt folgte und – ein Zeichen innerer Teilnahmslosigkeit – vierzehn Jahrhunderte über den Zeitpunkt seiner Entstehung hinausschaut ... Dies frohe Familienereignis war zugleich ein Staatsereignis, vor dem das persönliche Freundschaftsverhältnis zurückweichen musste ... Er [i.e., Goethe] hielt vierzehn Tage zurück, und als er endlich, auch von aussen gedrängt, nicht länger umhin konnte, ein Lebenszeichen zu geben, fand er sich mit den wenigen, fast inhaltslosen Zeilen ab.[2]

A complete assessment of the poem under discussion would require a fuller knowledge than we possess of the history of *Elpenor*. Work on *Elpenor* may have been begun in August 1781, in anticipation of the birth of a prince, and may possibly have been resumed in February 1783, in the hope of completing it in time for the duchess' return to her public duties. Gräf and Petsch subscribe to this theory. Kunz[2] is more judiciously reserved on the subject, and rightly so to judge by the evidence Gräf presents, which consists of little more than vague references, in connection with the birth of an heir, to an unnamed drama being written by Goethe.

It is true, of course, that Goethe's contribution to the occasion was conspicuously slim in the bulky dedicatory volume[3] as compared with the much more ambitious attempts at glorification of the occasion by Herder and Wieland, who wrote cantatas. But the relevant consideration for our purpose concerns the form chosen by Goethe, and it is reasonable to claim that the one most readily at his disposal at the time for this particular occasion was one that is used more frequently in the songs of sociability of later years. That the poem in question is primarily conceived as a song seems probable. It is a 'Ständchen' (l 10) and was sung at a 'Redoute' (Düntzer, p 24). The fourteen centuries objected to by Goedeke should be viewed in association with the other time units of fourteen (days, years) mentioned in the first line of each stanza and constituting a sort of refrain in reverse ('Vor vierzehn Tagen... / Nach vierzehn Jahren...' etc.). Aside from formal considerations, there may be another factor involved in Goethe's response to the birth of the prince: when the total production of Goethe's occasional utterances is surveyed we find that of all common occasions, births are the least often celebrated or remembered. In fact, I am unable to cite another poem expressly dedicated to the birth of a child, although the opportunities for writing them must have been numerous. And if silence is being used as evidence, are not the following lines from the birthday poem for Count von Brühl of July 1785 tantamount to silence of the voice that we may recognize as the poet's own: 'Doch übergross / Lässt ihn das Glück die Lust empfinden, / Einmal auf der Geliebten Schoos / Ein artig Murmelchen zu finden. / Nun fühlt er seinen neuen Stand / Und fügt sich in den Vater-Orden...' (WA I IV 225). In attempting to account for this situation I surmise that birth constituted an uncongenial occasion. To go beyond this meagre assertion would either lead to sweeping generalizations about Goethe's personality or towards a highly detailed investigation. The latter does exist, embedded in Eissler's psychoanalytic study.[4] Here, the birth of the heir, *Elpenor*, and Goethe's relationship with Fritz von Stein are brought into consideration. Inevitably, the conclusions are sombre and radical: '...Goethe's despair at not having a child ... the birth of a boy to his friend, the arousal of jealousy, the ensuing impulse to destroy the infant...' Would different answers issue from an equally thorough study of this question based on different assumptions? To have enabled us to ask this question constitutes in itself a contribution to our knowledge about the poet which we owe to Eissler.

There is some truth, to be sure, in the assertion that the existence of an infant son determined to some extent the contents of the masque of 30 January 1784, the *Planetentanz* (WA I, XVI 200–7). Yet the suggestion of Pniower and Andreas[5] that this work constitutes a belated and more adequate celebration of the event of almost exactly a year before does not appear warranted to me. It is not impossible, but neither is it verifiable, that Goethe was subjected to some pressure in connection with his poetic contribution to the general rejoicing. Only in the letter of Goethe's mother to the dowager duchess of 1 March 1783 ('Briefe von Goethes Mutter,' ed. A. Köster [Leipzig 1908] 72) could I find any evidence of urging of that nature. But it would be difficult to establish any relationship between 'Feier der Geburtsstunde' and *Planetentanz* comparable in any way to the antithetical or complementary relationships observed heretofore. I therefore regard the masque as a direct descendant of earlier glorifications of Duchess Luise, such as *Ein Zug Lappländer* and *Die weiblichen Tugenden*. Now, however, the distinction of having given birth to an heir adds to the height of the pedestal on which the object of the tribute is placed. If *Planetentanz* had revealed new structural characteristics of note it would have had to be examined in conjunction with *Pantomimisches Ballett* and *Aufzug des Winters*. But as far as could be discovered, no principle of organization is at work here other than the one imposed on the work by the choice of the planets as its thematic thread. This is not to say, however, that the execution of the plan does not bear the stamp of Goethe's personality as a poet.

The point has now been reached where the court of Weimar ceases to be the principal site and cause of occasional utterance for quite some time, and the remaining poems written before Goethe's Italian journey about to be examined may be labelled 'Karlsbad' poems. 'Ein munter Lied! Dort kommt ein Chor...' (WA i IV 223–6) was written during Goethe's first stay in that resort during the summer of 1785. 'O Schöne mit dem weissen Stabe...' (pp 226–7) and 'Abschied an den Herzog Karl August' (pp 227–8) originated during the second visit in August of the following year. But the use of 'Karlsbad' is meant to suggest more than common geographic origin; it will have to serve to designate a mood or tone of the poems involved that will by no means be rare in Goethe's later work. The poems are tributes to individuals, social gifts placed at the service of sociability and conviviality. They show definitely the physical distance from the stresses and strains and the obligations of Weimar, although, of course, poems similar in tone were written there, too. They are private utterances, or at any rate, they show a mingling of personal and public attitudes. The definition used here is purposely broad and tentative in order to hold within its compass at least one aspect of the most important group of poems written in Karlsbad, those collected later under the group title *Im Namen der Bürgerschaft von Karlsbad* (WA i XVI 311–29). This group included the four poems addressed to Empress Ludovica of Austria in the summer of 1810 and the three addressed to her, her husband, Francis I, and his daughter, Empress Marie Louise of France, in the summer of 1812. These poems transcend by far the private sphere sketched above, but they are, nevertheless, unmistakably linked to it. In fact, they might have proved impossible to write outside the mellowing atmosphere of the spa, although the fact that the poet speaks in the name of the Karlsbad citizenry is, of course, no more than a fictional device. The far-ranging theme of this group of poems, the over-riding question of Napoleon's European rule, is controlled and held within bounds by its development in the healing and relaxing influence of the spa, and its presentation on behalf of the non-political dispensers of the boon of physical well-being. These observations share common ground with a comment of Staiger, who attributes to them the quality of 'innige Förmlichkeit.'[6] He arrives at this characterization by looking at the 1810–12 poems from the vantage point of 'Geheimstes' of *West-Oestlicher Divan* (WA I VI 63), which also concerns Empress Ludovica. The conventions of the submersion of the personal element on the one side (by speaking on behalf of a group), and of its concealment on the other, form the poles between which the mode denoted by Staiger's felicitous phrase is cultivated.

It finds its supreme expression in *West-Oestlicher Divan*, revealing an intricate relationship between the poet and the ruler and beloved. *Noten und Abhandlungen zu besserem Verständniss des West-Oestlichen Divans* is the principal source of clues to this question. I shall explore it in a later section of this inquiry (ch. 9).

While the concept of 'Karlsbad' poetry as a whole prompts us to look ahead, at least one of the pre-Italian poems, being used as a point of departure, is actually more closely attached to the past, and evokes memories of such names as Gleim, Uz, and Ebert[7] more strongly than any documents of Goethe's artistic growth since the Leipzig days. For 'Ein munter Lied!...'[8] we may use the 'Neujahrslied' of 1769 as a point of comparison because both are 'Bänkelsänger' songs. But whereas the earlier poem had utilized that form as a veil for the expression of a mood that was found to range from fierce to self-pitying, we are now dealing with a poem of the utmost geniality and extroversion. Whether or not it was chorally performed, it was certainly written for that purpose, and in that sense may be regarded as a gift to a group as well as to the count. And whether or not Goethe looked back deliberately to the older forms of eighteenth-century social poetry is a moot question. But it is worth noting that the poem has some affinities with a group of songs of the first decade and a half of the new century which are dedicated to the advancement of conviviality in the small groups that Goethe gathered around him in those years. The 'Bundeslied,' an early member of this group, and its emergence from a 'Hochzeitscarmen' have been previously discussed (pp 35–7). Others, showing varying degrees of exuberance, are 'Stiftungslied' (1801), 'Tischlied' (1802), 'Vanitas! vanitatum vanitas' (1806), 'Erog bibamus!' (1810), and 'Die Lustigen von Weimar' (1813).[9] Looking farther ahead we perceive once more the *West-Oestlicher Divan*. Biographically speaking, I suggest a certain analogousness of 'Karlsbad' to the journey of 1814 to southern Germany. What is probably the earliest *Divan* poem, 'Erschaffen und Beleben' (WA I VI 16), may serve as evidence of the connection suggested. These songs of sociability have found no more well-disposed reader than Benedetto Croce,[10] who ends his discussion of this group by comparing their spontaneity and good cheer favourably with the deliberate literary traditionalism of the *Römische Elegien*. It might be well, however, to temper Croce's enthusiasm on this subject with the following comment by Schiller:

Es ist eine erstaunliche Klippe für die Poesie, Gesellschaftslieder zu verfertigen – die Prosa des wirklichen Lebens hängt sich bleischwer an die Phantasie, und man ist immer in Gefahr, in den Ton der Freimäurerlieder zu fallen, der (mit Erlaubniss zu sagen) der heilloseste von allen ist. So hat Goethe selbst einige platte Sachen bei dieser Gelegenheit ausgehen lassen; wiewohl auch einige sehr glückliche Liedchen mit unterliefen, die aus seiner besten Zeit sind.[11]

'O Schöne mit dem weissen Stabe ...,' written in August 1786 for Caroline von Staupitz (WA I IV 226–7), the seventeen-year-old daughter of an officer from Dresden, embodies other qualities of what I am attempting to define as 'Karlsbad' poetry. But that designation must now be widened to include the other spas of Bohemia and cover the area which forms the subject of Johannes Urzidil's[12] valuable study. His sensitive delineation of physical and social settings and of the poet's mood, and his literary, scientific, and political activities as they were affected by the site helps, as well, to cast a simultaneous glance upon the relationships with the women Goethe encountered in the spas during the decades from 1785 to 1823. So far omitted from the consideration of occasional poetry is the vast number of album ('Stammbuch') verses or quotations which constitute some of the earliest Goethe documents (September 1766, DJG I 165). The practice of presenting such mementos was universal and it is probable that a detailed examination of

Goethe's numerous contributions to it would produce a characteristic cross-section of his poetic evolution. In this instance, the general scheme, i.e., the statement of a general nature applied to or dedicated to the individual in question, often with a humorous twist, is being used with special and exemplary skill. The solemn and 'visionary' expectation of the first line is drawn immediately into the area of the familiar, 'Du kleiner, guter, holder Schatz'. the solemnity of the figure equipped with the white staff is modulated to convivial chaos in '... Stäbe, / Die schwarz und braun, so bunt als schön, / Gemodelt aus dem Holz der Rebe...'; and at the end we find an emotional, Anacreontic 'Pointe' blunted by the use of grammatical terminology, 'Der, wenn er im Plural gesprochen, / Sich doch den Singular gedacht.'

If we survey the lengthy array of Bohemian poems addressed to women we find that, in one way or other, they touch on the theme of rejuvenation inherent in the nature of the locale. This involves a free and non-commital tone and a flirtatiousness which the visitor could be said to owe to himself and to the place as part of the regimen. Seen in this context, Ulrike von Levetzow stands in direct line of succession to the ladies addressed in 1785 and 1786. (The first of them was Countess Brühl: 'Warum siehst du Tina...' [July 1785, WA i IV 223].) Some at least of the small poetic offerings to Ulrike (e.g., 'Es ist nicht gut, die Formen...' [WA i IV 256]) correspond closely to the numerous earlier ones presented to more casual acquaintances. Distinct traces of this mode of communication remain perceptible in the anguish of 'Elegie.' That poem, seen in this perspective, may be said to mark the collapse of a convention of occasional utterance under the weight of the poet's existential situation, of forces which overwhelm the dikes of social control. It is no longer a matter of periodic recreation and rejuvenation, but of sheer survival 'wo Tod und Leben grausend sich bekämpfen...' (l 118). This is not the place to recount the progress of this crisis, except to note that in its poetic resolution in *Trilogie* there enters another element of occasional poetry which may be said to counteract the breakdown of a convention suggested above. The original purpose of the first component of the trilogy, 'An Werther' (WA i III 19–20), was simply to act as an expression of the author's authorization and blessings to the publisher and the public for the issue of the fiftieth-anniversary edition of the novel (cf. letter to Rochlitz, 30 April 1824). It is almost a commissioned poem. Its composition was not completely detached from financial considerations – much like all the 'Hochzeitscarmina,' baptismal embellishments, and funeral dirges of a professional occasional poet. I venture to suggest that 'An Werther' may be regarded as a sort of safety net in which the impact of 'Elegie' was caught and softened, dealing as it does with a tragic situation safely caught between the covers of a book.

'Abschied an den Herzog Karl August in Namen der Engelhäuser Bäuerinnen' (WA i IV 227–8) is the last poem Goethe wrote before setting out for Italy. The poem's obvious parallelism with the first Weimar poem discussed, 'Durchlauchtigster!...' offers too tempting an opportunity for comparison to be ignored. It will be recalled that the latter was found to be a 'private' poem in which the poet conveyed a message to the duke that could not be transmitted openly because it contained criticism of the bystanders. The poet had assumed the mask of Sebastian Simpel for that purpose. Now it could be said (and this applies to some extent to the Karlsbad poems of 1810 and 1812 *Im Namen der Bürgerschaft*...) that, by speaking in behalf of a group of peasants and by apparently attempting to adapt his idiom to theirs, the poet makes the poem an altogether public one to the point of blotting out the personal relationship between himself and the duke. 'Public' in this instance refers, to be sure, to the circle around the duke and Goethe, who shared the minor joys and sorrows of life in the spa. So departing vacationers are wont to look back on fellow guests with amusement or relief ('Gurofsky'), on local delicacies ('Kollatschen'), and on the details and the success of the regimen ('Wie vom heissen Sprudel-Trieb / Dir niemals was im Leibe blieb'). In the mouths of the 'Nymphen' of Engelhaus these matters all sound innocent and jolly. It seems inadvisable to pursue the comparison beyond this point, since the later poem is so limited in every respect, and it is easier to discuss features it does not exhibit and a substantiality it does not possess, and thus incur the suspicion of asking the poet for a work he never intended to write. Its unity of tone reminds one, by contrast, of the sharp division within the early Weimar poem. At that point the poet had turned his back on the bystanders and guided the duke into the realm of the 'Zauberschloss / ... wo eine gute Fee regiert.' This section, more than any other, had given the poem the private, indeed conspiratorial character that makes it now, in retrospect, appear as an experiment in occasional poetry. The absence of any such elements in the later poem could be treated as at least symbolic evidence that Goethe's notions of the desirable range occupied by an informal occasional poem addressed to the duke had undergone a measure of clarification. Biographically, this poem marks the end of a phase in his relationship with his master. However strong the bond between the two men remained, its articulation was henceforth no longer to be interchangeably public and private. If we shift the perspective a little we may regard the poem as evidence of Goethe's growing willingness to keep a controlling eye on his own production – the rigorousness of 'classicism' did not after all begin on the day he crossed the Italian border. It is necessary, however, to add that it would be a dreadful distortion to imply that the poet made his painful way from the first poem to the duke through *Lila, Der Triumph der Empfindsamkeit*, the masques, 'Auf Miedings Tod,' and 'Ilmenau' to arrive at the one now under discussion. The absurdity of this notion may well serve as a warning against the teleological fallacy in the discussion of poetry.

·7·

The Poet and His Public

Goethe's first journey to Italy will undoubtedly persist in imposing itself as the great caesura in his life as a poet, regardless of the clear lines of continuity which force themselves upon the observer's eye with growing distinctiveness. But the critic who attempts to confine himself to that part of the poet's work which can in any way be designated as 'occasional' is all the more encouraged to draw a heavy line under September 1786, since the months of absence from Weimar did not produce a single work that he would feel obliged to examine under this heading. If occasions arose in Italy, they were decidedly ignored, and it can safely be said that at least a modest portion of the happy sense of liberation that engulfed Goethe after he had crossed the Alps was caused by the state of freedom from the obligations of this sort. Although I have not attempted to dispose of any of the works so far considered by abusing the notion of 'Amtspflichten,' I have not glossed over the circumstance that several of Goethe's works of the latter seventies and eighties do owe their existence to a sense of obligation towards his courtly environment. It is not easy to decide now whether it was that sense of obligation or the obligations themselves that faded after 1784, but there is no doubt that the idea of the public, of a wider, national audience gradually superseded the court as the objective of literary activity at that time. Before this process set in, as pointed out earlier, 'Auf Miedings Tod' occupied a position of eminence which enabled us to observe the motivations and methods of the Weimar period to best advantage. If the Italian interlude now seems to be a void with regard to occasional poetry, it can hardly be surprising that we should look for a similar peak on the other side of the chasm equally useful for a survey of the situation characteristic of the post-Italian decade.

No elaborate search is really required. 'Euphrosyne' is a poem which immediately qualifies as 'occasional' in the most conventional sense. Goethe's one extended utterance on its occasion has frequently been quoted. It is a passage from a letter to Böttiger written on 25 October 1797, from Switzerland:

> Dass gute Zeugniss, das Sie unserm Theater geben, hat mich sehr beruhigt, denn ich leugne nicht, dass der Tod der Becker mir sehr schmerzlich war. Sie war mir in mehr als Einem Sinne lieb. Wenn sich manchmal in mir die abgestorbne Lust für's Theater zu arbeiten wieder regte, so hatte ich sie gewiss vor Augen ... Die Nachricht von ihrem Tode hatte ich lange erwartet, sie überraschte mich in den formlosen Gebirgen. Liebende haben Thränen und Dichter Rhythmen zur Ehre der Todten, ich wünchte, dass mir etwas zu ihrem Andenken gelänge. [WA IV XII 345]

One justification for quoting this passage once more is the inclusion of the first sentence, usually omitted. It responds to some reassurance from a rather stern observer (who was never wont to hide his critical light under a bushel) concerning the maintenance of artistic standards at the Weimar theatre during the prolonged absence of its director. It also reveals that, in Goethe's mind, the kind and level of excellence he recognized were closely linked with the presence in the company of Christiane Becker-Neumann and severely threatened by her death. The phrase 'in mehr als Einem Sinne' (a favourite turn of speech of Goethe at the time) therefore propels us to the cluster of questions relating to Goethe and the theatre after Italy. We may feel reassured about travelling on a main road by the fact that, aside from 'Euphrosyne,' the bulk of Goethe's occasional works of the decade consists of theatrical prologues and epilogues, several of them recited by Christiane Becker-Neumann and therefore presumably written with her in mind.

Goethe's assumption of the co-directorship of the court theatre in 1791 is at the same time a link with activities before Italy and a new departure. It seems fairly clear that he undertook the work at the urging of the duke (and probably of Anna Amalia) without great hopes or enthusiasm. The economic and temperamental difficulties were foreseeable to all. Someone had to do it and Goethe had not been doing much in the eyes of Weimar society since his return. As the duke wrote to Kirms 'Behandeln [sie] nun das Geschäfte ganz öffent. u. mit Göthen: ich werde dadurch aller zudringlichkeiten loss, u. schiebe alles lezterem zu' (17 January 1791).[1]

An obscure point in the situation is the apparently general agreement that the contract of Bellomo and his troupe should not be renewed and that a permanent theatre should be made part of the governmental establishment. Wahle rightly doubts the genuineness of the 'Vergnügen' with which Goethe claims in the *Tag-und Jahreshefte* to have assumed his duties. To be sure, in a long perspective the decision can be seen as an aspect of the turning towards the public referred to above. Other reasons may have been more immediately involved: mere obedience to Carl August's wishes, a mixture of personal loyalty and the point of honour of earning his keep. If the latter sounds too simple, the reader is referred to the collection *Goethe in vertraulichen Briefen* ....[2] Apparently the feeling that his status on his return from Italy was that of a parasite was fairly wide spread. He had lost the desire to entertain society and his scientific activities were largely counted as an unsociable pastime. In the same vein, it may be relevant to remember that by this time the Ilmenau mine enterprise was beginning to look completely moribund. This was an official responsibility carried over from earlier days and we know that Goethe felt a strong sense of commitment and a correspondingly strong sense of frustration towards this scheme which had largely sprung from his initiative and in which were merged three typically eighteenth-century impulses: enlightened economic planning, scientific interest, and get-rich-quick efforts. This field of activity, incidentally, is akin to the theatrical enterprise in having produced occasional writing in the form of addresses to the 'Gewerkschaft' (WA I XXXVI 365 et seq.). Their appeal for help, dedication, patience, and indulgence, the tone of encouragement and renewal of hope, is presented with traditional rhetorical means much in the manner of the earlier prologues. But while nature sustains the hope of yielding its riches by the generous application of knowledge, funds, and persistence (at least until it gives its final negative answer), the maintenance of a healthy theatrical organization by a poet is a more demanding challenge from the beginning because Antonio is, by definition, haunted by Tasso and the 'Direktor' can never lock out the 'Dichter.' And furthermore, the 'Dichter' will not, even if he could, return to 'Die Zeiten ... da ich noch selbst im Werden war ...' (WA I XIV 14).

In social terms, this inability to resume where things had been left off about ten years before means that the primarily courtly, personal, and dilettante medium in which dramatic activities had been conducted could not be recovered and was not worth recovering at that. The habit and the ideal of objectivity had to encompass Goethe's dealings with the theatre as much as any other sphere of endeavour. The object in this case is the public. It is only a little less impersonal than the ore of Ilmenau and just as reluctant to become a tangible asset. It must be defined a little more accurately in Goethe's terms. An early reference comes from the extensive correspondence with Kayser concerning *Scherz, List und Rache*: 'Als ich das Stück schrieb, hatte ich nicht allein den engen Weimarischen Horizont im Auge, sondern den ganzen Teutschen, der doch noch beschränckt genug ist ...' (20 June 1785, WA iv vii 68). Inquiries about Vienna (to C.B. von Isenflamm, 5 November 1785) and Munich (to Knebel, 18 November 1785) as a market for the 'Operette' point in the same direction and are compatible with efforts expressed in those letters to help his protegé, Kayser. The opinions of local musicians are noted, as well as those of Herder, Wieland, and Einsiedel ('Die Musici gelten bey mir am wenigsten ... doch sind sie das nächste Publikum und nicht zu verachten' (to Kayser, 22–3 December 1785, WA iv vii 145). *Scherz List und Rache* is to be one of several works of this kind with which the public is to be conquered and held, as various references to the next 'Singspiel,' *Die ungleichen Hausgenossen*, indicate. The conquest of the public is seen as facilitated by close co-operation of poet and composer. Indeed, subordination of the poet is acceptable ('Die Delicatesse und Grazie, womit der Componist gleichsam als ein himmlisches Wesen über der irrdischen Natur des Dichters schwebt' (to Kayser, 28 June 1784, WA iv vi 318). There is no rash and isolated surrender of artistic autonomy. The idea of co-operation always comes to the fore when works are undertaken which aim at an immediate impact upon the public. *Xenien* is a case in point and 'gemeinsames Arbeiten' is extolled in the explanatory note 'Ueber die Entstehung des Festpiels zu Ifflands Andenken' of May 1815 (WA i, XL(I) 90). The most conspicuous manifestation of public-mindedness is undoubtedly the commitment implied in the 1786 contract with Göschen for the publication of the *Schriften*, which determined the direction of Goethe's literary activity for the next three years, that is, principally during the decisive period of his sojourn in Italy. Goethe undoubtedly underestimated the amount of work of revision and completion that this step entailed (cf. the various estimates concerning the date of dispatching the complete *Iphigenie*), but it is not easily conceivable that he took the step without an awareness of the burdensome responsibilities involved. It is no overstatement to regard the fragmentary works in his luggage as the only means of identification of the traveller who had shed his position, his closest human ties, as well as his name. In any case, it is not beyond verification that the public was very much on his mind during the early weeks in Italy. It occupies the Verona amphitheatre: 'das erste Monument der alten Zeit, das ich sehe ... will leer nicht gesehen seyn, sondern ganz voll Menschen, wie es der Kayser und der Papst gesehen haben. Doch nur damals that es seine Würckung, da das Volck noch mehr Volck war als es ietzt ist. Denn eigentlich ist so ein Amphitheater recht gemacht dem Volck mit sich selbst zu imponiren, das Volck mit sich selbst zum besten zu haben ...'[3] 'Volck' here and in the following passage is clearly the equivalent of a public as a higher form of collective humanity than a random accumulation of spectators. After a brief 'natural history' of the amphitheatre we are given a glimpse of this transformation:

Dieses allgemeine Bedürfnis had der Architeckt zum Gegenstand, er bereitet einen solchen Crater durch die Kunst, so einfach als nur möglich und dessen Zierrath das Volck selbst ist ... Da es sonst nur gewohnt ist sich durch einander laufen zu sehen, sich in einem Gewühl ohne Ordnung und ohne sonderlich Zucht zu sehn, sieht das vielköpfige, vielsinnige, schwanckende schwebende Thier sich zu Einem Ganzen ... gestimmt, in Eine Masse verbunden und befestigt, und zu einer Form gleichsam von Einem Geiste belebt. Die Simplicität des Ovals ist iedem Auge auf die angenehmste Weise fühlbar und ieder Kopf dient zum Maase wie gros das Ganze ist. Jetzt wenn man es leer sieht, hat man keinen Maasstab, man weiss nicht, ob es gros oder klein ist.[4]

The conviction that the theatrical building itself is an important factor in the civilization of an audience ('das Theater als moralische Anstalt' with un-Schillerian literalness) never left Goethe. Occasional works prompted by the inauguration of new or renovated buildings recur regularly and will be scrutinized farther on (esp. p 139 et seq.). Vicenza with its 'divine' *teatro olimpico* of Palladio ('ein Theater der Alten realisirt,' 19 September 1786) suggests a comparison of the theatre of the ancients with its modern counterpart: the former, 'ein vornehmes, reiches, wohlgebildetes Kind,' the latter, a clever businessman far less well endowed in all these respects but more knowledgeable about the use of his means. This trend of thought, as well as the decision to make Vicenza the home of Mignon (22 September), suggests the world of *Wilhelm Meisters Lehrjahre*. In Venice he ponders the public in relation to his own work:

Auch hab ich mir überlegt, dass ich mit dieser Truppe und vor diesem Volck wohl meine Iphigenie spielen wollte, nur würd ich eins und das andre verändern, wie ich überhaupt hätte thun müssen, wenn ich sie auch unsern Theatern und unserm Publiko hätte näher bringen wollen. Aber ach. Es scheint, dass der letzte Funcken von Anhänglichkeit ans Theater ausgelöscht werden soll. Du glaubst nicht, wie mir das alles so gar leer, so gar nichts wird...[5]

Other quotations could show that these utterances – all modified in, or omitted from *Italienische Reise* – have political and religious overtones. I merely want to indicate, however, that during the first weeks in Italy when memories of Weimar were still sharp enough to colour new impressions there are frequent references to the anonymous 'Volck' as a public. Goethe is by no means uncritical of it, but it appears to be closer to the ideal of cultivated receptivity than he had hitherto encountered, i.e., more 'natural' and more alive.

While the utterances quoted above have thematic significance for the decades to follow, they cannot be regarded as representing an area of passionate involvement during the larger part of Goethe's stay in Italy, nor in the years immediately following. During the latter, Goethe wavered between utmost contempt for German theatrical life and the hope of being able to influence it for the better by writing some suitable plays. The resolve, 'alle Jahre ein paar spielbare Stücke zu schreiben' (to F.H. Jacobi, 20 March 1791, WA IV IX 253) is less firm even than his earlier plans to help along the 'Singspiel' in the same fashion. The mixture of awe and misgiving with which he beheld the industry of Schiller, who came closer to the practice of a regulated dramatic output, is a more reliable indicator of his feelings on this subject.

The prologue of 7 May 1791 (WA I XIII 155) mirrors this mood; the new theatrical enterprise is approached with suspicious care. Public and performers are groups that must be alternately humoured and disciplined to prevent excesses and Goethe's tone of voice betrays the resigned strictness of a long-suffering parent. Any improvement of behaviour is to be rated as a windfall. When J.F. Reichardt had apparently expressed high amusement over the rules on moral behaviour issued by Schröder to his Hamburg troupe, Goethe had answered:

Von Kunst had unser Publikum keinen Begriff, und so lang solche Stücke allgemeinen Beyfall finden ... warum soll ein Direktor nicht auch eine sittliche Truppe wünschen, da er bey seinen Leuten nicht auf vorzügliches Talent zu sehen braucht, welches sonst allein den Mangel aller übrigen Eigenschaften entschuldigt. [28 February 1790, WA IV IX 180]

And, true to this assessment, Goethe asked Schröder for a copy of his rules along with advice on organizational matters as the spring season approached.[6]

This attitude then accounts for the singular plainness, indeed bleakness of the prologue of 7 May 1791. The practice of using prologues itself was a symptom of the disease that afflicted theatrical life. When Schröder took charge again of the Hamburg theatre in 1786 he promised that 'neither extensive programs nor prologues of any kind, perpetually repeating the same thing, will attempt to suborn your favour or your money.'[7] The prologue does, of course, attempt to attract the favour of the audience, but it does anything but suborn. One might almost say that it remains barely within the confines of common courtesy, so anxious is the author to avoid fawning. The final line invoking 'Billigkeit' and 'Strenge' cannot easily be imagined as being accompanied by a reverential bow. It would be idle to call the piece un-Goethean, but there can be few lines in his work of equal sobriety and lack of animation. It is a patient and pedantic elaboration on the commonplace 'aller Anfang ist schwer.' In effect it is a pedagogical trap set for the audience, but especially for the actors. Through the mouth of one of their own they are made to pledge abstention from what was surely the most irksome of their habits and the most deeply rooted, that of upstaging their colleagues, burying each other and the play in the process. Since this practice could only thrive on the low instincts of a barbaric public, note Goethe's sly use of his authority in serving notice on the audience through the mouth of one of the perpetrators that both accomplices must now consider themselves under restraint. Goethe sent the prologue to Schröder telling him, somewhat triumphantly, that he had used the opportunity 'dem Publico und den Acteurs zu seiner Zeit ein Wort sagen zu können' (24 May 1791, WA IV IX 262).

The reins on actors and public are noticeably slackened in the second prologue (WA I XIII 157) spoken by Mme Gatto upon the return of the company from Lauchstädt and Erfurt on 1 October 1791. The previous summer had not brought any catastrophes, and the flow of minor irritations had been stemmed by the distance from Weimar: 'In Lauchstädt geht es ganz leidlich. Es fügt und schickt sich alles. Kleine Inconvenienzen werden nicht gerechnet, sie machen nur Herrn Fischer zu schaffen' (to Carl August, 1 July 1791, WA IV IX 275). The first prologue had ushered in an abbreviated season of one month. Now the regular winter season lay ahead and the patronage of the public was perhaps worth a more gracious appeal. Once again, however, any show of conventional humility was studiously avoided; the argument of enlightened self-interest is as far as the master will go: 'Oh, seid nicht karg / Mit eurem Beifall! denn es ist ja nur / Ein Capital, das ihr auf Zinsen legt.' The treatment of the public on more equal terms than five months before is emphasized and, at the same time, qualified in the middle of the prologue:

> ... bedenkt doch ja,
> Dass unsre Kunst mit grossen Schwierigkeiten
> Zu kämpfen hat; vielleicht in Deutschland mehr
> Als anderswo.
> Von diesen Schwierigkeiten
> Euch hier zu unterhalten, ist nicht Zeit;
> Ihr kennt sie selbst, und besser ists vielleicht,
> Ihr kennt sie nicht.

It must have occurred to some of the audience that certain of these difficulties were caused by the very people to whom the prologue was being addressed.

In these two prologues an anonymous audience was being addressed by an actor or actress who spoke entirely on behalf of the collective. This method was not only in keeping with tradition but served the mood and attitude of the director towards all concerned. The following four theatrical addresses differ from the earlier ones by confronting the audience with an individual; the speaker of the prologue or epilogue is no longer interchangeable at will with any other member of the troupe. The association with one member, Christiane Neumann, brings about a fundamental change in the relationship of director, actors, and audience. It must be added that this does not apply quite as clearly to the epilogue of 11 June 1792, but the external evidence linking it to her is weighty and is strengthened, I believe, by the considerations to follow. In the first of this group, the epilogue of 31 December 1791 (WA I XIII 159), Christiane Neumann appeared as the spokesman of the troupe. As the youngest active member she would enjoy a certain priority in the hearts of the spectators in any case. This is, of course, a gift outside the confines of art as it is a symptom of the audience's sentimentality, and the poet presents it with more than a grain of irony: 'Kinder, sagen sie, / gefallen, rühren immer; geht, / gefallt und rührt.' But at the same time, the speaker detaches herself from the troupe and enters into an alliance against 'Die Alten, die dahinter stehn.' A moment of dramatic action of sorts thus flashes up leading to an altogether conventional plea for good will and the expression of seasonal wishes.

The June epilogue (WA i XIII 161) too has a dramatic aspect. Taking leave from the Weimar public, the speaker is made sad beyond realization and loses herself in the evocation of a happy return: 'Mit leichtem Geiste flieg' ich über Tage und Wochen weg ...,' a goal made all the happier by the return of the duke. But the vision ceases: 'Ach wo bin ich hin gerathen? Mich mit süssen Bildern getäuscht ... Geschwind herunter mit dem Vorhang! ... nur geschwind herunter, dass von uns ein heitres Bild in eurer Seele bleibe.' A similar vision of peace and reunion is evoked in the prologue of 15 October 1793 (WA i XIII 163), but here, for once, 'Die Gelegenheit gibt mir das Stück.' Goldoni's *Der Krieg* was the one play, thus far, that was sufficiently esteemed by the director to be directly related to the prologue. Once again it is the impending return of the duke which serves as the core of a vision of better and more peaceful times to come.

It will doubtless be felt that 'vision' is an excessively solemn designation of these modest projections of hope for a happier future. But in comparison with the directness and plain functionality of the earlier prologues we sense in those associated with Christiane Neumann the director's willingness to let the imagination of the audience be engaged, at least in modest flight. The stage of sober admonition and appeal for support has been passed, and at least some sparks of a flame which would join the performers and audience by its warmth and light are beginning to be perceptible. What is known of the situation of the Weimar theatre during its first five years under Goethe's direction leads to the conclusion that in this process of elevation above the level of pastime the talents of Christiane were a highly important, perhaps a decisive factor. Whether this recognition occurred in connection with her portrayal of the role of Arthur in the *King John* performances of the winter of 1791–2, or whether this episode was assigned crucial importance in 'Euphrosyne' only retrospectively need not be decided here. For the revelation of her talents and of her function within the troupe her rôle as the niece in *Der Grosskophta* (first performance in December 1791) may have been no less decisive.

It has become customary to lump together *Der Grosskophta*, *Die Aufgeregten*, and *Der Bürgergeneral*, to assign them a collective low grade, and to move on to more rewarding subjects. *Der Grosskophta*, at least, deserves a more careful examination. The plan itself and the stage which was carried out in the summer of 1787, i.e., the outline of the comic opera *Die Mystifizierten*, marks the first attempt by Goethe to deal in dramatic form with social and political problems of his own time. Already it has been noted that his dramatic projects, even before his departure for Italy, had moved in the realm of opera and 'Singspiel.' In retrospect, we may say that the choice of the subject matter – the abuse and exploitation of irrational and religious impulses in the courtly setting of the age of enlightenment and scepticism – testifies to a considerable diagnostic insight into the historical situation of the period immediately preceding the Revolution. The failure of this project was undoubtedly due to Reichardt, the composer, rather than to the eager librettist. Even though we are not excluding the possibility that Goethe was constitutionally incapable of entering into that peculiar give-and-take relationship with its specific ratio of initiative and subordination which must exist between librettist and composer, we can at least imagine this libretto set to music by Mozart and feel convinced that we might have possessed a work quite commensurate with the magnitude of the phenomenon and the depth of its roots.

The later conversion into spoken drama (i.e., *Der Grosskophta* proper) which took place in the summer of 1791, shortly after the establishment of the court theatre, may be regarded as a retreat from the original, utopian goal. The impact of the work now depends almost entirely on the ability of the heroine to represent an uncorrupted world through her personality alone, without any of the subverbal resources of the orchestra. I suggest that the personality of Christiane Becker-Neumann remained the sole agent of the realization of the original objective – the one substitute, as it were, for the collaborator of Mozartian calibre who had not been found. This situation bears out Goethe's assertion that she mobilized his almost atrophied desire to write for the theatre.

To extend this argument to *Der Bürgergeneral* and *Die Aufgeregten* would carry us too far afield. The fragment *Das Mädchen von Oberkirch* is more to the point because it is embryonic and potentially either a libretto or a play. Marie would seem to stand somewhere between the niece of *Der Grosskophta* and Eugenie. And on the other hand, only the most passing reference needs to be made to the protracted work on *Der Zauberflöte Zweiter Teil* as the most direct, hence the most futile attempt at conquering irretrievable Mozartian territory. The two works in which the phenomenon of the Revolution is, by common consent, treated with greater success than heretofore are by their purely verbal character an implied admission of the failure of the earlier attempts. *Hermann und Dorothea* does not belong in our context at all, but *Die Natürliche Tochter* is more relevant, first, because of the reappearance of the girl victim, and, secondly because of its total and deliberate verbality, i.e., the absence of all musical and spectacular elements. Indeed, it seems altogether possible that the utter determination to exclude such elements helped to prevent the completion of this work.

The parallelism between the things represented by the idea of Mozart and of the presence of Christiane Becker at the Weimar stage leads to a definition of the common denominators inherent in these two factors. It must be sought in the problem of the viability of genius or the question of success in art. If the 'Direktor's' aim is 'der Menge zu behagen' and the 'Dichter' finds happiness only in 'Himmelsenge, wo nur dem Dichter reine Freude blüht' (WA i XIV 9, 10), the solution of the dilemma for one in whom the two functions are united will obviously be a work of art which the public, as it is, will accept enthusiastically despite itself as it were – and the same remains true if applied to the interpreter instead of the work of art. The actual and the ideal will then have converged in the realm of the possible ('Das Mögliche soll der Entschluss / Beherzt sogleich beim Schopfe fassen' [WA i XIV 16]); a proper moment, a 'kairos' has occurred. In this sense the presence of Mozart and of Christiane Becker are successes. For the Mozart operas we only need to know the frequency of performance at the Weimar theatre,[8] for the actress, the many parts played by her[9] and the maturation of the relationship of poet and public as reflected in the prologues written for her. Essentially, these phenomena are outside the reach of evolution and education. In abandoning itself to the genius of Mozart the public did not shed the habits and tastes for which Goethe castigated it. And what set Christiane apart from her colleagues were qualities which could not really be learned.

We know a good deal about Goethe's methods as a trainer of actors and it would seem that he succeeded in teaching many of them a great deal. The testimony of numerous reports in records of conversations and memoirs (*Regeln für Schauspieler*, WA i XL 139ff; *Weimarisches Hoftheater*, WA i XL 72ff, etc.) suggest that a large part of these efforts was a form of social training. Hamming, caricaturing – so strongly inherent in the middle-class drama of Kotzebue and Iffland – upstaging: all these thespian vices are forms of social misbehaviour which run counter to the social conventions of a prevalently aristocratic society or of a bourgeois one that is reasonably sure of its position and values. Even the rules of diction, clear enunciation, submission to the exigencies of a metre, can be defined as manifestations of consideration and respect towards oneself, one's partner, and the audience. But one quality cannot be taught by example and criticism because it is pre-social or transcends the social sphere. It is the doomed innocence that marks most of Christiane's rôles.

Translated into contemporaneous terms in Goethe's work, all the principal characters in *Wilhelm Meisters Lehrjahre* are involved in a process of learning, or should be. They are passing through a process of development in the flow of life, and if they do not, there is the conceivable possibility that they might have, all except Mignon whose life is subject to a different and mysterious set of rules. Mignon is set apart by youth, extraordinary origin, sexual indifferentiation, and behaviour not determined by the desire to extend and develop life. Wilhelm Emrich has observed these traits in Mignon and numerous related figures in Goethe's work so clearly that the reader may be referred to his observations.[10] He has rightly stressed in this connection the presence of a mode of existence which differs essentially from that of 'real' figures ('So lasst mich scheinen, bis ich werde'). The portrayal of characters partly or wholly of the Mignon essence equally is not within the range of the means of training and control that Goethe used on the Weimar actors. If present, it may be intensified (with a hot poker, if necessary),[11] but it cannot be 'acted' with the detachment that is at the core of the craft. This particular unity of performer and part allows us to understand the 'Arthur' passage of 'Euphrosyne' (ll 43–68) as an essential component of this commemorative poem. A strong element of irony enters here with regard to the goal of perpetuation inherent in the production of occasional poetry. Heretofore (as in 'Mieding') the motive was the desire to preserve the memory of a life well spent. But the life commemorated here found its fulfilment in the portrayal of death, in the denial of life (we must remember that Christiane Becker-Neumann's Arthur was only her first important rôle and that she later played Klärchen, Amalie, and Ophelia, as well, of course, as numerous other parts which do not bear on the present argument). A strong anticipation of the irony of 'Euphrosyne' is found in the striking passage of the prologue of 6 October 1794, the last and most personal of the series.

> Jakob soll ich heissen?
> Ein Knabe sein? – Das glaubt kein Mensch.
> ...
> Erst ist man klein, wird grösser, man gefällt
> Man liebt – und endlich ist die Frau,
> Die Mutter da, die selbst nicht weiss,
> Was sie zu ihren Kindern sagen soll... [WA I XIII 165–6]

To be sure, there is nothing whatever of Mignon about Iffland's Jakob in *Alte und neue Zeit*. It would be surprising if Goethe had seen him as anything but what he appears now, a rather awful little model of middle-class virtue. And so the prologue becomes an act of ironic insight into dramatic art, which is made possible by the presence of Christiane and her popularity with the public, and which carries the public above its own predilection for viewing itself in the distorting mirror of sentimentality held up to it by the likes of Iffland and Kotzebue. A psychologist would find sufficient material in the scant records of her life to produce a coherent psychopathological pattern and perhaps thus to enlarge our understanding of the 'Mignon' phenomenon on Goethe's work. We know[12] of her intensity of response when her father died and when her husband was accidentally injured by a fellow actor and of her purity and erotic intensity (her marriage was accounted for by her 'Mannswuth'[13]); having married at the age of fifteen she would have to be regarded as a child bride by any standards. Her unqualified popularity in the competitive and quarrelsome atmosphere of an eighteenth-century theatrical ensemble and in the extraordinarily strife-and-gossip-ridden Weimar of the period would also have to form part of a coherent assessment of her extraordinary position. There is also the factor of her obsessive dedication to her craft. By our standards of concern for physical well being, we are compelled to observe that she worked herself to death or was induced to do so. After several disabling illnesses she plunged back into work with an intensity which seems either compulsive and self-destructive or the result of a fatalistic attitude towards disease far removed from our own. In any case, the lament in 'Euphrosyne' over the inscrutable cruelty of fate which carries away the young could easily be undermined by thoughts on the possible avoidance of her fate, if we allowed ourselves to read this poem as we can read 'Mieding,' i.e., as a tribute to an individual and as the means of extending the presence of that individual. But in that case we would read 'Euphrosyne' in the spirit of naïve literalism of the Iffland admirers and the Iffland mentality for which Christiane was the antidote on the Weimar stage.

One is aided here by a further manifestation of the Mignon-Euphrosyne parallelism, Mignon's 'Exequien' in the eighth book of *Wilhelm Meisters Lehrjahre* (WA i XXIII 253 et seq.), this 'Trauerfeier aus dem Geist der humanen Weltfrömmigkeit' (Trunz, HA VII 648). It is commonly accepted that Goethe tended to react to death with a minimum of speech, and as often as not with silence. It was not in his nature to produce elaborate funerary tributes. The laconic description of the events following Werther's death is as effective as it is typical. Relatively speaking, 'Epilog zu Schillers Glocke' is laconic compared with the original plan of a commemorative pageant, which was abandoned. The commemorative orations for Anna Amalia and the lodge brothers are purposely lacking ornateness and the trappings of rhetorical splendour. The striking exceptions that come to mind are 'Mieding,' 'Mignon's Exequien,' 'Euphrosyne,' and the Euphorion threnody of *Faust* II. In the first case the motivation may be described as the desire to preserve the memory of a life which would otherwise have been forgotten immediately and irrevocably. It is thus primarily written for the benefit of the living, who would be impoverished by their failure to realize that there was something they had forgotten. The other three instances, on the other hand, deal with figures whose death is an essential component of their existence, not simply its termination. Now, as death moves towards the centre of attention, taking the place of achievements of life, an increase in abstraction and generalization is bound to occur, simply because there is something impersonal about the universal common denominator of humanity. With this drift towards abstraction we begin to see the emergence of a borderline between two types of poem, one fitting under the general title of 'on the death of ... ,' and the other to be more appropriately accommodated under the title 'On Death.' Euphrosyne owes its singular interest, indeed fascination, as well as its crucial position in the sequence of Goethe's occasional poetry to being carefully, and perhaps precariously placed on this very borderline.

This examination takes us into the sphere of traditions, conventions, topoi, etc., and before it is carried forward, a few preliminary considerations are perhaps in order, foremost, that this criterion does not carry any evaluative overtones. Notions of the primacy of originality and spontaneity over other forms of poetic expression where the fire of personal inspiration burns less fiercely have proved less and less tenable and useful, if only because antecedents, traditions, and conventions have been found to lurk behind even the most apparently spontaneous utterances.[14] But even after casting off such distinctions and habits of evaluation, one may still note the relative conspicuousness of such traditional elements in one phase of the poet's work as compared with others. If I proceed by induction, rather than take the shorter route of deducing from a master concept, such as 'classicism,' I do so in the hope that a more coherent picture of this aspect of Goethe's work will emerge, one that does not propel us to the conclusion that Goethe lost and recovered his 'true self' at one time or other.[15]

Proceeding from the outside, it is to be noted that the poem originated in a way which discloses hesitation and deliberateness. Recall the phrase in the Böttiger letter, 'ich wünschte, dass mir etwas zu ihrem Andenken gelänge.' There is a personal note here, but it can also be related to a passage in a letter to Schiller of exactly a month before: 'Herrliche Stoffe zu Idyllen und Elegien ... habe ich schon wieder aufgefunden und auch einiges schon wirklich gemacht.' The two attitudes implied can perhaps be paraphrased thus: 'I feel the urge to perpetuate the memory of Christiane Becker-Neumann' (this would presumably be applicable to the mood in which 'Mieding' was written) and 'there is an elegy to be drawn out of this situation.' The sketchy outline of the poem (WA I XXXIV 135) is thought to have been dictated during the return journey from Switzerland in November. The actual writing was not done until the following June and passages from the correspondence characteristic of that period are: 'das dringendste Bedürfniss wird immer der Almanach bleiben' (to Schiller, 12 May 1798); 'Meine Elegie auf die Beckern ist fertig und darf sich, hoff' ich, unter ihren Geschwistern sehen lassen ... hoffe vor Johanni, wenn die Stimmung so bleibt, noch mein Pensum für den Almanach zu absolvieren' (to Meyer, 15 June), 'Vergangene Woche habe ich mich besonders mit Arbeiten für den nächsten Almanach beschäftigt und wünsche ... dass Sie sich unter meinen diesjährigen Producktionen auch einige Günstlinge aussuchen mögen' (to A.W. Schlegel, 18 June); 'Mein hiesiger Aufenthalt war diesmal sehr fruchtbar, ich habe mein Contingent zum Almanach gestellt...' (to C.G. Voigt, 21 June); 'Mein Contingent zum Musenalmanach wird dies Jahr wieder starck' (to Knebel, 16 July). 'Euphrosyne,' of course, led the Goethean 'contingent' in Schiller's *Musen Almanach für das Jahr 1799*. Thus we can expand the imagined motivation to 'there is an elegy here which would help fill Schiller's next almanach.' The almanach was one of the chief means by which Goethe and Schiller pursued their education of 'the public' and the succession of Goethe's contributions to the annual issues from 1795 on reads like a sequence of courses in practical poetics (epigrams, xenia, ballads, elegies). It would lead much too far to linger over the corresponding theoretical endeavours in the essays and projects (e.g., *Ueber den Dilettantismus*, WA I XLVII 299ff) and the records of the workshop, i.e., the correspondence between the two poets. They are pervaded by the spirit of professionalism (with the corresponding contempt for pretentious amateurs), by experimental venturesomeness, and by an invariable orientation towards the public. There is also present a quantitative factor, especially in the *Xenien* and the 'Balladenjahr.' The experimental mood could be illustrated with the testing of subjects for their generic potential, e.g., the discussion of the Tell story and the approach to the *Achilleis*. Occasion[16] and response are thus relatively far apart at this stage and between the two lies a search for the proper means towards an appropriate execution. Even in this sense, 'Euphrosyne' is a poem in a context, quite different from the isolation of 'Mieding,' an aspect that will be elaborated on further.

The conventional components of 'Euphrosyne' have been pointed out, by Hehn and by Kommerell.[17] Both have made reference to antecedents of isolated passages. Beissner, dealing with the poem as a whole, emphasizes its place in the tradition of the threnodic elegy. He links what is to him 'the queen of Goethe's elegies' with 'the queen of Latin elegies,' Propertius' 'Cornelia' (Desine, Paulle, etc.)[18] And there is a resemblance as far as the object of commemoration is concerned, but he overlooks the much closer structural links with one of Propertius' 'Cynthia' elegies (IV vii, 'Sunt aliquid Manes...'). It is, to be sure, entirely different in tone – scolding – but the basic situation resembles 'Euphrosyne' closely. The dead girl appears to the poet and reproaches him for presumably having forgotten her as soon as she was gone; fear of being forgotten and reminiscence as a means of restoring memory dominate the poet. This resemblance is worth stressing in connection with the impersonal and professional approach on the part of the poet who presumably would make use of an existent structure rather than borrow the tone and spirit of a literary model. Knebel's translation of the Cynthia ode had been published in *Die Horen* shortly before. The encouragement and help given by Goethe and Schiller to the translator have been carefully traced by Lieselotte Blumenthal.[19]

'Euphrosyne' has had considerable attention from the critics. I myself owe a great deal to Bach's essay. Koberstein treats it as an occasional poem. Litzmann[20] approached it as a poem of vision through a useful comparison with 'Zueignung I' ('Der Morgen kam...,' WA I 1 1ff) which he regards as primarily epic in contrast to the essentially dramatic structure of 'Euphrosyne.' However that may be, the two poems have much in common. In both poems the apparition interposes itself between the poet and the daily cycle of nature. In 'Zueignung' it renders bearable the blinding arrival of day ('stand geblendet') (z l 24); in 'Euphrosyne,' it retards or reverses the inevitable escape of the sun. In both poems, the bewildered poet is reproached for failing to recognize the apparition: 'Kennst Du mich nicht?' (z l 33) 'Kennst Du mich, Guter, nicht mehr?' (E l 23). The poet of 'Zueignung,' then, after the act of recognition, becomes a partner in a dialogue which ends with the significant gesture, the *tableau vivant* comparable to the endings of 'Mieding' and *Iphigenie*. In 'Euphrosyne' there is no dialogue. The only time the poet speaks is when he misinterprets the vision and addresses the goddess, instead of recognizing Euphrosyne. After that we only hear Euphrosyne's voice, and yet a large part of her speech consists of a quotation of what the poet had said during her lifetime. Her recollection leads to the request that the poet not permit her memory to fade away. ('Lass nicht ungerühmt mich zu den Schatten hinabgehn!/Nur die Muse gewährt einiges Leben dem Tod,' ll 121–2). But in appearing and speaking she herself has spoken the words of perpetuation and has thus revealed herself as the Muse. The poet's seemingly erroneous recognition proves to have been the proper one after all. This is an exceedingly intricate tissue of ironies and reversals which conveys the sensation of a vision in a mirror where right and left are reversed, as are speech and silence – most fitting for the twilight zone between life and death. The release from this rather frightening world comes with a brief glimpse of something familiar. Hermes Psychopompos guiding the dead girl towards Hades has the familiarity of a visual topos. It evokes the calming presence and permanence of a classical funerary relief. ('Die Kunst hat alle ihre Mittel angewandt ... den Körper ... der Vergänglichkeit zu entziehen' [*Lehrjahre*, WA I XXIII 256].) 'Euphrosyne' exposes us to the most drastic interaction of individual portrayal and generalization. At the point when personal recollection becomes almost embarrassingly poignant (the girl in the arms of the poet), we are given a lengthy general meditation (about one-eighth of the poem, ll 69–86): 'und vergeht nach Gesetz... ,' so general that it could easily take its place in Mignon's 'Exequien': 'für die Lebensdauer ist kein Gesetz. Der schwächste Lebensfaden zieht sich in unerwartete Länge, und den stärksten zerschneidet gewaltsam die Schere einer Parze, die sich in Widersprüchen zu gefallen scheint' (WA I XXIII 256). The poem as a whole is also a treatment in reverse of the topos 'Dem Mimem flicht die Nachwelt... ,' which represents a firmly established tradition abundantly used in the eighteenth century.[21]

The principal purpose of the foregoing observations has been to show that 'Euphrosyne' is a poem more noticeably set in the context of tradition and the convention of literary and visual art than the earlier examples of occasional poetry. The occasional poem as part of a grouping or a canon is a new phenomenon, but not an isolated one. The Karlsbad poems of 1810 and 1812 coalesce into a group, as do three poems of diverse origin and occasion into the *Trilogie der Leidenschaft*.

It seems that Friedrich Schlegel was the first to detect the contextual aspect of the elegies. In his review of volumes I to IV of *Göthes Werke* (1806), which was published in 1808, he wrote:

Wir glauben, man müsse alle diese Elegien und Epigramme nicht als einzelne Gedichte ein jedes für sich, sondern sie alle als ein zusammenhängendes Ganzes betrachten, dem nur die letzte Einheit und Verknüpfung fehlt ... es dürften die allgemeinen Ansichten, welche einzeln überall hervorblicken, in der 'Metamorphose der Pflanzen' aber, wie in einem Kern zusammengedrängt sind, nur gleichmässiger entwickelt und entfaltet seyn, so würden wir ein *Lehrgedicht* vor uns sehen, das uns die

Ansicht des Dichters von der Natur und der Kunst, ihrem Leben und ihrer Bildung einmal vollständig darstellend ... Ein solches Ganzes scheint uns in diesen gehaltvollen Gedichten im Keime zu liegen...[22]

Strange to say, Schlegel does not mention 'Euphrosyne,' although this poem would have supported his argument effectively. 'Die Metamorphose der Pflanzen' was written within a few days of 'Euphrosyne' (17–18 June 1798). Remembering that 'Euphrosyne' in subject matter and in execution can be understood against the background of the complex 'Goethe and the public,' there is one segment of this complex which has not yet been mentioned – his scientific work, which, almost by definition, is not directed towards any one group, but at anyone and no one. 'Ach Natur, wie sicher und gross in allem erscheinst du! Himmel und Erde befolgt ewiges, festes Gesetz ... Doch über des Menschen Leben ... herrschet ein schwankendes Los.' 'Jede Pflanze verkündet dir nun die ew'gen Gesetze-Jede Blume sie spricht lauter und lauter mit dir' 'Euphrosyne,' ll 69–70, 77–8; 'Die Metamorphose der Pflanzen,' ll 65–6). In 'Euphrosyne' the poet had lapsed into silence, overwhelmed by the confrontation with the paradox that the law governing human life seems to be the absence of law. The release from this paralyzing awareness had only been achieved by the emergence of an image, a work of art depicting leave-taking. In 'Die Metamorphose der Pflanzen' the poet speaks to the beloved from beginning to end, pointing out to her the presence of a law in the apparent chaos of natural phenomena which crowd around him.

The connection between the two poems permits us to understand more clearly Goethe's insistence on rehabilitating and broadening the concept of occasional poetry. It does not suffice to restrict the idea of occasion to the isolated, extraordinary moment, be it tragic or joyful, and to give it meaning by lament or praise. The continuous flow of life itself under a law that can be comprehended and loved has the same climactic power as the isolated moment and can constitute an occasion as well. Perhaps the harmonious contemplation of the two poems helps us to find a higher world:

> ...damit in harmonischem Anschaun
> Sich verbinde das Paar, finde die höhere Welt.
> [Die Metamorphose der Pflanzen ll 79–80]

'Euphrosyne' has been called an encounter in a twilight zone –

'Begegnung im Zwischenreich' (Bach). In simplest terms, this is the territory between contemporary reality and mythological reality. Christiane Becker-Neumann could, or even had to be, placed in this territory because of her particular and exceptional human status as a sister of Mignon and Euphorion. But even in this instance, the translation is tinged with guilt, and the words 'Kennst du mich, Guter, nicht mehr?' ring through the entire poem because the dead cannot fail to represent a reproach to the living and every marked grave proclaims an accusation and a threat to those who would forget.[23] Thus, the possibility and admissibility of mythical translation is extremely limited. As a norm it would veer off into the extremes of quasi-necrophilic obsession (for which Goethe would undoubtedly have cited Novalis' Sophia), or, more commonly, into facile habit. Transfiguration would yield to obliteration of individuality, idealization of the departed would turn into his concealment behind a classical mask, into a masquerade, the purpose of which is to dispose of the memory of the person behind it. From here, there is only a short step to dispensing with the human shape and to using non-committal abstract shapes.

Da man in Deutschland die Neigung hegt, Freunden, und besonders abgeschiedenen, Denkmale zu setzen so habe ich schon lange bedauert, dass ich meine lieben Landsleute nicht auf dem rechten Wege sehe. Leider haben sich unsere Monumente an die Garten-und Landschaftsliebhaberei angeschlossen, und da sehen wir denn abgestumpfte Säulen, Vasen, Altäre, Obelisken und was dergleichen bildlose allgemeine Formen sind ... Wie man es denn, solange, die Welt steht, nicht höher hat bringen können als zu einer ikonischen Statue. [*Denkmale* 1804, WA i XLVIII 141–2]

Oeser's monument to Gellert with its small portrait medallion attached to a truncated column bearing a vase, once praised as more eloquent than any verbal tribute could be (cf. above, p 58), does not rate highly by these standards. It is particularly ironical that the enunciation of these revised principles is addressed to Baron von Diede, with whom Goethe had been in correspondence about a monument consisting of an altar and of a tablet bearing an epigram. The passage quoted above clearly anticipates the final phase of this progression towards obliteration of memory, the blasphemous abuse of funerary monuments in the cause of 'Garten-und Landschaftsliebhaberei' in *Die Wahlverwandtschaften*. It would lead us too far to relate this to the final episodes of the novel after the death of Ottilie and back again to Mignon and Euphrosyne.

The preservation of the iconic image, of individual humanity, seems to have impressed Goethe as being of special urgency in the case of outstanding men whose profiles are too quickly eroded by the tendency of posterity to turn them into myths of their own making and convenience. The tributes to Schiller and Winckelmann reflect this urge. *Winckelmann und sein Jahrhundert* (and, to a lesser extent, *Philipp Hackert, Biographische Skizze*) is a peculiarly informal and artful agglomeration of descriptions of incidents, general reflections, and authentic biographical raw material (the letters to Berendis) presented with clear commemorative, elegiac intent, and rightly evaluated as 'probably the most impressive monument ever dedicated to Winckelmann.[24] The incidental and occasional nature of letters turns them into 'dauernde Spuren eines Daseins ... für die Nachwelt immer wichtiger, je mehr dem Schreibenden nur der Augenblick vorschwebte' (WA i XVI 163–8); the seeming shapelessness of the work, the multiplicity of authorship, are means of creating the illusion of life and of process. Goethe's intentions and actions in connection with the publication of his correspondence with Schiller and Zelter are similarly directed towards the preservation of authentic and living images.

The poems dedicated to the memory of Schiller are perhaps the most intense expressions of the urge to hold fast the uniquely human and to follow Phorkyas' exhortation to Faust: 'Halte fest, was dir von allem übrig blieb./Das Kleid, lass es nicht los. Da zupfen schon Dämonen an den Zipfeln...' (WA i XV (1) 239). If any poem can be said to have a theme it is 'Epilog zu Schillers Glocke' (WA i XVI 163–8) with its recurrent 'Denn er war unser.' The portrayal of the man, the references to his fragile humanity (suffering, paleness, patience), recall more than anything else the portrait of Mieding, the silent sufferer who was so easily overlooked, and we seem to be made to feel that Schiller's very greatness could have the same effect. To observe and anticipate the fate of Schiller's image must have weighed heavily on Goethe. It is in the nature of Schiller's work that it should be particularly susceptible to fragmentation and misappropriation in the service of causes, good or bad. This, at least, seems to be one of the possible motives of one of the most powerful of Goethe's commemorative poems, 'Im ernsten Beinhaus war's...' (WA i III 93), the visionary attempt at recovery of iconic individuality and distinctive form from the jaws of death itself and from the levelling action of decomposition. Here is no plaintive request to be remembered ('Kennst du mich, Guter, nicht mehr'), but a powerful command emanating from the skull which defies the disappearance of the corruptible marks of individuality.

As an occasional poem, 'Im ernsten Beinhaus...' is perhaps the last instance in Goethe's work of the making of an occasion, one could almost say in defiance of the official one. The ceremony of deposition of the skull in the pedestal of the Rauch portrait on 17 September 1826 had been marked by a short address delivered, but probably not composed by, August von Goethe, in which the poet's absence was referred to at length. The poem itself was written about a week later, after the skull had been taken to Goethe's house. Thus the official function ('Würdig und heilig vollbracht...,' WA iii x 245) is neither the objective nor the point of departure of Goethe's own utterance. Like 'Euphrosyne,' the vision is an event at once altogether private and of universal concern, but not one to fit the confines of a restricted and officially qualified audience.

The poem on Schiller describes a sudden and overwhelming flash of insight in the most literal sense of the term, interrupting a meditation on the vanity of life. The function of the visual in Goethe's occasional poetry has occupied our attention from the beginning. The generalization may be ventured that its importance increases constantly and that the visual dimension tends to assume at least equality with the verbal one in dealing with occasions. This leads to the likelihood that the visual component will become an indispensable prerequisite to which the word attaches itself as a means of interpretation and enhancement. There is here no radically new departure which could be assigned to any period of Goethe's work. If there is any constant in his makeup, it is the primacy of the eye as the organ of perception of reality. It could be said, however, that the iconological passion extends itself more and more beyond the use of the human form, and that visual presentations, works of visual art, or simple objects offered as gifts become increasingly infused with this spirit of supercharged reality which is the essence of the outstanding moment or occasion. From the abundance of possible illustrations of this trend, a few are chosen, at decent chronological intervals. First, we return to the 'Epilog zu Schillers Glocke' and note its close link to a visual event preceding it. The poem starts with the word 'und,' which connects the evocation of the man with the strongly visual experience of the mimic representation of Schiller's 'Glocke' itself, the poem, perhaps, of all Schiller's works, which embraces most closely tangible, everyday reality. Goethe had planned a much more ambitious and comprehensive spectacle on the stage. Whatever may have prevented the execution of this plan we may wonder if the allegorizing and more abstract character of the original plan itself does not account for its abandonment in favour of 'Epilog.'

The second example, again a commemorative poem, is 'Trauerloge' ('An dem öden Strand...,' WA i III 65). Beutler[25] has pointed out that this poem, dedicated to the memory of Princess Caroline, is in some way a paraphrase of C.D. Friedrich's painting 'Der Mönch am Meer.' This is a comparatively impersonal poem and its poignancy and occasional nature are enhanced by the element of identification and tribute implied in the knowledge that the princess was fond of this painting and of other works of the painter, 'dass sie in seinem Geschmack zeichnete.'[26] It may be noted here, too, that some of the more elaborate occasional poems, that is, those which convey a certain solemnity of form (Stanze) and tone are poems of 'place.' I am thinking here of the series of Karlsbad poems of 1810 and 1812 (see above, p 100) and of the poem 'Herrn Staats-Minister von Voigt' of 1816 (WA i IV 15). In the former, the poet speaks on behalf of the citizens of Karlsbad, disguises himself as a native, as it were, and in this manner the landscape, genius loci – again the tangible and visual component – assumes a crucial rôle, and in the Voigt poem the sites of joint activity are evoked.

The combination of visual and verbal elements in an altogether different ratio is presented by the inscription on the Blücher monument in Rostock, 'Dem Fürsten Blücher von Wahlstadt die Seinen' ('In Harren...,' WA i IV 131), a minute verbal component of a commemorative enterprise in which Goethe took considerable interest.[27] The consultations with the sponsors and with Schadow give us insight to Goethe's thinking on matters touched on in connection with 'Euphrosyne,' but this time primarily from the visual side. There is the question of the classical garb and the problem of the degree of retention of biographical authenticity in connection with the relief tablets of the pedestal, a balancing of the iconological and apotheotic impulses. There are also references to the site of the monument pointing to the desirability of keeping the act of commemoration within the flow of life and to avoid its isolation. This problem is even more clearly expressed in Goethe's reaction to the Frankfurt project of a monument to himself (1821). One of his reasons for objecting to the plan as submitted was that the site would displace a 'heilsame Schwimm-und Badeanstalt' ('Betrachtungen...,' WA i XLII (2) 44). The final example to be offered is Goethe's contribution to the fiftieth anniversary of Carl August's accession. It consisted of 'Zur Logenfeier des 3. Septembers 1825' (WA I III 67–70), reminiscent of the songs of sociability he had cultivated at about the turn of the century and of pictorial decorations of his house for each of which he wrote an interpretive stanza. ('Adler, mit einer Leier...,' 'Beschildeter Arm...,' etc., WA I IV 132–40). This collection marks an extreme point at which the poem has become completely emblematic with a total dependence on a visual corollary. These are almost solutions of visual riddles. The pictures had been used for purposes of decoration once before – in 1814 for the celebration of the duke's return from the wars (Gräf III 622). But even without this chronological hint, the use of riddles and poetic codes gives an indication that there may be correspondences and sources of the trend noted here in the poetics of *West-Oestliche Divan*. The relevance of this work to our theme is more conveniently examined later (ch. 9). The series of emblematic poems mentioned became a useful form of social currency; Goethe had them engraved and used them to help him discharge his growing array of social obligations. It goes without saying that the choice of poems glanced at in the consideration of 'Euphrosyne' has been but one of a vast number of possible combinations to illustrate characteristic tendencies. Nowhere is the sense of *embarras de richesse* that any cross-section of Goethe's work induces more exhilaratingly distressing than in the contemplation of the scores of poems addressed to persons. Resort to oxymora seems inescapable here as we mount once more our familiar seesaw of the poet under the compulsion of occasions and the poet seizing them.

On the passive side – the poet compelled – the obvious consequence is that these verbal tributes to the social graces did not always bear the unmistakable signature of a genius. The balance implied in the concept of 'innige Förmlichkeit' was not invariably achieved or maintained throughout each of the vast number of such poems. In recounting an episode involving a parody of the poem with which Goethe acknowledged tributes rendered on the fiftieth anniversary of his arrival in Weimar ('Meinen feyerlich Bewegten...' WA I IV 269), Hecker, not a member of the debunking school, writes of 'vielen sorglos schlechten Gelegenheitsversen Goethes.'[28] I believe that a sympathetic detailed examination of the hundreds of versified personal messages would permit the replacement of the attribute 'bad' with 'appropriate' in many instances, and that we would gain new insights into the poet's shrewd and sympathetic response to the need of doing what was expected of him. Undoubtedly, he would have been thought rude and cruel had he deprived those around him of their message in verse. Thomas Mann has dealt with this question in a properly unmagisterial manner:

da ist auch das Concept zum Geburtstagscarmen an Excellenz von Voigt – Himmel, es will ja gemacht und mundiert sein, am siebenundzwanzigsten ist der Geburtstag, und viel ist es nicht, was ich habe, eigentlich nur ein paar Verse, wovon einer taugt: 'Ob nicht Natur zuletzt sich doch ergründet?' Das ist gut, das lässt sich hören, das ist von mir, das mag den ganzen Quark tragen, denn natürlich wirds ein schicklicher Quark wie so vieles, es ist nur, dass das 'poetische Talent' gesellig vorspricht, man erwartets von ihm.'[29]

Yet this is only one side of the ledger and the matter of fulfilment of expectations cannot be left as an undefined absolute lest it be bent into supine compliance with the rhythm of a powerful social machine for the sake of comfortable survival. Mann would hardly have wished to create this impression, but even the representation of the Voigt poem as containing one grain of wheat buried in chaff is, when left as the last word on the matter, too uncomfortably close to the many less affectionate indictments of the poet as one who squandered, perhaps abused, his gift.

The endearing motivation by goodness of heart must be balanced by a powerful active force, a poetic initiative that is no less intense than the forces impelling Goethe's other and more readily recognized poetic and scientific endeavours. This is the encomiastic impulse. I realize that devising a label that describes the cause in terms of the effect does not contribute to its explanation, but it does perhaps suggest that the phenomenon is central and deep-rooted. If, by chance, the listeners to and readers of Goethe's sweeping statements on behalf on the *Gelegenheitsgedicht* quoted on page 1 had pressed him for an explanation the answer might have been, 'because I am endowed (blessed?) with the encomiastic impulse.' Perhaps he would have added that this impulse is good for poets, poetry, and society and would have quoted from Rochlitz's letter about his supreme encomiastic enterprise, the *Maskenzug 1818*: 'Ja, Sie sind glücklich, Sie müssen glücklich seyn, im Bewusstseyn, glücklich zu machen' (see Appendix 2). But we need not rely on imaginary conversations to trace the encomiastic impulse. In 'Goethe und das Preisgedicht'[30] Katharina Mommsen has not only defined it and explored its classical and oriental expressions and sources, but has most convincingly demonstrated its intricate manifestations in the grouping of encomiastic poems performed by Goethe in the section *An Personen* of the 1815 edition of his works. Here, too, we find valuable clues to the questions of visual complements of verbal encomia and of the praise of self, questions which have been or will be touched upon in different contexts in this inquiry.

·8·
Weimar Skirmishes and Imperial Battles

THOSE WHO ARE INCLINED to see in Goethe's activities as a supplier of courtly entertainment a desertion of his higher calling will be gratified by the situation obtaining during the first two post-Italian decades. In our review of occasional poems of that period we had encountered a rather complex modification of earlier attitudes and practices. In the dramatic field, the task of tracing developments is easier and can largely be accomplished with negatives. I expressly propose to ignore Goethe's contributions to the 'Maskenzüge' of 30 January 1798 ('Der lang ersehnte Friede...' WA I XVI 208), 30 January 1802 ('Wenn von der Ruhmverkünderin...,' *ibid.* 210), and 30 January 1809 (*ibid.* 213), as not strictly representative of the main direction of development and as sufficiently trifling to leave it unaffected. In this period the court is no longer the setting of occasional dramatic entertainments. Although *Der Triumph der Empfindsamkeit* and *Iphigenie* had brought the theatre into the courtly environment, now, whatever courtly elements may be observable are brought to the theatre. We may refer back to the general considerations relating to the concept and rôle of 'the public' offered in the last chapter. It would be reassuring if these changes could be reduced to an overall explanation, such as 'Personal patronage was superseded by a free market ... a conglomerate of nameless consumers, the so-called "public." The work of art was subjected more and more to the laws of competition.'[1] And perhaps this would be adequate if we looked at the scene through the wrong end of a telescope. But we must take into account some humbler causes as well, even though they, in turn, may be linked with large and long-range historical phenomena. I am thinking of the absence of the head of the court, the duke, from his residence during much of the period which we are examining. The interplay of historical events and personal inclination in the dual rôle of ruler and Prussian general removed Carl August from the scene for periods of unforseeable length. He may thus have served his subjects in the best way he knew, but the element of continuity for which Goethe had pleaded in 'Ilmenau' 'Streue klug wie reich mit männlich steter Hand,/ Den Segen aus auf ein geackert Land' (ll 188–9) was hardly being attained. Occasional works of the kind now being examined call for some degree of reliability on the part of those to whom tributes are directed. When they cannot be counted upon to play their appointed part – of mere presence at least to produce a 'kairos' – embarrassment is sure to ensue. Goethe once complained about such a situation in connection with *Epimenides* ('Was haben wir nicht für Kränze gewunden, Die Fürsten, sie sind nicht gekommen...,' WA i v (1) 148).

Paläophron und Neoterpe is the one larger work of the period which was, at least originally, written for the setting of courtly amateurism. It shows thematic affinities with typical masque subject matter, time as such, and was written for the ever more remote and aloof household of the dowager duchess, which was rather conservative inasmuch as it clung to the spirit of the seventies and early eighties. And at that, through the use of masks this work was at the same time part of the deliberate educative program for the theatre and was easily transferred to the realm of the public stage.

The notion of scale seems the most serviceable as a criterion of Goethe's response to occasions in this phase. Three orders of magnitude are involved here. The first one is appropriate to his pre-Italian (or pre-revolutionary, which amounted to the same thing) productions: the initimate, closed court environment in which distances are measured by the length of one's arm, as it were. The concepts of court and household coincide more or less. There is no strict line of demarcation between performer and audience, between professional and dilettante (cf. the position of Corona Schröter), between patron and friend. While conflict and frustration are not absent from this setting, they are representable and manageable.

Secondly, there is the impersonal order of magnitude, the natural order which is faceless though by no means unrelated to the realm of human response. The range of social phenomena here is, theoretically at least, as limitless and faceless as that of natural phenomena. For instance, the public is an object to be observed and influenced, educated, much as a natural force is taken account of and perhaps controlled. Positively speaking, it is the Roman Carnival which is a state of being, rather than an event devised and performed by someone for someone. Negatively, it is the phenomenon of revolution, anonymous, overwhelming, and essentially beyond the possibility of personal confrontation. As such, it may be beneficial or harmful. But it is really outside ethical categories, and if at all controllable, then in the way a river is controlled, by patient and purposeful and protracted labour (cf. the 'education' of the theatre, i.e., of actors and public).

Thirdly, between the two, there is the realm of the large political unit, of kingdom and empire. This is, on the whole, the stage of imperfection. It is essentially sinister in character because it is neither measurable nor controllable by the length of one's arm, nor by the manner in which one deals with nature. Here human action is most likely to be corrupt and hypocritical. For Goethe – who grew up in an autonomous city, who had been chief minister of a miniature dukedom, who held that humanity had attained its summit in the city states of ancient Greece, who had taken one cold look at Berlin, and none at Paris, Vienna, or London – for Goethe, kingdoms and empires such as Prussia and Russia, Austria, and France were sinister and dangerous places unless they were transfigured by the presence of exceptional personalities, Frederick II or Napoleon, when they ceased to be themselves, so to speak. The France of Louis XVI, and of *Grosskophta* had little in common with the realm of Napoleon. Conversely, in the poem addressed to Francis I of Austria ('Ihro des Kaisers von Oesterreich Majestät, WA I XVI 323) the ruler is addressed as the master of the least conspicuous of his cities, Karlsbad, which is not a seat of power but a site where the healing forces of nature manifest themselves.

Three instances seem to me to bear out the validity of this view and they are chronologically so closely grouped that the silence of the first and the language of the other two combine to form an explicit statement. Goethe's failure to contribute to the reception in Weimar of Maria Paulowna (1804) impresses as at least as relevant to Goethe's political conceptions and to his rôle as a poet associated with a court as his silence on the occasion of his sister's wedding may have been to his psychological constitution (cf. above, p 38). This marriage of the heir-apparent linked the insignificant duchy with a dynasty of first European rank. As such, it was expected to and did bring not only prestige but also a most welcome and dramatic infusion of money. No doubt the pleasure over this equalled that of the emperor of *Faust* II on the occasion of his currency reform. The match also established a close dynastic connection with a probable parricide, the offspring of a monarch who was universally acknowledged to have been a lunatic and a line of descent which may well have been direct in name only. It must be stressed that this situation has little to do with the person of the princess. Maria Paulowna by all accounts, including Goethe's, was a sensitive, intelligent, and generous woman. I am concerned here with the possible causes of Goethe's response to a courtly occasion, nothing else. And I suggest that Goethe was unable to pay fitting tribute to an event which amounted to the impingement of vast and alien forces upon his environment. Presumably, the situation would have necessitated a reconciliation of the spirit of celebration with the awareness of forces which are not given poetic shape until much later and in the context of a hypothetical occasion: 'Mummenschanz' and the preceding court scene of *Faust* II. Here the poet could enlarge freely on the relationship of power and illusion, of penury and aspiration and the affinity between the imperial theme and the dangerous sport of playing with fire.

Since the political situation of Weimar lurks behind almost every work yet to be considered in this inquiry, some further observations on Carl August as a ruler are perhaps in order. When Goethe held him up as an example – 'So wende nach innen, so wende nach aussen die Kräfte Jeder, da wärs ein Fest, Deutscher mit Deutschen zu sein' (WA i I 315) – in 1789 or 1790, he was possibly expressing a hope concerning the duke's own future course, as well. The duke, in fact, had shown a certain inclination to upset the nice balance of 'innen' and 'aussen' as early as 1785 in connection with the 'Fürstenbund.' And while no prince large or small possibly could have stayed on the ground in the revolutionary and Napoleonic decades, Carl August walked the tightrope with considerable gusto and showed a total lack of the isolationist disposition implied in Goethe's lines. In his allegiances and actions he gives the impression of a persistent but resilient romantic. Thus he went to the Congress of Vienna with high hopes of acquiring the crown of Saxony, but was quite unshaken when he returned home with but 50,000 'souls' added to his realm.[2] If he was too solidly constructed to be a Tasso among the crowned heads, he was certainly no Antonio, either; and he was far too colourful and restless to correspond to the portrait of the duke of Ferrara. To return to the occasion of 1804, it seems that the principal poetic response to it, Schiller's *Huldigung der Künste*, is built on a solid foundation of Goethean silence. (cf. GES I 975–6).

The ominous and sinister aspect of courtly festivity in an imperial setting was not definitely articulated until the writing of the 'Mummenschanz.' But the very year 1804 yielded a treatment of the theme which could perhaps be regarded as a 'Vorform' of the 'Mummenschanz.' Goethe spent much of that year in the preparation of a new and supposedly more stageable version of *Götz*. This objective was not attained, as is borne out by the further history of the staging of this play. One reason was perhaps Goethe's inability to keep in focus the goal of purely technical improvement and that some modifications and additions were prompted by different considerations. Scenes 17 to 19 of Act IV (WA i XIII (1) 302–8) show a dress rehearsal of Adelheid's part in a court masquerade being held before Weislingen, who is in anything but a festive mood and rightly suspicious of his wife's intentions. The object of these is Charles, the imperial heir as Adelheid herself announces in scene 19. While parading before her husband, Adelheid recites her verses on love and folly, supposedly written by the emperor himself. We are thus given a glimpse behind the stage, but unlike the one granted us in 'Mieding,' it suggests intrigue, evil intentions, and abuse of the festive setting and mood, in short, corruption. The emperor busies himself as occasional poet when he is helpless in his task of mending the empire; the heir is the unwitting object of intrigue. In this respect, they anticipate the situation of the emperor in *Faust* II. A suggestion of depravity pervades these brief scenes that is almost un-Goethean. Rather, one is led to think of the dumb show of *Hamlet* or the masquerade scene in Brecht's *Galilei*.

Anticipated festivity which does not actually take place as far as the spectator is concerned, an event which does not wait for its proper time and thus dooms itself, draws our attention towards a more explicit treatment of the theme during this period. In order to be a beneficial social force, a courtly feast or any festive occasion for that matter must be held at a fitting time. It must conform to an established order according to the religious or secular calendar, or by intuitive recognition of the right moment in order to represent an analogue to the legitimate rhythms of nature. Here the concepts of 'occasion,' 'opportunity,' and 'kairos' converge. If by some corruption of order this fails to be accomplished, there is sure to be something rotten in the state, and time is out of joint. Cause and effect then become indistinguishable, as do symptom and disease. It is a tragic situation in which guilt in the sense of individual causation becomes irrelevant. If the reader is at a loss as to whether Ottilie in *Die Wahlverwandtschaften* (1809) is being discussed, or Eugenie of *Die Natürliche Tochter* (1803), this confusion is all to the good because I want to suggest continuity of this concern from the latter work to the former. But the courtly side of the matter dominates *Die Natürliche Tochter*. Considerations of the health of the monarchy and the theme of 'kairos' are explicitly present and tightly interwoven. The entire first half of the completed part of the work has for its dramatic focus the courtly ceremony of the legitimatization of Eugenie. In preparing for it she anticipates it by writing and reciting the sonnet coveying her declaration of loyalty and by dressing for the occasion. One cannot be certain that Goethe planned[3] the ghostly parody of the ceremony in prison when the sonnet would be removed from its hiding place. To execute such a scene Goethe would perhaps have had to recapture the brutal recklessness of his youth when he wrote the prison scene of *Urfaust*. But scenes 4 and 5 of Act II convey the tragic implications sufficiently:

Eine wirkliche Vereinigung von Schein und Wesen wäre erst beim Fest eingetreten ... Bei dieser Vorwegnahme handelt es sich um eine Fehlerscheinung ...[4]

Anticipation of an occasion has once again been used as the means of accounting for the impossibility of the realization of an authentic occasion, in which society would confirm and renew itself. In the present case there is brought into play an entire spectrum of causes from the ironic one of youthful rashness through greed, hypocrisy, ambition, and weakness to the impersonal one of social imbalance. One could regard this situation as an eloquent definition of courtly poetry, albeit one in entirely negative terms.

Passing reference must be made to an isolated and futile attempt by Goethe to create, *in vitro*, a social form analogous to a court through which conditions for social poetry could be created. These were periodic gatherings, organized by Goethe and including among others the ladies and gentlemen of the Schiller, Egloffstein, Wolfskeel, and Wolzogen households with Heinrich Meyer as the only untitled member. The poetic yield of these mock-mediaeval courtly sessions were several of Goethe's songs of sociability ('Mich ergreift, ich weiss nicht wie ...,' 'Was gehst du schöne Nachbarin ...'). (See *Tag-und Jahres-Hefte* 1802, WA i xxxv, 126) We need not take as gospel truth every nasty detail contained in Countess Henriette von Egloffstein's 'Bericht einer Theilnehmerin'[5] or enter into details of the whole intrigue for which Kotzebue was blamed by Goethe to conclude that this experiment which did not survive its first season, 1801/2, was a failure, that the circle as a social foundation of culture situated between the official court and the public arena was not viable.

Discontinuity has been emphasized, and silence and withdrawal noted as prevalent alternatives to social occasional utterance. There is, however, one region where these alternatives do not apply; indeed, one is tempted to think of a compensatory mechanism at work. Conflict with respect to the theatre as a local and as an exemplary institution elicited an elaborate, almost a voluble work in 1802. *Was wir bringen* (WA i XIII 37–88) was written for the opening of the new Lauchstädt playhouse in June of that year. Seen in retrospect, this is actually a modest occasion and therefore one point to be made about it is the disproportion between the occasion and the work written for it. But we must note the strong effect on Goethe of the opening of new theatrical buildings. They never seem to have failed to arouse within him hopes of a better world to come. Witness his elation in connection with the opening of the new house in Weimar in 1797, along with his share in Schiller's prologue to *Wallenstein*.[6] Even stronger evidence of this feeling may be found in later years, long after he had relinquished an active rôle in theatrical matters; the Berlin *Prolog* of 1821 (WA i XIII (1) 115 et seq.), and the outline of a *Vorspiel* for Hamburg (1827, WA i XIII (2) 240 et seq.). Conversely, recall his extremely violent emotional reaction to the Weimar fire of 1825. In another way, Lauchstädt is more important than it appears to be. The summer seasons there, as well as the visits to Halle and Leipzig, were financially much the most rewarding phases of the Weimar theatrical year and helped to reduce the deficits of the winter season in Weimar proper. This success explains, in part at least, the almost undisguised flattery of place and audience in *Was wir bringen* which appears even more strongly in the Halle prologue of 1811 (WA i XIII (1) 172 et seq.).

But practical considerations alone would hardly account for so elaborate an inaugural work as *Was wir bringen*. Why was Goethe not content to write a conventional prologue similar to those of the previous decade? Körner posed this question, albeit in a spirit of antagonism and in eager assent to Schiller's evaluation of *Was wir bringen* as 'Sterne auf einen Bettlermantel gestickt.'[7] And even this very faint praise seems less damning than the conspicuous absence of this work from the indices of some of the more ambitious works of comprehensive Goethe scholarship in our own century (e.g., Gundolf, Viëtor, Staiger). Goethe himself had not anticipated the proportions of this work 'viel weitläufiger geworden ... als ich gedacht habe' (to Schiller, 11 June 1802, WA iv xvi 91). This places his modest work, in this respect at least, in august company such as that of *Die Wahlverwandtschaften* and *Der Zauberberg* as one which sought and imposed its own proportions on its creator – a phenomenon which points to the assertion of creative forces involving the artist beyond his assessment of moment and occasion. There may have been a catalyst – relief over the relative ease with which the construction of the new building had been accomplished. Goethe had anticipated complications and delays which, for once, did not occur (cf. letter to Voigt, 16 February 1802, *ibid.* 35). Obviously, this explanation still does not add sufficient weight to the event itself; perhaps we are dealing with a combination of events. Mindful of the arbitrariness inevitable in such reconstructions, I suggest 2 January 1802 as the occasioning date of *Was wir bringen*.

On that day A.W. Schlegel's *Ion* was first performed in Weimar and Goethe noted Böttiger's behaviour: 'Schon bey der ersten Vorstellung rannte dieser Tigeraffe im Parterre herum, durch pedantische Anmerkungen den Genuss einer Darstellung wie sie Weimar noch nicht gehabt hat, zu stören' (to Wieland, 13 January 1802, *ibid.* 4). In this letter, and in one to Bertuch, the day before, Goethe saw to it by a naked assertion of his authority which has few parallels in his correspondence that Böttiger should not be permitted to write about *Ion* in any Weimar periodical. It is important to see clearly that he was not so much protecting the play as the performance. Böttiger had interfered with his long-range program of education of actors and public, the merit of the vehicle was a secondary consideration, and the standing and the feelings of the author were not to the point at all. Goethe does not rise in wrath to defend Schlegel, or the Romantics, but his own sovereign decision that the performance of this play was desirable at this time. This incident forms part of a protracted campaign, the 'B. and K. War.' Kotzebue was the other chief enemy and if there is anything in the correspondence to exceed the fierceness of the letters referred to above it is one of 3 March 1802 to Kotzebue's mother (*ibid.* 47), who had objected to cuts ordered by Goethe in the performance of one of her son's plays. Again, none of this was done for the greater glory of the Schlegels. The alliance with the Romantics, if this be the proper term for the relationship, was strictly tactical in nature. One of the invectives makes this quite clear:

Zwar wär' es billig, diesen frechen Vögeln
Auch tüchtig was am bunten Zeug zu flicken;
Doch Euch, ihr Musenlosen, wirds nicht glücken,
Drum, Flegel, bleibt zu Haus mit euern Flegeln.
['B. und K.' ll 5–8, WA i v (1) 171]

It is not my purpose to record in detail the skirmishes and battles of these days. The war had a second front in the region of the visual arts, as witness the sequence of the competitions for the Weimar fall exhibitions. But all the blows struck were essentially defensive and intended to protect the development of public art in a desirable direction rather than to demolish the enemy. It is indicative of Goethe's disposition and intentions that he did not content himself with keeping Bertuch's *Journal des Luxus und der Moden* unsullied by Böttiger's review of *Ion*. Only a week later he was at work on the essay *Weimarisches Hoftheater* (WA i XL 72–85), which filled the gap when it was published there in March. On the face of it, annihilation of the enemy is followed by a constructive programmatic statement. Actually, polemics and constructiveness merge almost impishly. Goethe himself referred to the essay as a 'Schnurre' in which he appeared displaying 'ein erstaunt ernsthaft Gesicht' (to Schiller, 19 January 1802, WA iv XVI 11), and, in doing so, anticipated the spirit of *Was wir bringen*. We are given a calm, historical account of the evolutionary phases of the Weimar theatre, but the very detachment of historical presentation becomes the agent of polemical challenge. A brief summary will illustrate this account. The theatre in Weimar had passed through several stages towards the goal of artistic perfection and would continue to evolve. It was up to the public to follow suit; it could rise similarly, or it could descend to the level of a mob. Various skills had been mastered, and the point had been reached where justice could be done to such diverse authors and dramatic styles as Lessing (in *Nathan*), Terence (in Einsiedel's *Brüder*), Gozzi (in Schiller's *Turandot*), and Euripides (*Ion*). This versatility had brought all manner of greater and lesser works within the reach of the company and the public. The level of accomplishment was not yet high enough to render tolerable the lowest forms of dramatic life (i.e., Kotzebue's farce *Wirrwarr*), but eventually this would come to pass, too. Much of this paraphrase could easily be adapted to *Was wir bringen*. The blending of Napoleonic aloofness with exuberant satire that we are more readily prepared to find in Tieck's dramatized fairy-tales is common to both works. One is tempted to suggest 'Was wir brachten' as an alternative title for the essay.

The sonnet of *Die Natürliche Tochter* ('Welch Wonneleben ...,' 1, 4) was to be the climax of a court ceremony which did not take place. It was to mark the beginning of the phase of truth in the life of a young woman in which her natural origin and her place in the structure of society would be in harmony. But when this daughter of nature, this nymph of the woods, awakens from her fall she finds herself in the bearpit of intrigue and weakness. Nymphe of *Was wir bringen* is in the happier situation of being able to recite her sonnet ('Natur und Kunst...' sc. 19) at the proper moment, marking a transformation that Eugenie ('neugeboren durch sein Wort,' 1 4) could only anticipate in her girlish daydreams. But then, the harmonization that occurs in *Was wir bringen* is that of nature and art, not of nature and society, and it can be accomplished by means of a renewal of which the political world is incapable. Enlightenment in *Die Natürliche Tochter* is violent and tragic: 'wenn aus geheimnisvollem/ Verborgnem Zustand ich, ans Licht auf einmal/ Hervorgerissen und geblendet, mich,/ Unsicher, schwankend, nicht zu fassen weiss' (1.5). In the comic context of *Was wir bringen* Nymphe can and does experience a liberating revelation: 'welchen Schleier nahmst du mir/ Von meinen Augen weg, indess mein Herz/ So warm als sonst, ja freier glüht und schlägt' (sc. 19). She has a guide capable of directing the process of metamorphosis, a benevolent Mephistophelean 'Physikus ... Philosoph ... Taschenspieler' (sc. 10). The situation, the transformation of the setting into the new thespian temple, constitutes a genuine improvement with an inherent potential of rebirth which is denied to Eugenie. Here, Goethe felt free to write in a truly comic vein – if we take the essence of the comic to be the reconciliation and integration of apparently hopelessly disparate elements in a sphere in which such integration is still possible, i.e., in his own theatrical realm. No one is excluded and driven into the wilderness.

Goethe presented the work to the public, in the *Allgemeine Zeitung* (WA i XL 249), as a review of all dramatic forms. The processional and the dramatic lines are brought together with great ingenuity; the action consists in the metamorphosis of all; the dramatic conflict is determined by the various degrees of reluctance to enter and reluctance to leave. The hope which has been expressed tongue-in-cheek in the essay that even Kotzebue, or rather the dramatic style he represents, would become tolerable and assume a rightful place is actually fulfilled. Even Mutter Marthe, who is the most reluctant to let go of what she takes to be her true and indissoluble identity ('Doch heute hat sie sich das Eine Bauernweib/ So fest in Kopf gesetzt, 'sc. 17), finally agrees to accept what one might call the comic equivalent of 'Der Dichtung Schleier aus der Hand der Wahrheit.' Merkur, rascal and prestidigitator, is the agent who releases the humour-ridden characters from their bondage, as Mephistopheles frees Faust from the confinement of his solitary obsession, and as Verazio-Magus dispels Lila's demons. It is no accident but an important juncture in Goethe's poetic development that in this modest occasional work we hear again for the first time the comic accents of the peak of Weimar sociability, especially of *Der Triumph der Empfindsamkeit* with its topical allusions. A reader familiar with the successful dramatic literature of the day, of Iffland, Kotzebue, etc., could undoubtedly detect a large number of fragmentary quotations from these authors in the early scenes. But the court is no longer the object of the therapeutic process and the partner in bringing it about. Instead, the object is the public at large, and literary rather than social postures are involved. Later on, when Goethe returned to the court with more elaborate productions (especially the 'Maskenzüge' of 1810 and 1818) the court tends to appear as part of the literary public and literature remains the theme and the object. This development is presaged even in the 'Maskenzug' fragment of 1802 (WA I XVI 210).

Within the intricate dramatic framework of *Was wir bringen* is a didactic and exhortatory prologue (sc. 16) apparently much like those of the early nineties, but in the present context it reveals make-believe and teasing, too, a 'Schnurre' like the straight-faced essay. The explicitness of Merkur's explanation that Märten's old hut stands for the old theatre, and the palace for the new, etc., suggests that it cannot have been intended as a solemn revelation of a heretofore opaque poetic purpose. At least it is difficult to believe so in view of the considerable sophistication of the audience assembled in the resort which happened to include such rather flexible minds as A.W. Schlegel, Hegel, Schelling, and F.A. Wolf (cf. Gräf VI 425). Goethe is paying his audience a compliment by making fun of the tightly controlled narrow allegorization which the bourgeois theatre of the era used in its hours of festivity[8] and which takes the spectator on a straight and narrow track from point *a* to point *b*. On so short a journey neither the landscape nor the traveller is likely to change much. The sole reward is the gratification of being able to say that things are much the same all over, or, to put it in the terms of the Ifflandian 'Vorspiele,' that virtue is to be found in the hut and in the palace. But *Was wir bringen* as a whole beckons the audience to embark on a bolder expedition for which the proper vehicle is the magic carpet of the fairy-tale;⁹ it is a summons to broaden one's sympathies and interests and to rise above oneself. The exhortation of *Weimarisches Hoftheater* had made that point:

Man sollte nicht gerade immer sich und sein nächstes Geistes-Herzens- und-Sinnesbedürfniss auf dem Theater zu befriedigen gedenken; man könnte sich vielmehr öfters wie einen Reisenden betrachten, der in fremden Orten und Gegenden, die er zu seiner Belehrung und Ergötzung besucht, nicht alle Bequemlichkeit findet, die er zu Hause seiner Individualität anzupassen Gelegenheit hatte. [WA i XL 82]

It is not difficult to see that in this battle against the stay-at-homes, the Romantics were welcome fellow travellers, and, at times, guides. *Ion* (January 1802), and in *Alarcos* (May 1802), were admitted to the Weimar stage as demonstrations of poetic and theatrical mobility. We may take at face value Goethe's repeated assurances that he accepted these plays not so much for their intrinsic value, about which he had as many doubts as the rest of the world (except, perhaps, for the Schlegel brothers), but rather as a means of broadening the horizon of the dramatically possible by the use of verse, new metres, and masks. As the setting in a Calderonian play can change while the actors continue to recite their lines, so the spectator was to surrender to the experience of being carried into new realms of experience without feeling lost and abandoned, but elated and transformed. It is a question of elasticity of taste, of getting the public away from itself, and of confronting it with an art that is something more than a mirror in which a rather imperfect society persists in seeking its own reflection. The closely knit youthful court circle of Weimar had possessed this quality and had been able to fit *Proserpina* into *Der Triumph der Empfindsamkeit*. One is tempted to say that Goethe now was trying to give his public some of the quality of a court audience: 'Der Deutsche ist überhaupt ernsthafter Natur und sein Ernst zeigt sich vorzüglich, wenn vom Spiele die Rede ist, besonders auch im Theater...' (*ibid*. 82). In view of Schiller's reaction to *Was wir bringen* noted above (p 139) one is led to wonder about the vitality of the 'Spieltrieb,' which plays such an important rôle in his aesthetic theory. Goethe says further:

wir finden auch solche Stücke höchst nöthig, durch welche der Zuschauer erinnert wird, dass das ganze theatralische Wesen nur ein Spiel sei, über das er, wenn es ihm ästhetisch, ja moralisch nutzen soll, erhaben stehen muss, ohne desshalb weniger Genuss daran zu finden. [ibid. 83]

This attitude, the desire to have make-believe taken seriously, not literally, retains considerable importance in the later occasional works, and not merely there. The contemporaries of the aged Goethe who could not rid themselves of the suspicion that they were being made light of, as well as their successors, such as F.Th. Vischer, are the descendants of B. and K.

That the passages quoted above were not the result of a momentary mood, or of an isolated feud engendered by the provocations of time and place, is demonstrated at least ten years later by the fact that Goethe wrote a survey of the German theatre, originally intended for inclusion in *Dichtung und Wahrheit*. This now bears the title *Deutsches Theater*. Here Goethe enlarges on the foes of this 'peculiar institution': the police, religion, and taste purified by higher moral principles:

Ein Drittes hat sodann eine fortdauernde und vielleicht nie zu zerstörende Mittelmässigkeit des deutschen Theaters gewirkt. Es ist die ununterbrochene Folge von drei Schauspielern, welche, als Menschen schätzbar, das Gefühl ihrer Würde auch auf dem Theater nicht aufgeben konnten und deshalb mehr oder weniger die dramatische Kunst nach dem Sittlichen, Anständigen, Gebilligten und wenigstens scheinbar Guten hinzogen. Ekhofen, Schrödern und Ifflanden kam hierin sogar die allgemeine Tendenz der Zeit, die eine allgemeine An-und Ausgleichung aller Stände und Beschäftigungen zu einem allgemeinen Menschenwerthe durchaus im Herzen und im Auge hatten. Die Sentimentalität, die Würde des Alters und des Menschenverstandes, das Vermitteln durch vortreffliche Väter und weise Männer nahm auf dem Theater überhand. [WA i XL 176–7]

Iffland, is of course, of the greatest interest to us because he inflicted this spirit upon the public through his own plays and made it more efficacious by his universally acknowledged ability as an actor. The mediocrity to which Goethe refers is concerned with the average and shies away from excess. It leaves no room for metamorphosis by the imagination, a power that does not conveniently reproduce a man of average size, but is both greater and smaller than human dimension. In *Was wir bringen* it presents itself as 'Ein schäckig

Knäblein ... ein Zwerglein...' (sc. 20),[10] apparently beyond all human control, and yet capable of serving man:

> Doch ist er auch zu bänd'gen. Ja, er bändigt
> Sogar sich selbst, sobald ich ihm den Stab
> Vertrauend überliefre, der die Seelen führt. [sc. 20]

Several features of *Was wir bringen* thus present themselves as distinctive and indicative of practices to be observed in later works. First, the spirit of reconciliation as the goal of the drama: satire is used as a means of bringing about the transformation of its object into forms which are compatible with other and higher forms of human and artistic activity, but without its annihilation. In his desire to attack without destroying or discrediting, Goethe stands apart not only from the B. and K. group, but also from the Romantics, whose craving for synthesis was a much more theoretical affair, counterbalanced by their youthful impatience and their urge to score conspicuously. The attainment of a final festive reunion of all manifestations of the human spirit and artistic forms could be theoretically conceived by them, but could not be given shape.

Next, we note the special rôle of music: in *Was wir bringen* this is not so much a matter of the use which is restricted to a few arias and presumably some incidental music not mentioned in print but to be taken for granted according to the practice of the time. It is, rather, in this instance, the special rôle assigned to Phone. Between her sisters, Nymphe and Pathos, she is the most genuine, least in need of transformation, least afflicted by misapprehensions about herself and her rôle, and hence possesses the greatest transforming powers and is on the closest terms with the new Psychopompos:

> Besonders aber strebt ihm jene Schöne dort,
> Auf des Gesanges raschem Fittig nach.
> Wär' er zu halten, diese hielt' ihn fest;
> Doch wollt' er bleiben, sie entliess' ihn gleich. [sc. 20]

Thirdly, we observe the uninhibited use of realistic, allegorical, mythical, and symbolic figures, unfettered by a classicist code of correctness and consistency. When Märten and Marthe appear to be Philemon and Baucis, when Merkur is thought to be the devil, they assume the functions of their alleged identity, so that these interpretations are not mere illusions and errors which have to be corrected, but rather are dimensions added to the characters in question. Again nothing is annihilated or discarded, but everything is placed in a condition of transformability. Croce's strictures on Goethe's misuse of the terms allegorical and symbolic[11] are out of place here, because the intention of the poet is to let them merge and interact, as is made amply clear by the playful use of these terms in scene 17.

Lastly, in recalling the disproportion of occasion and of the work dedicated to it, I suggest that Goethe approaches a festive drama which has no visible or clearly definable occasion at all, an autonomous occasional presentation, the 'Festspiel' per se which has no fixed place in the courtly or theatrical calendar, but which is, nevertheless, related to a given human or dramatic or historic situation.

With appropriate qualifications, we could say that a projection of the trends summarized in the last paragraphs intersects with all dramatic works written by Goethe in the remaining thirty years of his life. It may be argued that this is too long a perspective, but it should be granted that the road from *Was wir bringen* to *Pandora* is a direct one.

While we may regard *Pandora* as the 'Festspiel' par excellence and as the realization of a trend which became visible in the examination of *Was wir bringen*, the nature of this enquiry does not allow us to leave it at that, however strong the lure of poetic logic. Even if Goethe as a poet were more directly committed to an ideal of *poésie pure*, or putting it in contemporaneous terms, if he were more of a Romantic poet than he actually was, we would still want to be sure of not overlooking any threads which might link this work with external conditions, with tangible factors that elicited this grandiose project and the effort of its partial execution.

There is no reason to assume that the poet's orientation towards the public and his concern with the progressive exploitation of the potential of the stage ceased abruptly. Granted, the Weimar stage was no longer the site of realization of such aspirations. Practical and political considerations aside, a large stage, literally and figuratively, may have taken its place in Goethe's mind. Even in *Was wir bringen* Goethe was beginning to strain at the limitations of time and place. We must resign ourselves to the fact that suggestions about the tangible components of the motivation for *Pandora* must remain speculative. Goethe remained persistently silent on this score, perhaps because the work remained unfinished, perhaps because he wanted to create the impression of a 'Festspiel' in the pure and abstract sense. With some reservations I adopt Hankammer's suggestion: 'Es ist nicht unwahrscheinlich, dass Goethe das Festspiel von Pandoras Heimkehr als dichterische Feier für den allgemeinen Frieden geplant hat, auf den er hoffte.'[12] This is a properly utopian formulation envisaging no place and no time for the realization of the work. If we retreat a step from this extreme position we might properly ask in which direction the poet would look to find the least unlikely site of its realization. I suggest that it was Vienna and Austria. We may remain puzzled by the diary entries of 27 and 31 July 1806 (WA III III 147–50) which associate Frau von Levetzow and Pandora in the most obscure fashion possible and which are frequently thought of as the earliest reference to the dramatic plan. Yet we can still maintain that the making of *Pandora* is to a large extent linked with Karlsbad. Between 1806 and 1808 Karlsbad is to Goethe a place of peace. This is not to say that it was hermetically sealed off from the continent. The sounds of political change and dislocation were audible, but they were muffled by the rustling of the mineral springs and rendered tolerable by the cosmopolitan character of the spa. Presumably, the common concern with health set a sheltering screen between the harsh realities of Napoleonic Europe and the visitors. Goethe's contacts with the Austro-Bohemian aristocracy were becoming ever more numerous and close. He was being wooed. When he reiterated (to Christiane, 23–7 July 1807, WA IV XIX 372–5) that he was not going to Vienna, we sense that the temptation to go matched the apprehension such rumours must have excited in Weimar. What could have tempted him? First and foremost surely the interest shown by a group of powerful and understanding aristocrats who were likely to form the core of an enlightened public in Vienna. Secondly, the fact that Austria was showing signs of being and remaining at peace, the most likely setting of a 'Feier für den allgemeinen Frieden.' In 1807 he could not know that the half-way mark had been reached between the battles of Austerlitz and Wagram and he may well have felt that Austria was farther removed from the shock of defeat and more willing to come to terms with the conspicuous presence of Napoleon in western and central Europe than were at that time his duke, that reluctant and elusive member of the *Rheinbund*, or the monarchs of Prussia and Russia who had just signed the treaty of Tilsit (July 1807) with minimal enthusiasm. Later in the year, Goethe summed up the mood of the season in a letter to Reinhard:

'Uebrigens haben wir alle Ursache unsere innern Familien-und Freundesfeyertage recht fromm zu begehen: denn was die öffentlichen Feyerlichkeiten betrifft, so theilt sich die Welt wirklich in eine Tages-und Nachtseite, und leider befinden wir uns auf der letztern' (16 November 1807, WA iv XIX 454). If any European capital was likely to move from the dark to the bright side as far as *public* festivity was concerned, it was Vienna. The best that could be done for Weimar was a 'Familienfeier' of sorts, the *Vorspiel zu Eröffnung des Weimarischen Theaters am 19. September 1807...* (WA i XIII (1) 23 et seq.) celebrating the reunion of the ducal family which had dispersed before the catastrophic days of October 1806. This dispersion had various reasons. Cowardice was not one of them, but a spirit of resistance in the case of the duke and of Princess Maria Paulowna was. Goethe is likely to have regarded this spirit as unwillingness to recognize the presence of a demonic force embodied in the conqueror. Thus the tribute contained in the *Vorspiel* was conspicuously concentrated on the Duchess Luise, who had averted worse disasters by having stayed in Weimar, and on the memory of Anna Amalia. Beyond this tribute, we find little more than the emphatic exhortation, addressed to all, to settle down and accept reality.

There is also reason to believe that Goethe harboured some hope of seing his Weimar theatrical style and objectives taking root in Vienna.[13] Two actors, alumni of the 'Weimar-School,' Heinrich Schmidt and Friedrich Haide, were in that city at the time and the poet seems to have thought of them as possible missionaries of his theatrical gospel. This did not come to pass; Haide was caught in the crossfire between what may roughly be called the Rationalists (Schreyvogel) and the Romantics and returned to Weimar after one year. Leo von Seckendorff and Josef Ludwig Stoll took his side in their periodical, *Prometheus*, in the first issue of which they had begun publication of Goethe's *Pandora*. Thus, broader considerations and expectations may well have been involved when Goethe promised a contribution to these two residents of Vienna, both of whom had previous ties with Weimar when they asked Goethe to contribute to their new journal during their visit on 25 October 1807.

A decision of this kind is a moment of fusion of vaguely conceived plans with the assessment of the immediate situation. It marks the poet's perception of a propitious hour and represents a commitment to himself through a promise to an outside agency.

Such a conjunction of external and internal forces may also involve a reaction *against* a given trend or tradition. Again, we are necessarily in the realm of speculation, but the questions raised by the phenomenon of the 'Festspiel' without visible occasion make this necessary.

In the paralipomenon to *Dichtung und Wahrheit* quoted earlier (p 145), Goethe had found a connection between the state of the theatre (its ailments, as he saw them) and socio-political developments. As director and as dramatist he had attempted to devise antidotes to its underlying egalitarianism. Iffland's name on the list of outstanding actors who had personified and advanced this state of affairs was of special interest because he was also a dramatist and writer of festive occasional works. Even if Goethe had written specifically about this minor branch of drama he would undoubtedly have omitted Herder's name. For a long time he had maintained courteous and loyal silence about him, except to praise him. But he does have a place in the antecedents of *Pandora*.

The antagonistic relationship of *Paläophron und Neoterpe* and Herder's *Aeon und Aeonis* is beyond conjecture.[14] Herder reacted to Goethe's play with the characteristic bitterness and bluntness of his later years. *Paläophron und Neoterpe* was too bland ('betulich'), did not face the issues of the era seriously, and did not plumb the depth of conflict between old and new, corruption and rebirth. Herder was to demonstrate how the theme should have been treated. Aeon, eighteenth-century absolutism, flanked by the courtiers Rank and Tradition ('Ansehen und Herkommen') and their vain and silly spouses, dies, reconciled to be sure, to make way for the new era embodied in his daughter Aeonis, whose name shall be Agape and who is heralded by choirs of working men and working women. This work appeared in the first issue of *Adrastea*, Herder's own journal in which he desperately attempted to erect a dike against most literary movements of his day. *Aeon und Aeonis* may be regarded as the allegorical equivalent of the festive philistine drama. It can actually be called a cantata, with a minimum of scenic dynamics and a good deal of destructive satire, in conscious contrast to Goethe's use of the operatic elements of metamorphosis and reconciliation in *Paläophron und Neoterpe*. No one ever dies in Goethe's festive plays.

I suggest that an analogous relationship, but in reverse, and perhaps altogether below the threshold of conscious response, exists between Herder's *Der Entfesselte Prometheus*, published in 1802 in

Adrastea VII,[15] and *Pandora*. While Goethe had expressed mild agreement with Schiller's horrified assessment of *Adrastea* I, which included *Aeon und Aeonis* (to Schiller, 21 March 1801, WA IV XV 202), his silence was complete in this instance. A later reaction to *Aeon*, in the masque of 1818, is outside the present chronological context.

It may be that Herder's *Prometheus* did nothing more than to convince Goethe that the treatment of the *Prometheus* theme along the lines of his own earlier attempts, i.e., the fragment (WA I XXXIX 193 et seq.) and the poem (II 76–8), was not feasible. At the same time we must assume that the desire to give it shape was second only in staying power to that exerted by the Faust theme. It would appear that the small fragment assigned to 1795–7[16] was indeed an attempt to resume – with new stylistic means – where the pre-Weimar fragment and ode had left off. Broadly speaking, these stages all constitute attempts to carry on in the Aeschylean tradition, to elaborate on the triumph of Prometheus over his divine antagonist. Herder's 'Scenes' carry the logic of this approach to the point where they must have struck Goethe as a caricature of his own gropings. Had he expressed himself on this subject he would perhaps have used the attribute which he applied in 1819 to his own fragment, 'modern-sansculottisch' (WA IV XXXII 134). Herder's *Prometheus* has all the noisy and truculent boisterousness of a Hero of Labour. At this point (well beyond the attempted impartiality of the dialogue *Voraussicht und Zurücksicht* of 1795[17]) Epimetheus can be no more than a dupe of the divine enemy, a wrong turn, at best, on the upward path of humanity and as such he is dismissed briefly and contemptuously by Herder's hero, who is better able to distinguish between a trap set by the gods (Hermes, sc. 9) and a divine ally of man (Pallas, sc. 13). In the light of the Goethean Epimetheus, Herder's can hardly be said to exist at all.

Pandora, as treated here, includes the entire work, i.e., the executed part as well as the remainder in schematic form. This is justified, I believe, because unlike the sketches for the completion of *Die Natürliche Tochter*, the *Pandora* plan is sufficiently clear and unequivocal to permit us to visualize the work in its entirety. Having examined possible reasons for the work being undertaken one cannot ignore or dismiss as fortuitous the fact that it was not completed. A 'Festspiel' above all others depends on its presentation at some particular moment, and the poet's failure to complete it represents a more decisive abandonment than would be the case with another genre or a different type of drama. When Goethe sent the texts of his festive dramas or masques to his friends he rarely failed to point out that they were merely receiving the bare verbal outline, the shadow of the work in question. In this instance there was no performance whatever which would have enabled Goethe to stimulate his readers' imagination. Failure to complete it amounted to abandoning any chance of bringing it to life. Hankammer[18] holds that the work could not be finished in the spirit in which it was conceived because Goethe could not maintain the dramatic balance between the two brother figures which is essential to the conciliatory and festive nature of the scheme and of the genre. He believes that the poet's prevailing mood during those years was too Epimethean to allow him to create a Prometheus in keeping with and worthy of the original conception. This would in effect have led to the annihilation or at least an implied rejection of Prometheus and thus have produced a Herderian Prometheus in reverse. This theory can be complemented by a less personal consideration. If, as suggested, the 'Festspiel' was undertaken with some hope that it should serve as a celebration of universal peace, however remote, the lessening likelihood of a pacification of Europe would indeed affect the creative impetus of the poet, and, since I have ventured to locate these hopes in the direction of Austria as the least afflicted portion of the continent in the years 1807-9, I note (but do not claim as a decisive cause) that Austria was once again involved in war with Napoleon in 1809 when work on *Pandora* definitely ceased. However remote or utopian the occasion, there may be a level of dilution of the prospects of realizing such an enterprise beyond which the creative impulse is definitely affected. The elegaic mood embodied in Epimetheus would then indeed overwhelm the poet and eventually yield to a sense of tragedy in the face of the futility of human action. This explains, according to Hankammer, why *Pandora* remained unfinished and *Die Wahlverwandtschaften* did not.

There is yet another sense in which work on *Pandora* may well have produced a growing sense of being pursued in a vacuum. It is not necessary to decide on the exact place of *Pandora* in the streams of traditions of classical and Renaissance drama and of opera and cantata in order to be fully persuaded of what Josef Kunz calls its 'Angewiesenheit des Wortes auf die Musik,' (HA v 529). This condition is so pervasive that an attempt to demonstrate it would require a survey of the entire work and would yet strike one as a labour of proving the obvious. *Pandora* is an operatic libretto. It is indicative of the utopian character of the enterprise that Goethe seems to have made no effort to secure the participation of a composer – it may be that he hoped or assumed that one would come forward while the instalments of the work were being published in *Prometheus*, just as he may have anticipated that the directors of the Viennese theatres would be among the more interested readers and would approach him with proposals for the performance of the work. But I chiefly want to suggest as a contributing cause of the cessation of work on *Pandora* that in this sense, too, the poet came to feel more and more that he was working in a vacuum. We do not need to examine the question whether the metric intricacy of *Pandora* renders it intractable to musical composition. When Zelter undertook to set parts of *Pandora* to music in 1810[19] Goethe did not encourage him greatly, either because his own creative momentum had disappeared entirely by that time or because he did not regard his friend as likely to be up to the task. There were enough other reasons to hold him in affectionate esteem and to maintain close contact with him. But Zelter's intelligent admiration of this and of so many other of Goethe's works could not save *Pandora* from the fate of remaining unfinished in every sense. Hofmannsthal's description of *Der Zauberflöte Zweiter Theil* is applicable here: 'so wie es nun dasteht, gleicht es einem herrlichen Wasserwerk in einem alten Park, steinernen Schalen ... denen die Fluten, die in ihnen hinströmen, von ihnen aufsteigen und gen Himmel stäuben sollten, ausgeblieben sind.'[20] The contemplation of *Pandora* engenders an Epimethean sense of loss and thoughts of what might have been. One is led to wish that Hofmannsthal had regarded it as part of his cultural mission to induce Richard Strauss, the one composer who might have been able to do so above all others, to breathe life into this extraordinary creation.

The pattern of antecedents culminating in the decision to write *Pandora* had been largely invisible. In no other instance of occasional writing could it be said that the occasion itself was the primary cause of a work; in no instance could a command or a sense of social obligation be said to have wrung an utterance from a reluctant poet. This observation is most difficult to verify when the factor of personal obligation, especially towards the ducal family, must be reckoned with. All these considerations involve *degrees* of willingness, spontaneity, and pressures, rather than motivations different in kind. The genesis of *Des Epimenides Erwachen* does not involve altogether new factors, but the configuration of forces and motives is so different from that of *Pandora* that a juxtaposition will give a useful demonstration of the range of possibilities.

On 17 May 1814, Kirms visited Goethe in Bad Berka and reported on a letter which Iffland, in his capacity as director of the Berlin theatre, had addressed to him on 7 May (quoted in Gräf III 298–9). The Prussian king was expected to return shortly from the wars in the company of the czar, and the genius of Herr von Goethe was to be enlisted in the production of an 'Einleitung' of any length over twenty minutes. Since the presence of the czar was not altogether certain he was to be referred to as one among the allies of Prussia, the others being the Austrian emperor and the crown prince of Sweden. The only other stipulation was that the king not be directly addressed, except possibly at the end. Goethe's reply – addressed to Kirms for transmission to Iffland – is dated 18 May (WA IV XXIV 277 et seq.) but seems to have been dispatched on the nineteenth (in the next letter to Kirms of 20 May it is referred to as 'gestrig'). It contains as the result of twenty-four hours of deliberation a refusal of the invitation, mainly on the plea of the shortness of time. Goethe goes to great lengths in expressing sensibility to the honour of the commission, enlarges on his general willingness to write occasional plays, exemplified by the fact that he was actually engaged in writing one (i.e., the Halle version of *Was wir bringen*) and expresses eager interest in contributing to a later victory celebration in Berlin. It is a verbose letter written to create a certain effect, either to reflect the regret over a necessary but reluctant decision, or simply to remove from the decision the possible flavour of an affront. In the next letter to Kirms, dated 20 May (*ibid.* 284), Goethe announces his decision to comply with Iffland's request, the previous refusal is transformed into 'Zweifeln' and 'Zaudern,' and an outline of a project is promised for a few days hence. The diary entries recording this change of mind are somewhat vague; the second letter to Kirms is not listed at all. The last sentence of the diary section of 19 May (WA iii v 108) relating to activities and events reads 'Vorspiel für Berlin,' but the second section, which usually deals with correspondence, contains the notation 'Expeditionen wegen Ifflands Antrag.' I read this to mean that the decision to comply was made during the latter part of 19 May, assuming that the correspondence of the day was disposed of in the morning – the first activity recorded for the day is 'diktiert' – and before the day's visitors had arrived and the formalities of the day begun. This was Ascension Day, which accounts for the visit of 'Kinder und Honoratioren von Berka.' The diary continues: 'Geh. Reg. R. v. Müller. Locken. Müller, Riemer. Blieben zu Abend. Vorspiel für Berlin.'[21] We may be certain that this line covers the moment of decision. If Riemer had had any part in it he would have noted it in his own diary. The decision affected him, inasmuch as Goethe turned over to him the projected continuation of *Was wir bringen* for Halle. We need not commit ourselves to a binding answer to the question, whether two Müllers visited Goethe that day, i.e., the Weimar conductor as well as the 'Geh. Reg. R.,' or whether the later chancellor is mentioned twice in that entry. I am inclined to assume the latter in view of my understanding of the word which precedes the name. Having satisfied myself that 'Locken' is not a name, all that remains is a choice between a plural noun and a gerund, and the former does not recommend itself strongly.

To sum up: the decision concerning Iffland's offer is not likely to have been reversed without a new agency coming into play. On the basis of the available record one can conclude that Müller, on being told of the offer and the reply to it, produced arguments which induced Goethe to consider once more and then to reverse his decision. The arguments deduced from the views of the two men and from the nature of the work resulting from the decision had probably occurred to Goethe before and they now assumed greater and decisive weight as they were presented to him by a man whom he trusted and with whom he was in general agreement on political matters. It seems almost certain that they were primarily political rather than artistic in nature, given the position and the interests of Müller. His purely literary opinions would not have carried much weight. But Müller's lure alone could not have had its presumed effect if other factors had not predisposed the poet, not the least powerful of which must have been the prospect of immediate realization of a 'Festspiel' with human and material resources vastly superior to those available locally. If *Pandora* was utopian in the several meanings of the term set forth above, the Berlin project was topical in the same broad sense which includes the prospect of completion in every dimension, especially including the committed efforts of a composer, B.A. Weber, which would warrant the concentrated labour required without the period of quiet maturation that usually preceded larger enterprises.

Epimenides is in some respects an offshoot of *Pandora*. The choruses of Prometheus' warriors (I. 4) were taken over without change. The figures of Epimetheus and Epimenides share the meaning of their common prefix, Elpore and Hoffnung their redeeming mission. The later work would also seem to represent a resurgence of vague and disappointed hopes attached to the former. The temptation of speedy realization of a spectacle on a truly large scale should not be underestimated. The flow of detailed instructions about sets, costumes, and stage effects that Goethe sent to Iffland almost immediately, and the constantly reiterated willingness to adapt to the exigencies of Berlin conditions and personnel were probably more than Iffland had hoped or bargained for. The poet's annoyance over the perpetual delays caused by circumstances and perhaps intrigue springs from the same source. Zelter surely knew that his lengthy report on the performances[22] and his detailed descriptions of the realization of intended effects were most eagerly awaited by the author. It is quite moving to find that, when *Epimenides* had at long last been performed under the aegis of Iffland's successor, Count Brühl, Goethe thought of the event as the beginning of a fruitful collaboration in the course of which he would supply more texts for the stage (WA iv xxv 290 et seq.).

What exactly prompted Iffland to address his request to Goethe is unknown unless it was the obvious desire to dignify a juncture in the history of Prussia and the continent with a work of the most distinguished pen. To Goethe this invitation must have had the ring of a personal challenge which Carl August expressed in a letter to Duchess Luise on 20 April 1814, a fortnight after Napoleon's abdication: 'Que dira donc Göthe de son Dieu tutelaire?'[23] I suggest that among all the higher officials of the duchy the same ironic question could most easily have been addressed to Müller. He owed his rise to his dogged attempts to pick up the pieces in 1806-7 through a policy of accommodation with the conqueror. His tribulations in the frantic search for the duke in order to bring about a meeting of conciliation between the emperor and the late Prussian general border on the comic.[24] And it was not only his youth that earned him the suspicions of the establishment at the time (and of posterity: Willy Andreas speaks of 'Beflissenheit, die die Vorzimmertätigkeit des späteren Kanzlers bisweilen peinlich erscheinen lässt')[25] although it must be added that the duke himself recognized his services. It would be an oversimplification to equate the attitude shared by Goethe and Müller towards Napoleon and Napoleonic rule with outright hostility towards Prussia or its allies, but one might safely say that one who had failed to regard the ascendancy of Napoleon as an unmitigated evil would not now anticipate an uninterrupted flow of goodness to issue from the victorious powers. Saxe-Weimar was bound to appear now very much alone with its big neighbour to the north and at its mercy, especially at a time when another neighbouring power of middle size, Saxony, stood a good chance of being abolished altogether. Therefore, unless one had felt that nothing mattered but the removal of the Corsican usurper from the European scene, he was bound to experience a mixture of feelings, including a good share of apprehension in connection with the victory celebrations in Berlin. It is not a very bold surmise that this was the prevailing mood at Berka in May 1814. At that time, Goethe helped to engage G.F.C. Sartorius, of whom Voigt wrote to Goethe, 'dass man seinen Feuereifer gegen das preussische System zu mildern suchen wird,'[26] as consultant to the Weimar delegation to the approaching peace congress. Unbridled attachment to Prussia was not received with applause. Riemer's diary of 8 June 1814 relates: 'Mit Reg. Rat Müller ... nach Berka ... Wolfs Spässe, der aber wieder wegen seiner Kokarde und seiner Preussischen Gesinnungen geschoren wurde.'[27] If Carl August had to divest himself of illusions concerning Prussia, he had ample opportunity for doing so during the same spring of 1814 and, in the subsequent long months of the Congress of Vienna, of learning that not one of the Big Three could be relied upon to assure his realm even the minimum of reasonable advantages to which he felt entitled. Only constant manoeuvering among them yielded the eventual modest enlargements of territory. It was not, to be sure, that the Three conspired among themselves to oppress the small, it was the simple fact of their being big powers. I like to think that it was the early realization of this basic defect that earned Müller his reputation for anti-Prussianism which is alluded to as well known in Gersdorff's remark while he was labouring for further Prussian territorial concessions: '... Wünsche ich von Herzen, dass während ich mich bemühe in Paris zu bauen, Herr von Müller nicht in Weimar einreissen möge ...'[28]

Essentially, I am here retracing the attitude towards empires discussed earlier in connection with Goethe's contributions to courtly occasions in the early years of the century, and it is this shared underlying attitude that seems to have enabled Müller to nudge Goethe towards the decision to write *Epimenides* on Ascension Day 1814. When Wachsmuth enjoins us, quite properly, to study the Goethe-Voigt correspondence in order to understand *Epimenides*,[29] I would add that Müller not be ignored either. In the light of this outline of the situation one might venture to reconstruct Müller's argument that tipped the balance on 19 May: 'This is an opportunity to curb the exuberance of victory which can only foster attitudes towards the rest of the world in keeping with the natural behaviour of big powers. It is a chance to celebrate the event in a manner that will avoid gloating over the fall of Napoleon and lapsing into a trance of self-glorification. If Goethe does not seize the opportunity, some sycophantic nationalistic hack will be only too eager to take his place.'

I have lingered over this detail, not so much because it could lead to a new understanding of the work in question, but because, for once, the point of crystallization can be assigned to almost a precise hour, for I believe that the decision to write and the outline of the work came to Goethe more or less simultaneously. *Epimenides*, in this respect, represents a sharp contrast to the earlier celebration of peace, *Pandora*. Granting the validity of the considerations presented above, the moment in question may not rate as 'kairos' if this term is to designate the auspicious confluence of inner readiness and outer motivation.

On the whole, the interpretation of the work offered by Wilhelm Mommsen[30] invites agreement as altogether judicious and in keeping with Goethe's general attitude towards political matters. With it in mind, I would offer this summary: A triumph and celebration of victory was called for and Goethe did not stint with trumpets and cymbals fortissimo and with broad allusions to all who shared in the victory, as requested (the Poles were left out after due consideration). But victory over whom? Not over Napoleon, but over the nameless forces of guile and oppression which wrested power from the imperial warrior and which are identifiable with any large power. This position was made clearer in the later, Weimar version where uncomplimentary remarks about sly diplomats and meddling clergy could be made with greater freedom and where, from the vantage point of a small capital, misgivings about the inherent corruption of power on a large scale could be expected to be understood more readily. But it remains true that, in the Berlin version, too, the only figure that can be said to bear the features of Napoleon, 'Dämon des Krieges,' clad in the imperial toga and identified by allusions to specific historical events (eg, the continental blockade and the Russian campaign) is frustrated and displaced by other demons, those of guile and oppression, which can be as easily identified with opposing empires. The fact that they wear Asiatic costumes suggests a stronger visual association with Russia than with France. It was observed earlier that in Goethe's eyes imperial France was different in kind from other empires and that it was to him the embodiment of one overwhelming natural event. *Epimenides* traces the sad degeneration of this unique phenomenon as it falls prey to the corroding forces of traditional power from within. Nature is overcome by the dark and disintegrating forces of society. The larger portion of *Epimenides* is ambiguous, i.e., the allegory is not clearly assignable to any one individual or state. This ambiguity was recognized by Riemer (or pointed out to him by Goethe) when he expressed approval of the work for its 'Allgemeinheit des Genusses ...' (in reference to the operatic treatment) 'und der poetischen Ironie.'[31]

Epimenides seems to be a peculiar and somewhat sly mixture of execration and exhortation, of satire and encomium. A reader of the work unaware of the circumstances of its composition would detect a synthetic quality in the work, the use of ready-made elements brought together under the pressure of time. Methods and devices recall those of *Pandora* and *Faust II*, but the quality of the verse would probably strike him as lacking the ease and urbanity which form a balance to the intricacies and involutions of Goethe's *Altersstil*. One can once again refer to Emrich, who pointed out the situations and devices which recur in *Faust II*.[32] But *Epimenides* does not convey the delicate balance of vast scope and human closeness to be observed in the court scenes of *Faust* or in 'Klassische Walpurgisnacht.' *Epimenides* lacks that sense of involvement effected throughout *Faust*, the sense of following the fortunes of a kindred human being. There seems to be no point whatever in *Epimenides* from which such involvement could grow, which differentiates the present work from all others considered in this inquiry. The 'Lustige Person' which Goethe added to the Weimar version (1.8) is a grim little apparition which gains entry to the circle of clergyman, courtier, jurist, and diplomat by revealing himself as 'Böser Geist' and then disappears in a flash. In contrast, the Mephistopheles of *Maskenzug 1818* takes pains to dispel his reputation as an evil spirit. Having presumably succeeded in doing so he qualifies as the interpreter of Goethe's most dramatic creation.

Whether or not Goethe intended it thus, *Epimenides* does not contain a single three-dimensional character. It is not easy to be humanly touched by a figure whose main claim to fame is his unusual capacity for sleep. There is something faintly funny about

Rip van Winkle and his ilk, as emphasized by the jests of the youths who escort the hero (1.3). The earlier literary treatments of the Epimenides story with which Goethe may have been familiar were nearly all comedies or farces.[33] The question of self-portrayal in the figure of Epimenides need not be raised again. Mommsen's evaluation and disposition of the arguments is fully adequate. One regrets to find Burdach as the most notable representative of the 'pater peccavi' school.[34] A sober evaluation of the personal content of the figure can only range from the assertion of the necessity of healing sleep for the preservation of permanent values to the half-humorous envy of one who was given the privilege of aloofness by being made to sleep through all the turmoil and who readily accepts reassurance that this was an honourable fate.

·9·

A Midwinter Night's Dream

IN MORE THAN THE chronological sense, *Des Epimenides Erwachen* stands half way between the two remaining occasional works to be examined, the masques of 1810 and 1818. Both are what *Epimenides* is most decidedly not – celebrations of family events – and, as such, appropriate to troubled times (cf. above, p 149). While this concept will have to be broadened decisively for 1818, it neatly fits the earlier work. *Die Romantische Poesie* (WA i XVI 215 et seq.) was one of several celebrations occasioned by the engagement of Princess Caroline and it falls readily in the established pattern of observances of the birthday of Duchess Luise as the peak of the social season, although it was not performed until shortly after 30 January 1810. The notion of using the court of Landgrave Ludwig and the semi-legendary renaissance of poetry at the Wartburg as a framework for a dynastic tribute is in itself an almost obvious and, sooner or later, an inevitable one. But the treatment given this theme by Goethe calls for an examination of some of its immediate antecedents and its implications.

'Wartburg' and the associations attached to the monument are part and parcel of the broader theme of Goethe and Romanticism. In this 'Maskenzug' that vast question is largely focused on the person of Zacharias Werner. He was one of the fomentors of the Wartburg cult, or fad, which, in turn, was a component of the mediaevalism that had taken root in Weimar during the years following the 1806 catastrophe. His two Wartburg poems of November 1807 are said to have been liked by Duchess Luise.[1] The second of these, 'Der Mönch und die Nonne,' based on an etiological tale of hapless love connected with two rocks, gives a hint of the semi-religious eroticism of the Romantics of which Goethe was so strongly aware and with which he dealt in *Die Wahlverwandtschaften* in his own way. These observations do not, of course, encompass by any means the phenomenon as a whole, nor do they exhaust the question of Goethe's relationship with Werner, one so largely determined by recognition of the sheer talent of his younger admirer.

Goethe's interest in mediaeval Germanic literature between 1808 and 1810 is well documented.[2] Here I simply wish to observe that his interest in this literary phenomenon accords with his desire to control its social effects, which tended towards forming an amalgam of a cult of nationalism and of gyniolatry. He wanted it treated with due historical detachment:

Ich will diese ganze Rücktendenz nach dem Mittelalter und überhaupt nach dem Veralteten recht gerne gelten lassen ... aber man muss mir nur nicht glorios damit zu Leibe rücken. [to Reinhard, 7 October 1810, WA IV XXI 394]

The gyniolatric side of mediaevalism contained a dangerous potential of social and political upheaval:

Die sogenannte romantische Poesie zieht besonders unsere jungen Leute an, weil sie der Willkür, der Sinnlichkeit, dem Hange nach Ungebundenheit, kurz der Neigung der Jugend schmeichelt. Mit Gewalt setzt man alles durch. Seinem Gegner bietet man Trotz. Die Weiber werden angebetet: Alles wie es die Jugend macht. [to Riemer, 28 August 1808, GES II 329]

This uncongenial view of social relationships, and especially of the relationship of the sexes, must have filled Goethe with particular apprehension insofar as it was connected with a certain fanaticism vis-à-vis Napoleon, hence a threat to the pacification of the continent. The hositility of women of the ruling houses and of the aristocracy can often be described as virulent and as involving a deep-seated feeling of personal violation. The connection between a sense of chastity and revulsion before Napoleon found its fiercest literary expression in Kleist and struck Goethe as pathological. Perhaps impressions of this kind prompted Goethe to write almost a decade later of women as 'immer die heftigsten, unversöhnlichsten Feinde der Feinde ...' (WA i XII 96). Goethe himself was, of course, quite incapable of regarding Napoleon's ascendancy as the Rape of Europe. Conversely, erotic mediaevalism opened the gate to the kind of corruption of society which in Goethe's poetic and political book was both practised and symbolized by the sly power-wielding cleric (*Götz*, *Faust*, *Epimenides*, etc.) for whom the devout female is much the best tool for the attainment of his unspiritual goals. *Die Romantische Poesie*, like *Epimenides*, harbours encomium and execration under one roof. Romantic attitudes and interests are not rejected, but modified and directed into more desirable channels.

Arthur Hübner surmised that the outline and details of this masque were put before Goethe by President von Fritsch: 'vermutlich um zu verhindern, dass der Dichter der Hofgesellschaft, die nun einmal dem altdeutschen Zeitgeschmack huldigte, wieder antikisch kam.'³ If this was the case, the sponsors had not reckoned with the poet's ability to conceal some boobytraps in the commissioned work, as illustrated by three aspects of the 'Maskenzug.' First, is the introduction of the stock figures of corrupt courtiers (secular and clerical) as a reminder of the dangers inherent in the tendency to treat mediaeval attitudes and forms as more than historical phenomena, as a compass to steer by in the nineteenth century. The language assigned to these characters (ll 169–93) is almost delphic and altogether sinister. A second aspect is the use of the Elberich riddle (ll 193–200). I have already referred to the close similarity of this dwarf to the powerful leader of souls in *Was wir bringen* (cf. above, p 145) and am satisfied that the two figures (close cousins of Knabe Lenker and Euphorion in *Faust* II) are as identical as two poetic creations can be. Among the many scholars who have addressed themselves to the solution of the riddle which Bertuch called 'eine von den Walfischtonnen, die Goethe dem Publikum hinwirft und selbst nicht löst ...'⁴ Unger has pointed out that there was a powerful dwarf in Werner's Nibelungen parody written and performed for the duchess' birthday a year before:

> *Louisa* wird genennet der Hort, der unser Hort!
> In aller Herzen Schachten, da brennt er fort und fort;
> Ein riesenstark Gezwerge steht ihm zur Hut bereit
> Der Engel Frauenwürde, der auch dem Blitz gebeut!⁵

Unger calls Goethe's dwarf a variation. I think that it represents a counter-figure placed in the 'Maskenzug' in a spirit of necessary contradiction. 'Frauenwürde,' as the Romantics defined it, could not in the eyes of Goethe be elevated to the status of semi-mystical supremacy, in view of the mischief that was bound to issue from it. Besides, Werner's dwarf had appeared in a parody, and, although I do not doubt that Goethe was receptive to its wit and skill, the phenomenon of parody as such was unacceptable and had to be reacted against. Finally, the presentation of epic and lyric literature in the masque avoids modes of human behaviour specifically associable with Romantic attitudes and steers spectators gently and imperceptibly into more congenial regions. There is no indication of the unapproachability of woman, of romantic agony, or of the submissive and protracted longing of 'Minne' – the men and women presented are simply enjoying the pleasures of love and of the seasons – reminiscent of the cyclical pattern of life pointed out in the review of the poems of J.H. Voss of 1804 (WA i XL 263 et seq.) – and the one instance of unconsummated love introduced into the work, Brunehild's, elicits the amused comment, 'O seltsames Vermählen.' In the King Rother section (ll 113 et seq.) there is a drift towards oriental regions and the fairy-tale, away from the austerity of a more northerly setting in the direction of romance and adventure, of the bizarre and of the world of Oberon.

Yet in tracing the polemical undercurrents of this 'Maskenzug' one risks distortion if one fails to say that the work, as a whole, is still a cordial and cheerful tribute to the ruling dynasty, and, especially, to its women. That Goethe should have succeeded in blending these elements without impairing the mood of festivity and without displaying ill nature is yet another indication of his ability to sound the right note appropriate to the occasion, not only without compromising his convictions but also without being obliged to shelter them in silence.

The first observation about *Bei Allerhöchster Anwesenheit Ihro Majestät der Kaiserin Mutter Maria Feodorowna in Weimar Maskenzug* must be that among the works written specifically for the court it requires superlatives. It is the longest, involved the largest number of persons and therefore called for the largest material investment in costumes and props, but above all, elicited from the poet the most protracted period of time spent on writing and preparation. He went into retreat at Berka for several weeks for this purpose alone. All these factors combined towards a total mobilization of resources, and there is no unequivocal answer as to why this happened, although it was by no means certain from the beginning that it would be so. There is, to be sure, no evidence of indecision as to whether or not to contribute to the festivities required by the prospective visit of the Dowager Czarina, Maria Feodorowna, once it was definitely known that it would take place in November and December 1818. It seems certain that the poet's participation in principle and his supervision of the series of festive events was formally requested by Maria Paulowna through her court marshal, von Bielke, on 16 October (WA i XVI 486). Goethe's outline of a 'Redouten-Aufzug' dated 17 October (*ibid.* 487) is a first reaction. His accompanying letter to Bielke the following day attempts to limit his involvement in the execution of this or other plans by the reminder that he is no longer connected with the theatre and is getting on in years in any case (WA iv XXIX 312). The outline itself gives no indication of the magnitude and character of the work that we know. Title ('Der Winter mit seinem Gefolge') and description point to a rather conventional Winter and Night procession, appropriate to the reception of a guest from dark and chilly regions. In fact, the list of characters (Night, Dreams, etc.) suggests close similarity to the modest *Aufzug des Winters* (WA i XVI 191–4) of 1781, so that one is inclined to think that Goethe made a survey of stock-in-hand and found the earlier work to be the most suitable for adaptation to the needs of the coming event.

Within a week, approximately, this scheme began to develop and expand; why and exactly how cannot be fully traced. We cannot be sure whether the command of Maria Paulowna referred to in 'Vorläufige Anzeige' of 1 December to present 'einheimische Erzeugnisse der Einbilungskraft und des Nachdenkens' implies a rejection of the original proposal, or whether there was a suggestion to add these domestic products to the original scheme, or whether consultations with Riemer, who was at work on extensive contributions of his own to the festive season, Meyer, and Chancellor von Müller are the source of *Maskenzug 1818* as we know it now. In any case, the original scheme can be regarded as essentially superseded when Goethe reported to Meyer (22 November, WA iv XXXI 13) that the road had been clear since he threw out Winter and his suite. Then work proceeded quite smoothly; the diary gives us the various stages of composition, indicating even growth. As far as can be determined, Goethe showed little of the nervous eagerness to get the job out of the way and to return to more essential tasks that can be observed in connection with earlier and less demanding enterprises of this kind. He gave close attention to the printing of the text immediately after the performance. Repeatedly, he expressed satisfaction that something substantial had been accomplished in spite of the transitory nature of the enterprise.

genossen wir jedoch des allgemeinsten Beifalls, welcher freilich durch den grossen Aufwand ... der denn doch aber zuletzt, in kurzen Augenblicken, wie ein Feuerwerk in der Luft verpuffte, theuer genug erkauft wurde. Ich habe mich persönlich am wenigsten zu beklagen, denn die Gedichte, auf welche ich viel Sorgfalt verwendet, bleiben übrig ... [to Zelter, 4 January 1819, ibid. 44]

This feeling may have been strengthened by the fact that this was not a libretto. The reader needs to contribute only an effort of visual, not aural, imagination.

Two connected reasons for this acquiescence in the task suggest themselves. First, its 'voluntary' nature. Although it had been actuated 'durch Vorsatz, Drang und Muss' (to Sulpiz Boisserée, 12 August 1819, *ibid*. 258) the masque clearly rose above these exigencies. A feeling of release enters into the situation. This was the last masque Goethe would write for the court. He expressed this relief shortly after completing the work: 'ich aber, will's Gott! von solchen Eitelkeiten hiedurch für immer Abschied genommen' (to Knebel, 26 December 1818, *ibid*. 38). But this hope is reflected much more strongly in the work itself. Its retrospective, comprehensive, and elegaic character makes it the celebration of an era with no intimations of future activity on the part of the one surviving poet presented in the procession. The sense of marking the beginning of a new era and the end of an old was surely reinforced by the fact that *Maskenzug 1818* also constitutes the celebration of the birth of a male heir to Maria Paulowna. It had occurred on 24 June and is conspicuously referred to in the work. This feeling must have been strengthened by the birth of the poet's first grandson in April. As it turned out, *Maskenzug 1818* was indeed Goethe's final gift to the ducal family, though not to its individual members. In retrospect it fills the gap left by his silence in 1804 (see above, p 135). It is really his own 'Huldigung der Künste.'

The second factor which may account for the magnitude and the spirit of the work and the mood informing its preparation is the fact that it was, or proved to be, thoroughly compatible with Goethe's principal concern at the time, the *West-Oestlicher Divan*, or rather the writing of *Noten und Abhandlungen*. Before we examine this close relationship we must, however, place the occasioning event, Maria Feodorowna's visit, into the context of its time. This step is justified and necessitated, I think, by the assumption that the visit to the court of Weimar was not purely a family affair, and could not be, even if those concerned had so desired. Such an assumption is based on facts of political life of the age in general, on the generally acknowledged fact that Maria Feodorowna possessed a strong personality and was not without influence throughout the reign of her son, Alexander I, and lastly on the observation that for at least two daughters to be visited on this journey, Maria Paulowna and Katharina of Württemberg, their rôle as wives of their respective spouses had by no means displaced or weakened their awareness of being the czar's sisters.

One of the entertainments offered to the imperial visitor in

Weimar was a mythological 'Vorspiel' presented at the theatre on a theme which Julie von Egloffstein called 'Ceres, die ihre Tochter in der Hölle aufsucht.'[7] This may not have been the actual title, but the choice of subject seems to have struck some members of society as amusingly apt, especially with regard to the daughter's husband. Looking beyond personal matters, one is led to reflect that the grand-duchy had indeed the reputation of a fiery place in the minds of many European observers. The bonfire of the 'Wartburgfest' of October 1817 was regarded by some as capable of starting a destructive conflagration throughout the continent, by others as the source of a cleansing flame. I need not and cannot enlarge on the question of Goethe's attitude to this event – it would lead into a jungle of details involving his relationships with Jena University, its faculty, the 'Burschenschaften,' the liberal periodicals, especially *Isis*, the behaviour of Oken and Luden, the question of censorship, and more. It is one of the ironies of the situation that the students on the Wartburg had been doing exactly what Goethe had recommended in a brief essay (*Zum Reformationsfest*, WA I XLII (2) 32–4) in which there are some interesting generalizations on the spirit of festivity, i.e., to combine the observance of the anniversaries of the Reformation and of the battle of Leipzig.

Interested outsiders blamed Carl August for permitting dangerous activities on the Wartburg and charged him with excessive tolerance of, indeed sympathy with, the 'Burschenschaften.' A reprimand was considered insufficient punishment for a Jena lecturer who had given an address during the 'Wartburgfest.' The correspondence with Voigt indicates that Goethe held a position somewhere between tolerance of such youthful activities and an inclination to sacrifice freedom of expression to the maintenance of peace and order. During his stay in Karlsbad in 1818 Goethe had contacts with the men who were most worried about such activities – Metternich, Gentz, and Prince Schwarzenberg – but he seems to have felt more attracted to and impressed by the company of Count Capodistrias, the Russian minister with decidedly liberal leanings. After Goethe's return from Karlsbad the statesmen who had been there and their monarchs converged on Aix-la-Chapelle. The chief visible result of that gathering, the reinstatement of France as an equal among the leading powers through the removal of restrictions imposed upon her after 1814, is likely to have pleased Goethe as an indication of the continuing pacification and increasing stability of the continent. (He had just obtained – not without trying – the golden [officer's] version of the de-napoleonized Legion of Honour.) It is unclear whether he was fully aware of the ulterior motives pursued by the participants of the Congress (especially Metternich's desire to prevent too close a rapprochement between France and Russia and his policy of counteracting lingering liberalizing impulses in and influences upon the czar). These matters indicate that the imperial visit of November-December was not solely illuminated by the gentle light of family affection. A homage to the dowager czarina could not but be a message to the czar, and to Russia as well, at a time when the czar had not yet taken a firm position at the extremes of the political spectrum, between reaction and liberalism. There seems to be agreement that this did not happen until the assassination of Kotzebue and the Karlsbad conference in the following year (1819). However, it was not a question of pointing out a particular position that Russia ought to assume. Rather, it was a question of presenting to the spectator a Weimar which was unique for other reasons than those which had recently attracted European attention to it – the 'Wartburgfest' and the true or imagined subversive stirrings which formed the content of the Kotzebue report and the Stourdza memorandum. The publication of the former by Luden had created the impression of a state where chaos was just around the corner, and the attack on Jena University in the latter was, after all, an attack on the patrons of the institution. Considerations of this kind may have prompted Goethe to describe as one of the effects of the 'Maskenzug': 'haben wir die alte Ehre Weimars gerettet...' (WA iv XXXI 37). If such reflections appear too extrinsic, it may be recalled that the content of the 'Maskenzug' itself is largely political. More than anything else, it deals with political matters, power, kingship, liberty, loyalty, and order.

Chancellor von Müller reports that on 24 February 1819, Goethe read from the *Divan* 'den Goethe zum Vehikel seines politischen Glaubensbekenntnisses und mancher, wie er's nennt, Eselbohrerei, zu brauchen scheint...' (GES III (1) 102). The reference is almost certainly to *Noten und Abhandlungen*, which occupied the poet throughout the winter. Müller's observation could just as easily refer to *Maskenzug 1818*, for *Noten und Abhandlungen* may be regarded as commentary on that work as well. Goethe himself forged conspicuous links between the two. He gave the masque a place in the section 'Künftiger Divan' (WA i VII 133) and he incorporated one of the *Divan* poems in *Maskenzug 1818* ('Wenn vor deines Kaisers Throne' (ll 209–14)). An examination of *Noten und*

Abhandlungen sheds light both on the meaning of *Maskenzug 1818* and on Goethe's political attitudes on which this political work is based. This is clearly not a question of discovering whose side he was on because the notion of taking sides is alien to the work and to Goethe's manner of looking at the world. However, neither is the opposite notion of non-involvement, of aloofness, or of neutrality an adequate key to the basic orientation of the spectacle. Gentz thought that neutrality was a label applicable to Goethe:

eine lange Unterredung mit ihm über den Studentenunfug ... wobei er sich durch ein affektiertes Streben nach Neutralität ziemlich linkisch benahm, ob er gleich seine tiefste Indignation gegen alles, was sich seit Jahr und Tag in Weimar und Jena zugetragen hat, nicht verbarg. Er ist nun einmal ein seltsamer Mensch, aber wahrlich kein interessanter. [18 August 1818, GES III (1) 77]

One would like to know whether Gentz would have passed the same stern judgement after reading the passage of *Tag-und-Jahreshefte* for 1817:

Ein Symbol der Souverainetät ward uns Weimaranern durch die Feierlichkeit, als der Grossherzog vom Thron den Fürsten von Thurn und Taxis, in seinem Abgeordneten, mit dem Postregal belieh, wobei wir sämmtlichen Diener in geziemendem Schmuck, nach Rangesgebühr erschienen, und also auch unsrerseits die Oberherrschaft des Fürsten anerkannten, indessen im Lauf desselben Jahrs eine allgemeine Feier deutscher Studirenden am 18. Juni zu Jena und noch bedeutender den 18. October auf der Wartburg eine ahnungsvolle Gegenwirkung verkündigten. [WA i XXXVI 131]

This is not neutrality but an act of understanding brought about by the almost simultaneous evocation of two scenes and pointing to a reality which is not encompassed by either one in isolation. The symbolic force of each is enhanced by the perception of the other, and the absence of reference to words uttered on either occasion enhances the impact of both. It is an example of the 'Revue' technique so vigorously used in *Faust* II and of the phenomenon of 'Spiegelung der Teile' as an instrument of understanding.[8] Thus the understanding of attitudes and positions taken is inseparable from understanding the means employed for their presentation. There are no references to phenomena comparable to the student gatherings in *Noten und Abhandlungen*, but we read a great deal about the poet before the throne. For the sake of convenience and clarity I shall sum up and interpret those parts of *Noten und Abhandlungen* that shed light on *Maskenzug 1818* without full regard to the order in which they appear, and merely indicate the sections which contain longer passages thus used.

Goethe finds the greatest obstacle to the appreciation and appropriation of oriental poetry to be the spiritual and physical submissiveness ('Unterwürfigkeit') of the oriental poet to the ruler and the ruling class. He attempts to overcome this inhibition by distinguishing between submission and servility or venality and by analyzing the assumptions on which this occidental sense of revulsion rests (*Despotie*). This involves a general definition of the poet's function as distinguished from that of the prophet or ideologue as naturally and primarily encomiastic. Western sensibility does not take umbrage at this posture in erotic or religious poetry; the hyperbolic praise of God is part and parcel of religious tradition (*Einrede*). Encomiastic excess in love poetry is properly regarded as a measure of intensity and wealth of feeling. Convention allows the poet to attribute all superlatives of perfection without measuring the degree of justification on the person of the adored because the erotic (or religious) impulse itself is recognized as worthy of hyperbolic expression. In the socio-political sphere, however, we have come to reject this attitude and have substituted a restrictive convention of 'Bescheidenheit,' which is an adulterated form of the general and natural need of self-assertion, of 'Anmassung' (*Künftiger Divan. B.d. Unmuts*). The effects of this inverted snobbery on society and on the poet are all bad. It disguises and distorts true power relationships (cf. once again, the stereotype of the hypocritical, powerful cleric) and casts a grey uniformity over their expression, thus removing shape and structure from the image of society. This is a process of impoverishment in which all concerned are losers. The poet is impoverished because he is prevented from giving. Wealth and variety of the world of which he is more aware than his less articulate fellow men cease to be within his gift to the ruler and to the ruled when he is prevented from articulating them. The ruler is deprived of the opportunity to display his noblest function, that of translating power into protection and reward when social convention forces him to hide his power. The fruitful interdependence of those who praise and those who are praised which raises the poet to a lofty and necessary place in the social structure vanishes. Moreover, society is deprived of two means of potential improvement. The idealization of the ruler is conventional, not entirely dependent on his real worth, The poet, in need of something or someone 'higher' as object of his panegyric impulse, addresses the ruler *as if* he were endowed with all imaginable virtues. In doing so he places before the ruler his ideal image and acts as a spur for him to seek greater perfection.

Secondly, the encomiastic posture gives the poet greater freedom to criticize through irony, when the distance between the actual and the ideal speaks for itself, or by satire and invective, which is the reverse of the encomiastic and made possible by it (*Einrede*). Some years later, Goethe drew attention to a poem addressed to Rudolf von Habsburg in which praise and invective alternate regularly (*Lob-und Spottgedicht...* WA i XLII [1] 5). By donning the mask of absolute submission the poet forces the ruler to assume the mask of the worthy object of submission. Aside from the social content, Goethe enlarges on another obstacle to occidental appreciation of oriental poetry, the greater freedom of association of disparate and seemingly mutually exclusive elements. One is led to think of similar trends in baroque or metaphysical poetry, its hyperbolic propensities and its freedom of association fed by a spirit of absolute acceptance and praise as opposed to the selectivity of a classicist code of proprieties (*Allgemeinstes*). And – returning to the social effects of such an approach – the poet possesses the power to impart on society the vital impulses of change and mobility. As the indispensable slave or subject he nullifies the abyss between high and low, between the exceptional position of the ruler and his share in common humanity as a human being. But the poet's power of giving is inseparable from his willingness to receive. By imposing on and eliciting from the ruler the ideal of pure humanity he transforms sheer power into a viable social force and, in the process, restores the unity of the erotic, the political, and religious impulses. This approach could almost be taken as identical with the evocation of the mediaeval ideal by the Romantics, but the reader of *West-Oestlicher Divan* is unlikely to confuse Goethe's East with Novalis' *Die 'Christenheit' oder 'Europa.'* The difference lies in the presence of 'Geist,' the mature detachment and the use and awareness of the mask that characterizes Goethe's vision (*Allgemeinstes*).

Goethe's exposition of the social rôle of poetry is thus carried to its ideal terminal point because *Maskenzug 1818* presents these relationships from this direction, as befits an Ideal Masque. It operates on the assumption that an ideal ruler in possession of supreme power is present in whom power and humanity are fully balanced and made interchangeable. By virtue of this presence, human desires, aspirations, and dreams are being fulfilled. But the presentation of this condition of dream fulfilment would be altogether static, not to say dull. Movement, the dramatic element, is supplied by the demonstration of reconciliation of opposites, and by the disappearance rather than the absence of conflict. Thus the negative forces which usually constitute the anti-masque[9] episode do not here appear as a group that threatens the ideal state in a crisis, but rather as an aspect of each phase of fulfilment which is either overcome or removed from view. In this way the poet creates or seizes opportunities for comment on the world outside.

In the light of the preceding considerations it is not difficult to think of *Maskenzug 1818* as an experiment in orientalizing dramatic poetry, just as *Divan* may be regarded as one in other poetic categories. The imperial guest, incidentally, seems to have entered into the spirit of oriental largesse by rewarding the poet with her portrait on a jeweled box worth at least three thousand Thaler (GES III [1] 96).

The Genius of the occasion in pilgrim's garb guides the participants into the realm of night and fulfilment and Nacht proclaims the presence of supreme power and the conciliation of opposites in an extravagantly oriental address. She may linger in the presence of the imperial splendour because 'Die Majestät ist milder als die Sonne' (l 23), but the task of doing justice to the apparition is too great. 'Wo ist ein Gold zu Fassung der Juwelen?' (l 31). Three months of fulfilment are invoked – October as the month of the wine harvest and of the birthday of Maria Feodorowna; November as the month of fulfilment of hopes for the auspicious imperial journey and arrival; and December as the month of winter solstice and of fulfilment of mankind's hopes. At this point the vista is expanded in two directions, towards all humanity in the redemption shared by all and in the gentle equation of imperial motherhood and of humble divinity. It is worth noting how Goethe avoids even the suggestion of religious sentimentality, cant, or possibly, in the light of religious sensibilities of his age, sacrilege, by modulating into the world of the child to whom Christmas seems ever so far away and Christmas gifts represent the literal fulfilment of all wishes and dreams. The equality thus brought about covers the social sphere, but, beyond it, suggests the attainment of the innocence of childhood.

And thus yet another gap, that between old and young, is closed. The central position of the child is put to further use as the prologue continues. The variety of human wishes had converged in the mind of the 'Weihnachts-Kind.' Now Sleep as the vehicle of desire comes in as a sleepy child rubbing its eyes, as it were, and reluctantly aware of the brightness and splendour of an adult festivity (ll 91-8), and now there radiate from its mind the universal wishes and aspirations that reflect and move society (ll 99-123). Dreams are powerful rulers of human affairs inasmuch as they release forces affecting stability and change in the life of society. 'Denn Sehnsucht hält von Staub zu Thron,/uns all' in strengen Banden' ('An Hafis,' WA i VI 43, written a few weeks before). They are also the image of the world as it appears in the child's innocent imagination. In the hour of fulfilment there is no danger of these two aspects conflicting.

It is well to recall that all that the gathering has been shown so far is part of a prologue which has for one of its purposes the creation of a strong, expectant feeling about the arrival of the procession of masks proper. It is a common characteristic of such processions that they require interpretation in order to reveal their significance and relevance to the occasion. An extreme of this quest for meaning is the charade where the audience itself is challenged to undertake this work. But this is more of a parlour game than a significant tribute. One of the entertainments devised by Riemer for the imperial visit was to have three groups representing successively the meanings 'toi,' 'son,' and (d')or' which led to the solution toison d'or (Düntzer 134). On any level above that of visual and verbal ingenuity the services of an authorized guide to the riddle, a herald, are required. This interpreter is a participant in the event, hence must enter into its spirit. He must be involved, even, as in the case of the 'Mummenschanz' of Faust II, to the point where he reaches the limits of his competence. Involvement and detachment must hold each other in balance. In this case, that function is assigned to Epos and Tragödie. Both deal traditionally with persons and events of highest rank and impact and are therefore fit interpreters of the occasion. Both, too, deal with the intensified and magnified exactions of blood and sorrow that conflicting desires or the collision with impersonal forces produce in their lofty subjects. On this occasion they can and must abdicate this latter rôle. This means that, remaining themselves 'ohne ihren Charakter abzulegen' ('Vorl. Anzeige' p 236), they find themselves changed, 'wir sind verändert' (l 161). It is by virtue of their being changed, by their adopting a mask, that they can be active participants in an event which proclaims universal change through the presence of majesty. Komödie, paradoxically, does not qualify because she does not need what is required of all. She cannot participate in the act of transformation ('Ich brauche nichts zu thun, es ist gethan,' l 152).

Epos ends her first speech describing her old and new rôles with the words: 'Die Grossen sehn sich, einen sich, vereinen' (l 140). Düntzer (p 161), quite rightly, I think, believes that this is a reference to the Congress of Aix-la-Chapelle. A line such as this, understood by the audience as topical and accentuated through position and rhetorical emphasis, renders visible the world outside in a rapid flash of light; the ideal state conjured up by the spectacle as a whole must not lull the community into a drowsy sense of having been transported into a never-never land. Here, and elsewhere, the poet is anxious to remind those present that the state of fulfilment can have its roots in the here and now. This delicate balance of utopia and the suggestion of feasibility of attainment is maintained throughout the work and finds its most interesting expression towards the end of the procession in the *Demetrius* section. Topicality in a slightly different sense is reinforced by the rôle assigned to Ilm. The presence of the *genius loci* assures us that transformation of reality takes place where the poet is permitted to unfold his powers, where giving and receiving interact harmoniously.

Giving and receiving are acted out in the 'Festzug' proper. The products of the land ('Landeserzeugnisse') are placed at the feet of the ruler; at the same time, this ceremony is a formal act of presentation with the full implications of the most strictly courtly meaning of the term. Being named before the sovereign constitutes recognition and the conferral of status and implies an undertaking on the part of the sovereign to give future access and hearing to those thus singled out. The poets who, in keeping with ceremonial tradition, are about to appear in strict order of seniority cease to be subjects or slaves and could be said to assume the rank of ambassadors of a mighty power. There are several references to such rites in *Noten und Abhandlungen* and a formal letter by the Shah of Persia to the Russian imperial court is quoted in full (WA i XII 241 et seq.). But the language of power and the language of poetry are not always the same; in this sense, the 'Festzug' is a procession of riddles which require interpretation by Epos, Tragödie, and Ilm.

What are the components, what is the structure of this procession which constitutes fulfilment and commentary on the miracle of the humanization of power and the infusion of power into the arts? As suggested before, the ceremonial character determined the order of appearance. The choice of works through which the poets speak is less easily accounted for. We cannot exclude such practical considerations as the one put forward by Düntzer (pp 180–1), namely that *Mahomet* and *Götz* were included because the costumes and the actors wearing them had remained ready for use from a masque of Goethean works and characters presented in January 1818. And it is useful to recall that practical matters could hardly be ignored when it was a question of costuming, choosing, and rehearsing about 150 amateurs because each work that was presented and elucidated by a single character involved a dozen or so silent figures, and, no doubt, all manner of social and personal factors and preferences had to be taken into account. But if considerations of this kind affected the composition of the work, they were assimilated in the process and need not be regarded as standing in the way of the poet's grand design.

There are two sections within the procession: the presentation of Wieland, Herder, and Goethe and the presentation of Schiller. In the first, the presentation and reconciliation of opposites continues to dominate. I have thus far drawn attention to opposites of great and small, of powerful and humble, few and many, old and young. It is the last of these that is once again brought into ascendancy.

As we turn to Wieland's *Musarion*, we recall that the poet had used the figure of Hercules at the crossroads in the discharge of his own courtly responsibilities (cf. p 42). It has been suggested earlier that Alexander I in 1818 was still sufficiently uncommitted in his attitude and actions to leave the world in doubt about whether he would be the mainstay of the rejuvenation of Europe or of the restoration of the old. A 'Jugendfürst' of uncertain identity had appeared as the fulfilling vision in *Epimenides*. Goethe now recalls Phanias, a young man of quality and promise and the manner in which he overcame the paralysis of the crossroads. Musarion represents the assertion of the erotic impulse and its harmonization with political and religious aspirations against the reduction of choice to two ideologies, the Scylla of immobility and the Charybdis of frantic exultation. Wieland's own progression from 'enthusiast' to detached giver of delights may be hinted at here, too. In the post-Napoleonic period he would undoubtedly have prescribed the substitution of a Musarion for Baroness de Krüdener, who was to exercise such great influence on Alexander.

Phanias' difficulty is rather a simple one, a natural phase in the attainment of maturity which can be overcome by the proper conveyance of the insight that 'Die Menschen sind, trotz allen ihren Mängeln,/ das Liebenswürdigste was es gibt' (ll 278–9), but the stage of human life is not filled with human beings alone. All-powerful majesty can command harmony – provided it knows its nature – in all spheres, so the fable of the masque continues and the reconciliation of Oberon and Titania is within its power in this propitious hour. However, it is not brought about by the imposition of law, but by the release of undivided loyalty to that which deserves love ('Gott, seinem Kaiser, Einem Liebchen treu', l 327).

Phanias of *Musarion* and Hüon of *Oberon* are young men; their lives unfold in the realm of fable and of early, semi-mythical civilizations. Herder's perspective reveals above all the unchanging nature of the human condition through the identity of human aspirations regardless of distance in time and space. ('Die ältesten, die neusten Regionen ...,' 'Vom Paradies bis heute gleich gemeint ...', ll 333–45). But the broader the perspective the greater is the danger of discouragement over the ever receding goal of fulfilment of these aspirations. The evocation of harmony in history and in the face of the ever present forces of violence and chaos is contained in *El Cid*. In the life of this young hero, man's essential goodness and lovableness are rooted much more deeply than in the figure of Hüon. The epic imposes a much severer test upon the poet than does romance, hence achievement must weigh more heavily, too. *El Cid* also articulates collective or national aspirations, and in the hands of a German poet this impulse reveals its positive side without lapse into nationalistic distortion of human striving. But what if the poet himself grows weary and bitter under the strain of the task of uncovering the essential nobility and validity of human desires in the face of their corruption in his own time? Bitterness and frustration prevent him from fulfilling his essential function of giving and praising; they clog the channels through which he imparts his wealth and impoverish him and the society which depends on him and on which he depends. As was suggested earlier (p 150), *Aeon und Aeonis* is not free from this defect, and in order to remedy it Goethe makes full use of his sovereign power as the Prospero of this midwinter night's dream. He introduces Aeon, the eighteenth-century tyrant, who dies in Herder's festive centenary play and thus pays his debt to time in a setting in which time should be suspended. Gently, Goethe leads us back from *Aeon und Aeonis* to the work which it was intended to contradict:

Er fühlt sich besser als in besten Zeiten,
Ist neubelebt und wird mich froh begleiten ... [ll 401–2]

The magic revival of Aeon in the presence of majesty is at the same time the transfiguration of Aeon into Paläophron.

Where does the poet derive the authority to perform this pious annulment of an existing work? For one, there is the general authority of the occasion which puts everything into a state of flux so that it may be bent to the theme of the celebration. Secondly, there is vested in the poet the power of advocacy before the throne which puts the motivation of an act on a par with its execution. This power will stand the poet in good stead when he presents himself ('im höhern Sinne war es gut gemeint,' l 454), but it is already invoked in Herder's case, though not directly applied to his problematic personality ('Sie meinen's gut und fromm im Grund ...,' l 351), and it will finally be invoked by Ilm on behalf of all who have appeared ('Hört er öftermal die Flöte/ Seiner Dichter treu und gut,' ll 877–8). Lastly, *Maskenzug 1818* is, in addition to its other aspects, an act of friendship performed by the surviving poet:

die eigentlichsten Vorzüge trefflicher Männer auszusprechen, deren Vollkommenheiten man erst recht empfindet, wenn sie dahingegangen sind, wenn ihre Eigenheiten uns nicht mehr stören ... [*Noten und Abhandlungen* WA i XII 133]

The self-presentation of the poet in any context could be a highly precarious and delicate undertaking. The ease with which it is accomplished here attests to the solidity and viability of some of the basic assumptions on which the entire work is based. Goethe's presentation is founded on the ceremonial character of the whole which provided for an assigned place and on the validity of the encomiastic function of the assembly. The ceremonial mask protects one and all from the debilitating and distorting effects of 'Bescheidenheit.' The only departure from established procedure consists in the omission of the name itself. Goethe presents himself as a man of the theatre, as translator, director, and playwright. Of the three plays used in the procession two, *Mahomet* and *Götz*, were specifically adapted to the Weimar stage and are thus 'Landeserzeugnisse' in the proper sense. They constitute extremes of dramatic styles and hint at the ideal of variety and universal competence to which Goethe aspired as director of the theatre. A reference to the recent unpleasantness which had terminated Goethe's connection with the theatre in the preceding year can be detected. The matter is dismissed with a sovereign gesture ('Allerlei mag unterlaufen,/ Womit ich mich nicht befasse ...' (ll 474–5).

The *Mahomet* and *Götz* episodes together convey two different messages. First, they present as equally valid two poles of dramatic presentation, the classical and the Shakespearean methods, and imply thus the denial of any nationalistic or ideological scale of evaluation. Therefore they measure the dimensions of the modest court theatre of Weimar. Secondly, they evoke two contrasting situations of political upheaval and oppression: the ruthlessness engendered by, or at least associated with, prophetic zeal, and the jeopardy in which instinctive humanity and virtue ('That Recht und Unrecht in Verworrenheit,' l 534) are placed in an empire where the erotic, political, and religious impulses have been hopelessly dissociated and perverted: '... Scepter, Krummstab, Schwert,/ Feindselig eins dem andern zugekehrt' (ll 523–4). 'Des Pfaffenhofes listgesinnte Macht,/ Gewandter Männer weltlicher Gewinn/ Und leidenschaftlich wirkend Frauensinn' (ll 540–2). The gypsies, however, introduced as the representatives of ultimate chaos and disorganization, proclaim the antidote. Because they are outside society they can see through the trappings of empire to the essential sources of social coherence:

> Gold und Perlen und Juwelen
> Können solcher edlen Seelen
> Himmelglanz nicht überleuchten.
> Der allein ist's der uns blendet.
> Aber wenn wir abgewendet
> Stehn betroffen, lockt uns wieder
> Mutterlieb' so süss vom Throne,
> Zu der Tochter, zu dem Sohne;
> Doch sie steigt vom Throne nieder
> Und beseligt niedre Hütte... [ll 564–73]

The assurance of continuity and of order through the infant prince ('Eine Gegengabe Gottes,' l 579) moves the spectacle forward to the greatest challenge to the force of harmonization. The phase dedicated to Wieland had dealt with youth, Herder's with youth and age. But there remains the seemingly insuperable obstacle, the overriding fact of the loss of youth, of the subjection to the tyranny of time. Only the most potent magic of poetic imagination can master this challenge. Here the themes of political power and of mastery over time converge. Wise rule provides the magic circle in which magic works beneficially. Mephistopheles himself may avail himself of the plea of good intentions, as had the poets before ('böser Geist mit bestem Willen,' l 593) in this secure place:

> Wenn scharfes Aug' des Herrschers die Verirrung
> Stets unter sich in kräft'ger Leitung hält;
> Und wir besonders können sicher hausen
> Wir spüren nichts; denn alles ist dadraussen. [ll 596–9]

The poet who had experienced the miracle of rejuvenation under the celestial arch of 'Phänomen,' 'Sind gleich die Haare weiss,/ Doch wirst du lieben' (WA i VI 17) now assigns this white magic to Mephistopheles: 'Im Alter Jugendkraft entzünden ... Das ist gewiss nicht schwarze Kunst' (ll 647–9). Like Epic and Tragedy themselves, Mephistopheles is changed, 'ohne seinen Charakter abzulegen.' In the festive setting of the court he is allowed to shed the burden of paradoxical nature of being part of a force 'die stets das Böse will und stets das Gute schafft.'

This double feat, the domestication of Mephistopheles and rejuvenation, marks the farthest point of dream fulfilment, and the great ease of expression, the almost conversational relaxation, indicates and helps to produce a feeling of the disappearance of social distinction and of the strain of unfilled desire. It is the celestial condition of 'es ist gar hübsch von einem grossen Herrn, so menschlich mit dem Teufel selbst zu sprechen,' with the parts reversed. But this point also marks the end of the rule of Nacht. The final section, devoted to science and social pursuits, passes on review under the auspices of Tag, and this is plausibly explained by the poet through that figure: 'Doch diese hier [i.e., sciences and arts], kein wandelbar Ereignis/ Der Pflege sollen sie empfohlen sein.' These endeavours require patronage, but they do not set in motion the specific process of giving and taking that poetry and poets require and offer.

But what of the Schiller section? It is set aside from those devoted to the three older poets in that Schiller is not presented by Ilm and his works are placed in the realm of Aurora, who also utters his name. Here, if anywhere, is proof of the deliberate seriousness of the poet's intention to produce an authentic representation of the essence of the Weimar renaissance 'dass von nichts weniger als von einer weimarischen Poetik ... die Rede war' (to Klinger, 20 December 1818 WA IV XXXI 20). It would certainly have been more convenient to have maintained the same pattern throughout, and there is a glimpse of the difficulty of the poet's task when we find that the larger part of Aurora's speech (ll 666–89) was left to the last and written on 15 December, three days before the performance (cf. WA I XVI 472). In what way, then, is Schiller's poetic identity presented as different from the others', and by what means is this heterogeneous component fitted into the work as a whole? One possible answer which comes to mind is neither misleading nor, however, fully exhaustive. It suggests a scheme in which poetry as an instrument of transformation and dream fulfilment represents one pole, the realm of Night, the sciences and arts the other, the realm of Day and the work of Schiller with its strong philosophical and historical orientation a middle region, far enough removed from the analogy to natural phenomena and process, to not be amenable to presentation by the river nymph. The universality of philosophical concepts and the broad stage of European history of Schiller's work were not rooted in Weimar's soil. His activity enjoyed, instead, the protection of Weimar in the way the sciences and arts do in the 'Maskenzug.' The necessity of reiteration of 'Denn er war unser' in Goethe's commemorative poem (see above, p 127) makes a similar point. To put it more broadly, Schiller's entire relationship to 'nature' could not be accommodated in the concept of a protective divinity that is implied in Ilm as *genius loci*.

With almost shocking consistency, Goethe draws a line between himself and Schiller by introducing him through a work which is diametrically opposed to his own genius, one which he would have been least capable of writing. *Die Braut von Messina* is the most abstract of Schiller's tragedies, in which not the slightest attempt is made to give human shape to the cause of tragedy and thus to suggest the possibility of human transformation. It is thus the antipode of *Iphigenie*, where the dramatic effort had been devoted to avoiding the tragedy of fratricide by recognition of the illusory nature of an arbitrary divine command. In presenting *Die Braut von Messina* Goethe put this situation in the most poignant terms he knew, those of nature deserting man. Dawn can present the survivors of such a tragedy only by the denial of her own fulfilment. The depth of misery, conveyed by the denial of sunlight after the promise of dawn, can only be gauged by recalling the effect of the healing powers of sleep and dreams in the wake of tragedy in Faust's contemplation of the rising sun:

> Hinaufgeschaut! – Der Berge Gipfelriesen
> Verkünden schon die feierlichste Stunde,
> Sie dürfen früh des ewigen Lichts geniessen
> Das später sich zu uns hernieder wendet.
> ...
> Und stufenweis herab ist es gelungen;
> Sie tritt hervor ... [WA i xv (1) 6]

The hope, the promise of this fulfilment is voiced by Aurora, too:

> So aus der Tiefe dieser Schlucht der Peinen
> Blick' ich hinauf zum schmalen Himmelsklar!
> Schon wird es besser! ach ich durfte weinen,
> Ein Sonnenabglanz heilt und hebt mich gar. [ll 658–61]

But here, Night does not yield her place. She usurps the place of Day and offers only a fiery message, as on a scroll in a mediaeval vision of hell:

> Doch wenn von dort, woher wir Heil erflehen,
> Ein Blitz, ein Donnerschlag erschreckt,
> ...
> Uns Nacht am Tag umgibt, der Himmel flammet
> ...
> In Schreckenszügen Feuerworte mahlt:
> Das Schicksal sei's, das ohne Schuld verdammet. [ll 666–73]

As mentioned before, Goethe put off writing this part to the last probably because the only remedy of this alien situation was one alien to him: 'Alsdann vernimmt ein so bedrängtes Flehen/ *Religion* allein von ew'gen Höhen' (ll 688–9). Religion here is an abstraction with no suggestion of the personal divinity which can be harmonized with erotic and social impulses.

Now that an extreme point of reference has been established, the work of Schiller too can be brought into the conciliatory context of the masque. The means used in turn reflect the essentially rational nature of Schiller's achievement. There is a symmetry about this section undetected in the earlier phases of the procession. The unclosed abyss of the action of fate in *Die Braut von Messina* is also formulated in terms of an insoluble riddle: '*Ganz gleich ergeht's dem Guten wie dem Bösen!*/Ein schwierig Räthsel, räthselhaft zu lösen' (ll 690–1). But this is an evening when riddles must be solved, if the procession is not to disband in disorder, and the impasse is compensated for by at least one work of Schiller whose happy outcome depends on the solution of riddles – *Turandot*. Hyperbole can come into its own once again. Such is the auspicious power of the occasion that all riddles are solved before they are set:

> Denn wie Ihr schon die Träume wahrgemacht,
> So lös'tet ihr auch jedes Räthsel auf.
> Und welches Wort sie immer sucht und wählt
> In Redeknoten listig zu verstricken:
> Zum Beispiel *Majestät* und *Häuslich Wohl*,
> *Thron* und *Verdienst* und *rein verbreitet Glück*,
> Das alles findet sie vor Augen klar ... [ll 844–50]

Restored, too, is the easy conversational tone. Once Atoum has discharged his responsibility as dramatic character of a happy royal father he cannot stop himself and addresses the gathering with the exuberant garrulousness which recalls the charming informality of Christiane Becker-Neumann's prologue to *Alte und neue Zeit* and makes a reluctant exit, prompted by his decorous daughter.

Die Braut von Messina and *Turandot* are both fictions, one a hypothetical construction, the other a fairy-tale. They contain and mark the limits of the historical dramas. The historical group consists of *Tell*, *Wallenstein*, and *Demetrius*. The last of these might be called indispensable in view of the nationality of the visitor. Besides, its incomplete state left convenient room for an ending in the spirit of the occasion. But each of these plays is filled with the display of conflict and of the use and abuse of power, and none is conducive to a final *tableau* in which power has been assigned its proper place, permitting the harmonization of society. Therefore each one must be given a utopian turn, wrenched from its historical moorings, in order to serve the occasion. This is most difficult in the work which occupies the centre – *Wallenstein*. Here the forces of disintegration are most closely linked with highest personal endowment. Wallenstein's failure is the most frightening because of the greatness of his gifts. His fall from grace is a betrayal not only of duty, not only of pure souls like Max and Thekla, but of nature itself. The climactic lines are: 'Dem Irrthum leuchten, zur verworrnen Bahn / Gestirne falsch, die noch so herrlich blinken' (ll 734–5). A man capable of deriving such sinister guidance from nature at its most beautiful is truly beyond redemption. He has placed himself outside the realm of Night of fulfilment, which contains within itself all celestial splendour

> Dass nur in mir die hellste Sonne strahlt
> Auf dunklem Grunde blinkend, lieblich stille
> Sich Stern an Stern in ew'gen Bildern mahlt. [ll 26–9]

Only a few months before, in February 1818, the poet had exalted the unceasing sympathy between the heavenly bodies and personal fate in 'Um Mitternacht,' where the boy expresses it in simplest, child-like words '... Stern am Sterne / Sie leuchteten doch alle gar zu schön (WA i III 47):

In the case of *Wallenstein*, then, transformation is impossible. This vision must be exorcised ('Es war ein Bild. Das Herz ist wieder frei,' l 737). Although resolution outside, or in spite of history cannot be effected, there remains at least the possibility of a new beginning. In *Wallensteins Lager*, aspiration and loyalty do not yet clash in the simple hearts of the lowly soldiers who look straight ahead, do not gaze at the stars at all, and can thus remain true to themselves ('Sich immer treu geblieben'). Once again, Mephistopheles, this time disguised as sergeant-major, presides over an act of rejuvenation of a sort, clears the air of the oppressive 'Grillen, Phantasien und Spintisirerei' (l 626) and their fateful consequences in the mind and actions of a powerful man. The invocation of Russia's knightly saint 'es lebe St. Georg der Held' (l 768) and the passwords 'Manneszucht' 'Subordination' (ll 775–6) point at least to the possibility that the same tragic road need not be travelled over and over again, always provided 'die Herrscher wissen, was sie wollen' (l 772).

The discovery and definition of the proper function of the ruler dominates the transformations brought about on the two dramas flanking Wallenstein. In *Tell* this is simply a matter of changing the mechanism of the attainment of the ideal ends proclaimed in the play. Once the ruler has discovered his true function as a source of good, bloodshed and violence yield to deliberation ('Was sie entrissen wird gegeben,' l 703), but it is made clear that the goal itself ('der Freiheit aufgeklärter Blick,' l 702) remains unchanged. But the circle of beneficiaries has widened. The ideal is reached at no one's expense ('Ja sogar die Gestalt Gesslers wagt es, versöhnt, under seinen Widersachern aufzutreten' ('Vorl. Anzeige,' p 241). Nowhere, up to this point, has the spectacle touched so explicitly upon the immediate issues of the time, the frustrations and hopes of the half decade following the fall of Napoleon. This central portion of the Schiller section of the 'Maskenzug' comes close to being a *speculum principum*, a statement of the duties of monarchs, which is not at all at odds with the broader view of kingship developed from the beginning of the work, but is clearly focussed upon its political aspects. With an eye to a corresponding impression to be found in the *Demetrius* passage it should be noted that at this point the specific form of the relationship is not as clearly outlined as one might have expected in view of the associability of the entire passage with Carl August and Weimar. 'Die mit dem Fürsten sich berathen' (l 706) could, but need not, imply the existence of a constitutional arrangement. In any case, the idea of submission to a circumscribed rôle of the throne (as distinguished from absolute freedom of the ruler) is put forward clearly enough.

While the revision of *Tell* for the purpose of the occasion is utopian, *Demetrius* offers an opportunity of locating fulfilment in time. History and utopia can be made to coincide, provided the ruler in question seizes the opportunity to do so. This is brought about by means of a gentle adjustment of chronology reminiscent of, but not identical with, the device used in connection with Herder's personality and work. The discursive portion of the *Demetrius* episode deals with the chaos preceding the establishment of the Romanov dynasty. But the passage announcing the release from these afflictions ('Bis nun erscheint ... ein Heldenspross...,' ll 810–11) breaks the historical continuity because the regeneration of the country proclaimed here can hardly be associated with the reign of the first Romanov (Michael, 1613–45), especially in view of the far from tranquil and harmonious two centuries through which Russia passed under his dynastic successors, the Peters, the Elizabeths, and the Catherines. The 'Heldenspross' then is bound to be the present ruler – not so much for what he has achieved, as for what he might accomplish. It is up to him to bring about the fusion of history and utopia. How this may come about is clearly stated by the use of the full range of meaning of the verb 'fügen':

> Er wird sich in's Geschick zu fügen wissen,
> Es fügt sich ihm dass alle, sich bewusst
> Des eignen Heils, dem Herrscherwort sich fügen... [ll 813-15]

Thus, once again, the active and passive functions of the ideal ruler, one who gives and who receives, are set before the visitor. Here is a gentle emphasis on the notion of enlightened self-interest (especially through the word 'bewusst'), on a relationship of ruler and ruled which is much closer to a contractual and constitutional idea of monarchy than the messianic notions to which Alexander inclined.

It was suggested earlier that the character of the Schiller section of the 'Maskenzug' is more abstract, conceptual, and hortatory than the other parts of the work. The absence of Ilm in this phase is symptomatic and significant in this respect. By the same token – and in spite of the considerable space alotted to the practical arts in the final section – the return of the river nymph marks the re-emergence of elements which had characterized the early parts of the work and which dominate it to the end. The themes of adulthood and childhood, strength and weakness, vastness and smallness had already been introduced when Ilm justified her entrance before the assembly: 'Denn ich muss am besten wissen, / wie das Räthsel sich entsiegelt' (ll 225–6). The solution of the mystery involves her own transformation, which is also an alignment of nature with society through the identification of the stream with the human procession ('Sonne mich im Jubel-Saale' (l 893)). Now she has attained the rank of a great river alongside the Rhine and the Danube: 'und als Fluss, zum erstenmale, / Geb' ich mich dem Thal zurück' (ll 895–6).

The time has come for the tribute to Weimar itself, whose smallness seemed even more absurd on the map of post-Napoleonic Europe than it had thirty-six years earlier when the poet had written: 'O Weimar! dir fiel ein besonder Loos! / Wie Bethlehem in Juda, klein und gross' (WA I XVI 134). This is a tribute to a dynasty, to four generations from Anna Amalia to the infant Carl Alexander, towards whose cradle the royal visitor from the East is now being led. With the same delicacy of allusion which had marked the earlier reference to the messianic season the poet now makes the briefest modulation into another dynasty, 'the stem of Jesse.' Considering that Goethe had looked for models of the relationship of ruler and poet and of king and subject in the Orient, it seems altogether consistent that he should find there, as well, the representation of the fulfilment of this relationship through the identification of the two, in the royal harper and psalmist and in the redemptive force that issued from him. The poet's wish for Carl Alexander, 'er sei ein Harfner' (l. 1002) distressed one of the few faithful readers of *Maskenzug 1818* to the point where he called for any interpretation that might possibly justify the poet (Düntzer, p 226). The messianic climax of the work can only be acceptable if we allow ourselves to perceive the visionary character of the work as a whole, as a dream where transformation and fulfilment are enacted. Without lingering over the question one might refer to Kerényi's exposition of the relationship of religious and festive attitudes.[10]

There are no more memorable, no more haunting places in Goethe's work than those which mark the end of a vision, of a dream and which give expression to the dreadful moment of awakening, to the jolting awareness of the passage of time and the irrevocability of a 'kairos.' Think of Egmont's awakening, Faust's despair after the disappearance of Erdgeist, Epimetheus' first monologue, or the first few stanzas of the Marienbad elegy. It is a measure of the high seriousness of the work under consideration and an indication of the high sense of responsibility of the poet towards it and towards his public, that we are not spared such a moment in a work which could so easily have been ended with a massive flourish:

> Ach warum schon unterbrochen!
> ...
> Soll uns das vorüber schwinden,
> Als wenn alles eitel sei?
> Klagend wir uns wieder finden:
> Alles, alles ist vorbei! [ll 1010, 1018–21]

'Vorbei' is hardly a word at all, 'ein dummes Wort' perhaps, and tantamount to 'reines Nicht, vollkommnes Einerlei.' In any case it is the ultimate cry of man as the object of time. If time is to be overcome it cannot be argued away, but must be banished with authority. Authority to counter it with 'Nicht vorbei!' (l 1022) is here derived from the alignment of poetry and power which is enacted in the *Maskenzug 1818*. Not only does the royal progress continue beyond Weimar and continue, too, as a mother's journey to her children, but the silence of the dead poets and of him who has now drowned his book of courtly entertainment is formed and transformed into the permanence of love: 'Das Verstummen, das Erstaunen / Bildet sich als Liebe fort' (ll 1032–3).

Evidence of this perpetuation of the magic night, proof that the procession had not ended with the break of day, came to Goethe in the form of a loving tribute to the work and to himself from one who was not present on 18 December 1818 and who was not concerned with the occasioning event of the royal visit itself. J.F. Rochlitz' letter (see Appendix 2) does not indicate that he was touched by the political facets and overtones of the work, and yet when he speaks of its wholeness he must have sensed its full range. In any case, he convinced Goethe that the essential act, the creation of love, had been accomplished. And this, in turn, elicited an exuberant expression of gratitude:

Es ist der Mühe werth! gelebt zu haben, wenn man sich von solchen Geistern und Gemüthern begleitet sieht und sah; es ist eine Lust zu sterben, wenn man solche Freunde und Liebhaber hinterlässt, die unser Andenken frisch erhalten, ausbilden und fortpflanzen. Nehmen Sie meinen herzlichsten Dank für Ihren herrlichen Brief, dessen ich mich als des schönsten Zeugnisses zu rühmen habe. [18 April 1819 WA IV XXXI 127]

There is no simple formula which would cover the various phases and examples of occasional poetry examined in this study. Nevertheless, 'Auf Miedings Tod,' 'Euphrosyne,' *Was wir bringen*, and *Maskenzug 1818* were each in its own way contiguous to all great orders of existence, nature, art, society, individuality, and all found their realization in a setting which numbered smallness among its positive qualities: a small duchy, a small court, a small theatre. This situation was favourable to the harmonious interaction of universals and individual forms which is so characteristic of Goethe's view of the world and which renders possible the existence of genius in society. Putting it in social terms: not to feel overwhelmed by what is large, not to feel demeaned by what is small is the mark of courtesy. Those who expressed displeasure at the time and energy Goethe gave to the social institutions around him, and especially to the court, would have done well to consider the possibility that these were natural and necessary activities for a man who was naturally courteous. I am not suggesting that this quality is doomed or stunted in an environment other than a courtly one, but it should be noted that the subsequent fate of occasional poetry suggests that courtesy as a formative force did not fare well in a widened world. Goethe served the cause of his own survival when he stayed on in his small town with a castle. Indeed, perhaps the principal clue to the whole question is the merging and the identification of the two observed by Mme de Staël: 'Ce n'était point une petite ville, mais un grand château' (*De l'Allemagne* I xv.) How remote such identification had become by the time Hauptmann wrote his centennial 'Festspiel' in 1913 and Rilke his thank you poems to his aristocratic hostesses, and how unattainable for K. of *Das Schloss*, as he marked time in his village!

·10·

Once More into the Breach ...

AT THIS POINT IT may be reasonably assumed that the reader is experiencing a certain weariness, one not engendered, it is hoped, by the drone of the guide's voice, but rather by the variety of sights inspected during the journey and by the vigorous air of the Goethean highlands through which it proceeded. It can be claimed that the journey went according to plan, a modest claim, because the plan was such a simple one: to progress, more or less chronologically, through a sequence of representative works written for occasions. It should not be regarded as a bold deviation from this simple itinerary if once or twice blank spots on the landscape were contemplated, points of interest in the negative sense that conspicuous occasions remained unmarked by occasional utterance. If now the guide still seems reluctant to remove himself from sight it is not in order to solicit a gratuity, but rather because of an irresistible urge to confide in the traveller concerning the circumstances of the tour. It must be told: a spectre has been haunting a considerable portion of this inquiry, not a vague shadow by any means, but an undeniably substantial and important work. *Torquato Tasso* was bypassed in the first instance on the technical ground that it could not and needed not be related to any occasion. This technically sufficient reason was gradually fortified by a sense of relief at not being obliged to include this elusive work in the compass of the enquiry. Is there any other work of Goethe that moves so clearly and determinedly away from the goal of reconciliation and festivity, opposite to the direction of all considered heretofore? Is there another work in the entire Goethe opus where so much agony and gnawing misery are heaped on the shoulders of the protagonist without the fellowship of suffering nature as in *Werther* or of the human community as in *Egmont*? The intensity of this anti-festive mood is, no doubt, largely owing to the unity of the courtly, hence potentially festive setting. Tradition no less than the desires of the characters in the play point constantly towards the goal of reconciliation and celebration. And yet, dark, nameless forces turn the court into a torture chamber where the antagonists are engaged in disposing of each other without the shedding of blood, as befits the age of the Inquisition. The bloodlessness is the agony of the play. One would almost be relieved to hear the report of Werther's pistol or see the flashing of Alba's axe. But no drop of blood is shed; the duel is fought with weapons designed to get under the enemy's skin. This is indeed a fearful stage on the voyage of art into the interior.[1] Within an hour, the site of courtesy and friendliness is tranformed into a seamless cell where the hero pleads for and plots his release.

Lest it be thought that I have taken leave of my sense of proportion or of Goethe and slipped into the agony columns of our own century with contributions by Sartre or Kafka, it should be noted once again that my objective is not the total illumination of any of the works under consideration, but rather a functional enquiry into one aspect of Goethe's work. The questions appropriate to it will have to be: what exactly turns the life of an honoured poet at an honourable court into a nightmare and what could have prompted Goethe to turn to this subject and treat it in this particular way? The task faced is chiefly one of fitting *Torquato Tasso* into various contexts, but in a larger sense the play will remain, at least to this reader, uniquely aloof, alone, elusive, ironic. Even the reader most determined to take the outcome of the play as denoting recovery and a new beginning would not claim that Goethe is disposed to give us a glimpse of the birth of a new community in which the poet might live in harmony with society. Perhaps a Nausicaa is about to welcome the shipwrecked man, but perhaps not.

In attempting to 'locate' *Torquato Tasso*, a glance at the terminal emblematic figures which appeared at the beginning of this enquiry may be of some help: Poet Seizing Occasion ('und ich verkannte sie nicht, ergriff die Eilende') and Poet Seized ('by the crown'). Thus far the poet in question was the maker of the works examined, but for the present, the poet is the principal component of the poetic object, Tasso, because he is a poet. Here we have the first of several ironic involutions. Here, too, perhaps lies the root of the palpably 'modern' elusiveness of the work, considering that poems about the making of poems are a specialty of the Romantic era in a definition wide enough to extend into our own time.

The act of seizing is inseparable from considerations of appropriate time, of 'kairos.' *Tasso* turns out to be an account of desperately bad timing by the protagonists manifested most poignantly, but by no means solely, in Tasso's attempt to seize 'die Eilende' at the point of catastrophe of the play. The second emblematic figure, the poet whom the angel takes by the crown and bears by the hair of his head, points to the related focus of conflict involving authority over the poet. Such an indication of the total subjection will engender the elation of ecstatic submission, provided there is complete assurance of the validity and legitimacy of the power so exercised. This is not the case in *Tasso*. The hero resists being possessed and in the course of the struggle becomes convinced that the higher power which claims him and his work is a destructive and demonic one. The members of an enlightened court must inevitably interpret this conflict in psycho-pathological terms. We, the spectators, cannot allow ourselves to join them in this secular form of exorcism.

The theme of authority over poetry comes into the play, before a word has been spoken in it, through the coronation of the busts of Virgil and Ariosto. Whoever performs this act and chooses the manner of the tribute by assigning laurel to one and flowers to the other assumes a responsibility and arrogates for herself an office, however playfully and in the spirit of private make-believe this may be done. Neither the courtly ladies nor we know at this point that the crowning of a poet is a deadly serious matter, and thus Tasso's passionate and visionary reaction to the continuation of the game is profoundly shocking.

The theme of time, of the proper moment, is also introduced at the earliest possible stage. The duke's first words are 'Ich suche Tasso, den ich nirgends finde...' (l 239). From the ruler's point of view, the right time for a member of the court to be present is any time. The readiness is all and withdrawal, absence, is a flaw ('ein alter Fehler...,' l 243), an ailment ('Wenn wir ihn heilen könnten ...,' l 329). The ailment of withdrawal deprives the court of the attribute of completeness. Ideally, the court community as the distillate of society should be constituted fully and intact at any and all times with each component member fulfilling his function completely. For a court poet in the straightforward and traditional sense of the term this would mean no more than that he be ready with a complete and appropriate contribution to be delivered on certain and predictable occasions, birthdays, baptisms, etc. No such relatively simple and manageable assignments are at issue in Ferrara – the court is too sophisticated, enlightened, liberal for that, and therefore much more demanding. We are left in no doubt that the duke and his sister take immense pride in nurturing a 'great' poet rather than employing a competent purveyor of conventional expressions of joy, sorrow, praise, or other respectable sentiments. There is much stress on forebearance, patience and, by implication, on the renunciation of conventional tributes. And yet the obligation to deliver remains; the duke's impatience and the poet's initial recognition of the obligation are elaborately presented. One may take it as part of the author's design that we are to share with the court the explanation of the painful reluctance with which Tasso delivers his poem as the nervous perfectionism of a young man who has some difficulty in relating to his environment. It is well to remember that the act of delivery and dedication has lost much of its weight and import since the period chosen by Goethe as the setting. Here the recipient and patron assumes a most powerful dual rôle as judge through his willingness to accept the dedication and as owner and disposer of the work. The delivery scene contains many references to the proprietary aspects of the situation: 'So halt' ich's endlich denn in meinen Händen, / Und nenn' es in gewissem Sinne mein!' (ll 393–4); 'Denn euch gehört es zu in jedem Sinn' (l 398); 'So konnt' ich sagen: Dieses Werk ist mein' (l 401); 'Und welchen Preis nun auch mein Werk erhält, / Euch dank' ich ihn, denn euch gehört es zu' (ll 422–3). A relationship in which the border between what is mine and what is thine is blurred is unsettling: 'Allein, war ich besorgt es unvollkommen / Dir hinzugeben, so bezwingt mich nun / Die neue Sorge: möcht' ich doch nicht gern / Zu ängstlich, möcht' ich nicht undankbar scheinen' (ll 384–7). The conventional court poet is much freer. He delivers his goods at the proper time and goes home to his wife or other private preoccupation. Here, on the other hand, the object delivered is the poet himself and the total content of his creative life, his central epic. To the totality of this claim on the poet there corresponds a totality of the poet's claim on his patron. The collision of these two constitutes the dramatic action of the play with respect to occasional poetry.

Two events follow the difficult delivery of the poem in quick succession. The first is the presentation of the reward, the transfer of the laurel wreath from Virgil to Tasso: 'Es ist ein Vorbild nur von jener Krone, / Die auf dem Capitol dich zieren soll' (ll 484–5). It is after this allusion to a place and authority beyond the court made with the kindest of intentions that Tasso speaks of the wreath with panic and terror: '... Er sengt mir meine Locken, / Und wie ein Strahl der Sonne, der zu heiss / Das Haupt mir träfe ... Fieberhitze / Bewegt mein Blut...' (ll 489–93). The second event is Antonio's return from Rome. Another member of the court is about to deliver the fruit of his professional labours, but he, by contrast, is very much imbued with a sense of a task completed.

It is necessary to examine the nature and value of these accomplishments. The play tells us at length about Antonio's, about the content and outcome of the negotiations conducted in Rome. The text is far less explicit with regard to Tasso's work. For a full understanding of the subsequent events and in order to activate the inconspicuous and most subtly conceived ironies which pervade the play, we are permitted, indeed obliged, to involve in its experience data not expressly conveyed to us within its compass. To put it very simply: in a play dealing with John or Jane Doe all we can expect or hope to know about the protagonist must be conveyed in the work itself by the devices available to the author. Clearly a different situation obtains in a play dealing with Torquato Tasso. In the case of an artist as the protagonist it is not only the circumstances of his historical existence that are part of the exposition offered us through the mere mention of his name, but his work, too, becomes an agent in the dramatic action. The Sistine ceiling and David, but not paintings and sculptures in general, would be component parts of a play or novel about Michelangelo. Indeed, still lives and cast iron constructions would be expressly excluded. In this respect one is led to think of *Torquato Tasso* as an historical play where the spectator is called upon to supply a framework of information within which the events shown are organized, supported, and given contextual significance. To use a more obvious example, the knowledge that the Netherlanders eventually obtained their freedom from Spain is an essential ingredient of the experience of *Egmont*. The availability of an historically innocent generation would perhaps now make a controlled experiment along these lines possible.

It is most instructive to follow the fortunes of the historical criterion in *Tasso* scholarship. In the earlier stages the work was likely to be regarded primarily as a document on the history of Goethe's life, especially his position at Weimar and vis-à-vis Carl August and Charlotte von Stein. The waning of positivistic predilections resulted in an almost total disappearance of these straight biographical equations in favour of investigations of the relationship of artist and society. A trace of the emergence of a different kind of historical consciousness appears in the comprehensive and perceptive study by W. Rasch, who reminds us that in Goethe's day

Tasso was still known as a great poet and that the work handed to the duke was not a fictitious product, but a well-known epic which had formed part of Goethe's own literary education.[2] A somewhat more closely defined view of the rôle of Tasso's epic in the play is achieved by Lawrence Ryan. In his analysis Tasso is seen as suffering from the effects of being situated in a transitional zone between poetry as the expression of the totality of the world (as reflected in the vision of Elysium [1 iii], with its identification of poet and hero, 'Wie gleiches Streben Held und Dichter bindet,' l 551) and 'modern poetry' which produces a personal, hence unencompassing and incomplete image of the world.[3] This is a suitable framework for our purpose, but the concept of totality used by Ryan needs closer definition with respect to Tasso's epic.

If we survey the epic tradition from Goethe's point of view, Tasso's *Jerusalem Delivered* appears as the first of a species of epic the last of which, Klopstock's *Messias*, was a literary event of his own lifetime. The middle link, less conspicuous on Goethe's horizon it would seem, is Milton's *Paradise Lost*. As a group they could perhaps be loosely classed as the post-Reformation epic in the Virgilian tradition.[4] A cautious generalization that may be ventured about them is that they aim at some distant goal of collective redemption and of a renewal primarily, yet not exclusively religious, a goal merged with aspirations of national fulfilment. Each in its own way represents an attempt to validate and recapture the Virgilian achievement in its own time and culture. A further common characteristic is likely to be noted, especially by a reader who is finding dramatic material in this poetic tradition. Each of these epic poets reflects in his life and each in his own way acts out the pursuit of this epic goal. These poets are not inclined to disappear behind their poetic creations (with the inevitable consequence that later generations have been inclined to take a more sympathetic interest in their lives than their works). We probably ought to look for the root cause of this situation in the very determination to remain in the Virgilian succession, as well as in the uncertainty as to the nature of epic heroism and its proper location with regard to the human sphere on the one hand and the divine on the other. The never-ending debates on the acceptable level of the supernatural in the epic that stretch from the sixteenth into the eighteenth century are symptomatic of these inherent difficulties. Or, one thinks of the discussions about the 'real' hero of *Paradise Lost*. It seems that traditional certainties concerning the boundaries between word and deed, art and life, maker and matter, poet and hero are beyond recovery. In any event, Goethe's Tasso is made to appear powerfully controlled by the vision of an identity as poet and hero. There is a correspondence to the literary link between Tasso and Klopstock in the fairly close association of the two poetic personalities in Goethe's literary education. Evidence of it appears in their almost simultaneous presentation in *Dichtung und Wahrheit* (I ii; WA I XXVI 123). Several passages in the letters to Cornelia from Leipzig (DJG I 93, 107, 117, 129) suggest that Tasso's work and life – the Koppe translation was accompanied by a biographical sketch – were subjects of lively enthusiasm and controversy between brother and sister. Similarly, a strong and personal response to Tasso, comparable to the Klopstock 'Erlebnis,' may be deduced from *Wilhelm Meisters Theatralische Sendung* (I ix). One is not likely to find a more telling description of the poet-hero syndrome with its comic and tragic potentialities than in the characterization of Klopstock in *Dichtung und Wahrheit*:

Im Ganzen hatte seine Gegenwart etwas von der eines Diplomaten. Ein solcher Mann unterwindet sich der schweren Aufgabe, zugleich seine eigene Würde und die Würde eines Höheren, dem er Rechenschaft schuldig ist, durchzuführen, seinen eigenen Vortheil neben dem viel wichtigern eines Fürsten, ja ganzer Staaten zu befördern und sich in dieser bedenklichen Lage vor allen Dingen den Menschen gefällig zu machen. Und so schien sich auch Klopstock als Mann von Werth und als Stellvertreter höherer Wesen, der Religion, der Sittlichkeit und Freiheit, zu betragen. Eine andere Eigenheit der Weltleute hatte er auch angenommen, nämlich nicht leicht von Gegenständen zu reden, über die man gerade ein Gespräch erwartet und wünscht. [WA I XXVIII 332–3]

For Alphons, the events of act I, scenes ii and iv, are a gratifying process of completion and perfection of his realm, a propitious time (to Tasso: 'machst mir diesen schönen Tag zum Fest,' l 392; about Antonio's arrival: 'recht zur guten Stunde,' l 564), a confirmation and celebration of his authority. His court and the world have become co-extensive. By an exact counter-movement, Tasso experiences a stunning realization of the incompleteness and fragmentary nature of the world where he finds himself, and consequently of the imperfection and inadequacy of his own artistic action. This realization – actuated, as pointed out earlier, by the mention of

Rome – is conveyed by a visionary gaze into the magic mirror at the source of the Virgilian epic tradition, the Homeric world. Incompleteness and isolation: '... Käme doch / Ein andrer ... O säh' ich die Heroen, die Poeten ... O säh' ich hier sie immer unzertrennlich ... So bindet der Magnet durch seine Kraft ... Wie gleiches Streben Held und Dichter bindet' (ll 542–51). Is he not saying to his ruler that if the poet be deemed worthy of the laurel, then the ruler must make himself worthy of it, too? Leonore, the perceptive outsider, seems to sense this challenge, this claim of totality on the duke, when she intimates that things are different now: '... Lass uns nicht empfinden, / Dass du das Gegenwärt'ge ganz verkennst' (ll 558–9).

The chasm between the duke's notion of completeness and accomplishment and that of Tasso widens and becomes ever more visible when we are told the proportions and quality of the work that Antonio places into his master's hands as the fulfilment of the ducal aspirations: '... Wir haben / Nun was wir wünschen, und kein Streit ist mehr' (ll 575–6). It is a miniature *pax Romana*, the end of haggling over a 'Streifchen Land ...' (l 619).

We are looking through the eyes of a poet who has committed himself to a labour of redemption and renewal in a clearly-marked historical setting, of a Roman and Catholic poet for whom the New Jerusalem is attainable through the liberation of a city known by that name and who has taken for his epic matter the anticipation of this redemptive act in history. The ethical values of Christian knighthood can, at this juncture, only be credibly realized by action, by the assumption of an heroic existence. Anyone who lives up to these ideals should automatically find himself on the road towards the Holy Sepulchre. The full effectiveness of the poem could only be demonstrated by the immediate departure for Jerusalem by those to whom it is dedicated. If this does not happen, the poem or the recipients, or both, are incomplete and imperfect. Thus the decision to write a poem of this sort imposes a standard of perfection to be satisfied by maker and recipient alike. If the poem does not do its redemptive work it flaws both. The recipient becomes guilty of degrading the work to an ornament of vanity, the poet of not having been able to summon the creative power to impart to it its true redemptive momentum. Thus the two are clamped together as in a vise because in the isolated situation of the court there is no higher authority, no Rome, to decide who is at fault. Some of this is made more explicit later in the play, e.g., when Tasso says:

Bescheiden hofft' ich, jenen grossen Meistern
Der Vorwelt mich zu nahen; kühn gesinnt,
Zu edlen Thaten unsern Zeitgenossen
Aus einem langen Schlaf zu rufen, dann
Vielleicht mit einem edlen Christen-Heere
Gefahr und Ruhm des heil'gen Kriegs zu theilen.
Und soll mein Lied die besten Männer wecken,
So muss es auch der besten würdig sein.
Alphonsen bin ich schuldig was ich that;
Nun möcht' ich ihm auch die Vollendung danken. [ll 2634-43]

It is important to identify the presence of these motivating forces in the expository scenes of Act I in order to see the roots of the conflict in the poet's original artistic commitment rather than in a progressive affliction of social disorientation that looms so large later on. By the time Tasso conducts his tearful and touching ceremony of disinvestiture (II iv), he has grasped through personal experience what intuition had conveyed to him at the moment of coronation – that the moment had not been a propitious one ('Zu früh war mir das schönste Glück verliehen ...,' l 1574), that the ambiguity of the laurel as a tribute to heroes and poets is a destructive one, that in Ferrara the knightly sword is as ornamental as buttons and braid and may never be drawn on pain of demerit points, that Alphons is not about to emulate his ancestor Goffredo, and that the valid verdict on the efficacy of his redemptive poem can only be cast in Rome. There alone can the ambiguity of the laurel symbol be resolved because it is the point of intersection between universal authority in space as well as in time. Thus the literary jury gathered there to which Tasso wishes to submit ('... Gonzaga hat / Mir ein Gericht versammelt, dem ich erst / Mich stellen muss ...,' ll 2654-6) appears, so to speak, as the visible church of poetry, the guardian of the Virgilian tradition.

Whether or not Goethe intended them, there are two significant ironies concealed in the Roman theme in its literary aspect. When Tasso was finally about to be crowned on the Capitol, the death of the poet necessitated the cancellation of the ceremony. Secondly, Tasso's continued craving for Roman approbation resulted eventually in the destruction of *Jerusalem Delivered* because Roman authority came to be more and more equated in the poet's mind with religious orthodoxy of which the Holy Office could be the only arbiter and thus, as far as Tasso was concerned, *Jerusalem Delivered* had to yield to an emasculated revision, *Jerusalem Conquered*, inferior by all accounts to the original. Frantic perfectionism had obliterated the poem.

The most telling illumination of Tasso's Rome-centred world comes through Antonio, who returns from Rome to the undoubted centre of his existence. He tells us that his achievement had been made possible only because of and for the sake of Tasso's aspiration and goal. Tasso cannot be deaf to Antonio's assessment of the cause of his success:

> ... der hohe Sinn des Papsts.
> Er sieht das Kleine klein, das Grosse gross.
> Damit er einer Welt gebiete, gibt
> Er seinen Nachbarn gern und freundlich nach.
> Das Streifchen Land, das er dir überlässt,
> Weiss er, wie deine Freundschaft, wohl zu schätzen.
> Italien soll ruhig sein, er will
> In seiner Nähe Freunde sehen, Friede
> Bei seinen Grenzen halten, dass die Macht
> Der Christenheit, die er gewaltig lenkt,
> Die Türken da, die Ketzer dort vertilge. [ll 615–25]

It is irresistible not to ascribe the violence of Antonio's baiting of Tasso in the following scene to at least a dim realization of the dependence of his hard-won achievement on the efficacy of the conceptual world, to the articulation and realization of which Tasso has dedicated his life. In this sense Antonio is Tasso's instrument, almost the servant of him whom he is at such pains to put in his place as a fellow-servant of junior grade. The achievement for which Antonio reaps ducal confidence and recognition was in fact made possible by the existence of a more universal pattern of activity, the Roman pattern. Indeed, history intensifies and enlarges this irony when it underlines the ephemeralness of the achievement. With the duke's death a few years later the entire dukedom, so conscientiously secured and enlarged, reverted to the pope. In this instance, Goethe seems to be guiding us towards a perception of an ironic pattern when we consider that one of the few historic components of the play invented by him is the territorial nature of the issue between Rome and Ferrara.[5] The work as a whole does convey a vague sense of fin-de-siècle, of dynastic discontinuity, through the isolation of the duke and the spinsterhood of the princess.

These considerations of Antonio's position would, however, fail to attain full relevance to the work as a whole in its bearing on this inquiry if they were confined exclusively to the social and political portions of the play. As we have seen, in several examples of Goethe's social poetry there is a climactic *tableau vivant* constituting visual consummation and the resolution of all the contending forces of the work. *Tasso*, ironic in this respect, too, begins with a visual synthesis: two poetic worlds, complementary and compatible in their courtly setting. If symmetry is to be taken as an insufficient reason for Ariosto and his flower wreath, his presence must be translated into a pervasive and dramatic one, an overtone not consciously perceived, but nevertheless essential to the play as a whole. This symmetry is brought about by the translation of the visual presence of Ariosto into a verbal one through Antonio's elaborate encomium (1 iv 733ff), which conveys to us not only a characterization of *Orlando Furioso* but also a demonstration of its poetic effect. The immediate dramatic purpose of this speech, i.e., as a means of provoking Tasso, has tended to obscure from critical attention the detection of the continued presence of the Ariostean mode of poetry throughout the play as an alternative to the Virgilian. Leonore has a small rôle in this, too, but it is Antonio's commitment to Ariosto that counts. Whenever he speaks or acts he proclaims implicitly the existence and viability of another avenue of major poetry in counterbalance to Tasso's passionate commitment to his way of poetry and life. Incidentally, the Tasso-Ariosto alternative appears to have been part and parcel of public and critical consciousness at least into Goethe's own time if we recall the episode related in *Italienische Reise* (WA I XXII 51–2) when he was asked to take sides. Needless to say, he acquitted himself in the detached and impartial manner that behooves the stranger and is in any event appropriate to such naïve pastimes which were to find their equivalent in the Goethe-Schiller games that prevailed in the lecture halls and parlours in the nineteenth century.

Antonio's Ariosto speech thus extends the Antonio-Tasso confrontation into the realm of poetics even when it appears to be exclusively a clash of opposing personalities and philosophies of life. The encomium, curiously enough, is also the one moment in this play about a poet when a work of poetry is immediately present through verbal evocation. The 'Verzückung' (l 737) that Antonio experiences (and, true to the spirit of Ariosto, immediately disclaims ironically) is brought about directly by the act of evocation and definition of *Orlando*. Tasso's flight of enthusiasm, on the other hand, is brought on by the social act of coronation with all its questionable legitimacy and disastrous consequences. The effect of poetry on the other members of the court is always a mixture of a surrender to the poetry itself and to affection for the poet or considerations of the social enhancement to be derived from the work. The immediate efficacy of Ariostean poetry points to the possibility of a coincidence of poetic activity and action, word and deed, art and life, that Tasso pursues so desperately in his endeavours.

Broadly speaking, Ariostean poetry, according to Antonio, reflects and constructs a world which is not in need of radical transformation through an act of redemption, but one that is being redeemed and made complete through the unifying power of the poet who grasps in their fullness those qualities which render man fit to function as a complete being in an harmonious setting. Contentment, Experience, Good Sense, Intellect, Taste, and a capacity for True Good mark the realm of the true courtier, and the realization of these qualities within the poem bridges the gap between their presence in the artist's vision and in society ('geistig ... und persönlich doch ...', ll 718–19). Such poetry is didactic by obliterating the dichotomy between instruction and delight ('So hüllt er alles, was den Menschen nur / Ehrwürdig, liebenswürdig machen kann, / In's blühende Gewand der Fabel ein,' ll 713–15). The poet's task and goal are the presentation of a civilized world for the purpose of civilizing, rather than of a fallen world for the sake of bringing about radical transformation. The power of this poetry is strong enough to contain forces which in a poem aiming at redemption are necessarily part of another, a demonic world in conflict with human existence. The grotesque forms of life are here means of enlarging the sense of the beauty and variety of the whole ('Der Quell des Ueberflusses ...', l 724) instead of being the figments of an anguished imagination in need of being purged. Finally, and most relevantly to the play, the poet's firm grasp on reality controls and overcomes the chaotic forces in his creation and within himself. Sovereignty over his own person and control of *furor poeticus* enable him to write his poem about obsession and madness, the *Orlando Furioso* ('Indess auf wohl gestimmter Laute wild / Der Wahnsinn hin und her zu wühlen scheint, / Und doch im schönsten Tact sich mässig hält,' ll 731–3).

It is essential to understand Antonio's words as a presentation and definition of an alternative to Tasso's poetic ideal, but it may be noted in passing that the life and personality behind the work thus evoked would also be exemplary in Antonio's eyes. Ariosto had the ability to separate his existence as a poet from his political assignments; the episodes of his embassy to Rome and of his term as governor of the bandit-ridden Garfagnana province were related by Ariosto himself in a spirit of self-deprecatory amusement; and finally, he achieved detachment from the court in the security and privacy of his little house in Ferrara. To a literate audience, the Ariosto image thus adds some weight to the juxtaposition.

Consideration of *Torquato Tasso* has now sufficiently advanced to attempt an answer to the question which must justify the inclusion of the play in this inquiry: how does *Tasso* bear upon the opus of occasional poetry considered earlier? Later I will return to the play proper and raise at least, if not answer, two more questions, namely what sort of poet Tasso is at the end of the play and what sort of play *Tasso* is, but for now the challenge of the biographical integration of the work must be met.

The history of the conception and composition of *Tasso* is lengthy and, fortunately, obscure – 'fortunately' because our ignorance of the exact stages of development and revision between March 1780, the time of the first verifiable recording of a project, and July 1789, the time of completion, allows the assumption that the complete work may be related to Goethe's situation at the time of initial conception.[6] Granted, at one time Goethe refers to the need to recast what had been written from the bottom up (February 1788, Rome WA iv xxxii 272), but even this is not sufficient reason to believe that the later execution diverged in essence from the initial impetus in the case of a poet who has rightly not met with disbelief when he claims that *Faust* was fully in his mind from its earliest beginnings.

The chronology, following Gräf is: reference to Tasso, March 1780; Act I and part of Act II written in the fall of that year; work resumed in the spring of 1781 and a further segment dispatched in the fall; last traceable reference indicating intention to work on the project in spring 1782; hiatus of a little under five years until resumption of work in Rome in February 1787; the plan declared 'in Ordnung' in March 1788; finally, starting a few weeks after the return to Weimar, a year's regular and systematic work – August 1788 to July 1789 (Gräf VI 288–320).

I now intend to show a/ that the *Tasso* project in 1780 appeared at a time when Goethe had reached a state of awareness of his situation as a poet and as a member of the court which was conducive to a detached consideration of the possibilities presented by the literary situation around him, and of his own position within and with regard to it; b/ that part of this 'crossroads' consciousness derives from a sense of an insufficient or diffuse employment of his creative energies and the attendant search for a more deliberately organized and productive use of them in a large-scale work that would engage his creative potential; c/ that this state of mind though detectable in 1780 extends over the full span of the composition of *Tasso*; d/ that cetain shifts in emphasis in the poet's socially directed, or occasional poetry, capable of being related to *Tasso* can be observed after 1780; and finally e/ that the manner of treatment of the Tasso subject as a play reflects the situation and spirit in which it was conceived and completed.

These propositions overlap constantly and it is impossible to keep them neatly apart in elaborating them, not the least difficulty being that I am endeavouring to define a mood, an attitude, a state of mind for which there can be little documentary evidence but for which the object of attention, the play itself, must serve as the chief witness.

The first mention of *Tasso* (or of Tasso in a context that suggests reference to a literary project) occurs in the diary entry of 30 March 1780, which begins 'hatt ich den erfindenden Tag,' preceded by the entry for the 29th referred to as 'aufräumender und ordnender Tag' and followed by an end-of-the-month assessment and a look ahead on 31 March: 'Es scheint das Glück mich zu begünstigen, dass ich in wenigen Tagen viel garstige mit geschleppte Verhältnisse abschütteln soll ...' A victory crown would seem to beckon: '... *Nemo coronatur nisi qui certaverit ante* ... in diesem Monat muss alles zurecht' (WA iii I 113–14).

This succession of themes or dominant moods in a cycle of three days ('ordnen,' 'erfinden,' acknowledgment of the presence of good Fortune) might be taken as accidental or a passing whim if it did not recall a parallel connected with the Swiss journey from which Goethe and the duke had returned in January. The three diary entries apply to the poet's day-to-day activity, the three elements of life which were to have been visually represented on the monument to the happy accomplishment of the ducal journey as outlined in the letter to Lavater (see above, p 75), Terminus corresponds to the act of organizing, of sorting out, Genius corresponds to invention or creation, and Fortuna retains her tutelatory identity as 'Glück.' A further indication that Goethe was sketching and testing a pattern of the rhythm of his own life is to be found in an analogous tripartite scheme in 'Meine Göttin' assumed to have been written in September 1780. It is not difficult to relate Phantasie of the poem to the Genius of the monument, Weisheit to Terminus, and Hoffnung to Fortuna. Yet another diary entry of March 1780, that of the 26th, suggests the prevalence in these weeks and months of the need and urge to discover and render conscious the inner laws of activity, this time with an almost physiological emphasis, giving the proper organic range to organizing, 'ordnen':

Ich muss den Cirkel der sich in mir umdreht, von guten und bössen Tagen näher bemercken, Leidenschafften, Anhänglichkeit Trieb dies oder ienes zu thun. Erfindung, Ausführung Ordnung alles wechselt, und hält einen regelmäsigen Kreis. Heiterkeit, Trübe, Stärcke, Elastizität, Schwäche, Gelassenheit, Begier eben so. Da ich sehr diät lebe wird der Gang nicht gestört und ich muss noch heraus kriegen in welcher Zeit und Ordnung ich mich um mich selbst bewege. [WA iii I 112]

Carl August's and Goethe's journey to Switzerland from mid-September 1779 to mid-January 1780 was a carefully prepared and carefully recorded undertaking, its very deliberateness a contrast and antidote to the exhilarating spontaneity of the first years of Goethe's stay at Weimar. The epistolary record of these months tends to put to the fore the therapeutic progress of the duke, who, in a sense, is engaged in a second 'grand tour' under the guidance of a competent governor. There is no reason to deny the validity of this concept because it does not negate the somewhat less overt function of the journey as a period of enlightenment and clarification for Goethe himself. This process of *aménagement*, of sorting out, of taking stock of the several forces, impulses, and activities in order to release the full potential of endowment and opportunities would, in the case of the duke, aim at a wise distribution of energies in order to integrate his human qualities with the responsibilities of the ruler (as reiterated some time later in 'Ilmenau': 'streue klug wie reich mit männlich steter Hand / Den Segen aus auf ein geackert Land

...'). For Goethe it could not be anything but a process of organization which would put him on a firm footing as a poet. This is the cardinal point and as such almost invisible at the centre when the intricate web of human relationships and public responsibilities is exposed in such fascinating detail in Goethe's various utterances of the late seventies and early eighties. Virtually inseparable from this central impulse, really another facet of it, is the silent quest for an Archimedean point from which the powers known to be possessed will be controlled and utilized in their very fullness. The possibility of a supremely concerted effort, of a magnum opus, looms large and is never directly articulated at the turn of the decade (except obliquely so in the *Tasso* project), but does come to the surface as a personal statement in the 'Zueignung' of August 1784 ('ich kann und will das Pfund nicht mehr vergraben ...').

In attempting to capture Goethe's prevailing mood and disposition in the span of approximately sixteen months in the middle of which we find 'Tasso Day' (that is, from July 1779, when the Swiss journey emerges as a plan, to November 1780, the end of the first stage of the writing of *Tasso*), one is aided by evidence a little more trustworthy than that provided by our empathetically cocked inner ear. The poetic crown of supreme achievement, inseparable from the *Tasso* conception of late March and the tripartite rhythm of organization-invention-triumph (*nemo coronatur* ...) makes a tangible appearance in the unique gesture of Goethe's dispatch of a laurel wreath to Wieland about a week before to express his appreciation and evaluation of *Oberon*. This seems to be a manifestation of the organizing impulse, the desire to put things in their proper place and rank, as is born out by Goethe's accompanying message:

meinen Beyfall und Vergnügen recht lebhafft zu bezeugen; es ist so mancherley was ich dir zu sagen habe dass ich dir's wohl nie sagen werde ... Indessen ... fällt die Seele bey langem Dencken aus dem mannichfaltigen ins einfache, drum schick ich dir hier statt alles, ein Zeichen ... [WA IV IV 196]

Again, as an isolated utterance this might be taken as a charmingly spontaneous gesture of a generous soul, but Goethe's response to *Oberon* is significantly related in time and in kind to the constellation of forces and attitudes in which are located the beginnings of *Tasso*. The significance of the dispatch of the wreath as a gesture of unqualified admiration can be interpreted in the light of evidence which indicates that Goethe thought that *Oberon* would probably not be granted its due as a supreme poetic achievement by a public which was conditioned to look for masterpieces of a different kind. This expectation can be found in the first reaction to *Oberon* of interest to us in the diary entry of 26 July 1779:

bat Wielanden mir dabey seinen Oberon zu lesen er thats zur Hälfte. Es ist ein schäzbaar Werck für Kinder und Kenner, so was macht ihm niemand nach. Es ist grose Kunst in dem Ganzen ... Es sezt eine unsägliche Ubung voraus, und ist mit einem grosen Dichter Verstand, Wahrheit der Characktere, der Empfindungen, der Beschreibungen, der Folge der Dinge, und Lüge der Formen, Begebenheiten, Mährgen Frazzen und Plattheiten zusammen gewoben, dass es an ihm nicht liegt wenn es nicht unterhält und vergnügt. Nur wehe dem Stück wenns einer ausser Laune und Lage, oder einer der für dies Wesen taub ist hört, so einer der fragt *a quoi bon*. [WA iii 191]

Here is the germinal cell of Antonio's tribute to Ariosto because if *Tasso* reflects basic outlines of the literary situation at the time of its writing then the presence of Ariosto can only point to its sole equivalent in that situation, the author of *Oberon*.

A year later there is a spirited defence of *Oberon* and of Wieland against one 'der für dies Wesen taub ist,' namely Lavater. It tells us much about the defender's need to defend his position the more agitated the exchange grows. In its progress there occurs the famous tribute 'so lang Poesie Poesie, Gold Gold und Crystall Crystall bleiben wird als ein Meisterstük poetischer Kunst Geliebt und bewundert werden'[7] (3 July 1780 G-L 119). The point Goethe is making with ever-growing fervour and exasperation in the course of this debate is that there is such a thing as pure art, but that its appearance in German literature is being perceived only darkly, if at all, through the glass of ideological or religious prejudice which attaches extra-artistic expectations to the work of the artist. Goethe draws clear lines of demarcation in this assessment as he mentions two non-poets: Lavater himself ('bist ... deswegen auch kein Poet ...') in connection with his *Offenbarung* (5 June 1780 G-L 115) and Bodmer ('Bodmer ... ohne Dichter zu sein ...' 3 July 1780 G-L 119). The controversy comes into focus and a barely muted explosion takes place (24 July 1780 G-L 125) after Lavater had granted that Wieland was a great 'Talent' (15 July 1780 G-L 123), i.e., a rung below 'Genie,' admirable, but imitable by anyone, e.g., Lavater, circumstances, time, and inclination permitting, that is if one were inclined to invest one's energies in such frivolities. In attempting to stave off Goethe's wrath Lavater broadens the discussion to become part of the pervasive eighteenth-century one about the beautiful versus the sublime (5 August 1780 G-L 130), continued in the next century as 'Schriftsteller' versus 'Dichter.' Goethe dropped the matter after that, resigned, one imagines, to the impossibility of Lavater ever being found among the 'Kinder' or the 'Kenner' who would sense the full dimensions of Wieland's achievement.

The vigour of Goethe's appreciation and advocacy of *Oberon* must be explained at least in part by his awareness of the difficult route by which Wieland arrived at this peak of consummate artistry. We can and need not do more than refer to Friedrich Sengle's description of this ascent in his Wieland biography and in 'Wieland und Goethe,' where he traces the points of contact and interaction between the two poets.[8] Suffice it to recall that Goethe was well aware of Wieland's youthful involvement in the pursuit of the post-Reformation epic goal in the company of and in opposition to the principal theorists and practitioners, Gottsched, Bodmer, and Klopstock. Thus, the apparition of a short, unpretentious, perfectly wrought narrative poem, the result of a visible acquisition of mastery of the craft extending over a quarter of a century must have touched Goethe deeply.

Goethe tried to explain this appreciation to Lavater when he singled out a conspicuous quality of *Oberon*: 'was man nicht leicht an so einem Werke schäzt weil es so selten ist; dass nemlich der Autor nichts hat machen wollen ... als was eben da steht' (WA IV IV 259). Although this represents a technical aesthetic appraisal, in the first instance it is, in its full implications, a criticism of all literary activity that uses poetry as a tool for an allegedly higher purpose, be it the goal of messianic redemption or that of social liberation, with the consequence that poetry can never appear perfected or completed until it has demonstrated its perfection by perfecting the world. And so we are back in the garden of Belriguardo.

Once the need to take stock, 'ordnen,' has been recognized as paramount in the field of forces where *Tasso* originated, the dominant note of detachment is perceived clearly. All the expressions of praise for *Oberon* (as well as the encomium in the play) are those of a highly elated and articulate reader-critic contemplating an object without a trace of identification or, conversely, rejection. It is seen, recorded, and defended as a manifestation of major poetic endeavour and achievement and thus capable of occupying an important space on the map of major poetic provinces that Goethe was drawing for himself from 1779 to 1790. How symmetrically convenient it would be if there were a similar objective detachment with regard to the Virgil-Tasso side of the tableau, but, of course, there cannot be. Here the progress of the play itself is the manifestation of a process of objectivation of 'ordnen.' To be sure, we can lift off quite easily one or two strata of the organism, or rather watch the poet wield the scalpel in doing so. In terms of the epic tradition associated with Tasso, Goethe's was never a prophetic voice and the Klopstockian stance ('auf Prophetenstelzen') had never tempted him. But the prophetic trend was conspicuously spread over the literary landscape – the urgent sense of the need for redemption through the propelling force of the written word. This view was quite different from that of literature as an ornament and instrument of the improvement of life which left the redemptive task, if any, to the traditional or to newly emerging religious organizations or groups. The full range of the prophetic sense of mission attached to literature includes its expressions in the secular areas of society and politics. Indeed by 1780 the process of secularization of the prophetic impulse had advanced far enough to give the goal of national and social redemption at least equal rank with the religious one. This situation is referred to here only to suggest that its existence would not have impelled Goethe to erect the complex structure of *Tasso*, however strong was the urge to survey, 'ordnen,' in the period under examination. These phenomena do have the function of a negative background. The sense of failure, of futility, that had grown along with the slow growth of the *Messias*, the stridency of secular and religious messianism in Klopstock's own work and that of those who were inspired by him, whether they acknowledged it or not, cultivation of pietistic inwardness or vociferous denunciation of present ills – the awareness of all this orchestrates *Tasso*. However, it could not by itself have elicited the theme from the poet, because he was an aloof observer, protected from it in the magic circle of Weimar (the 'Zaubermärchen-Land' of 'Ilmenau').

So the strenuous and intricate labour of 'ordnen' could not be called forth solely by a state of affairs that Goethe already saw as a pattern, albeit not a pleasing one. It had to be something that involved his own situation. These remarks are put circumstantially and laboriously in order to locate the figure of Tasso at the right distance and in the proper relationship to Goethe. In the earlier examination of the play Tasso was established as an historical figure, safe through his historicity from facile identification with Goethe. In attempting to account for the origin of the work that distance must be shortened, but what should be brought closer to Goethe is not the person of Tasso but a Tassoesque condition or state of mind.

The projected biography of Bernhard of Weimar has imprinted faint tracks upon the literary biography of Goethe but deserves some attention here mainly for illustrative and symptomatic use, although it seems to have had some catalytic force in the making of *Tasso*, as well, because it rises to its highest point of visibility during the weeks and months examined above. It attracts attention as the only subject of epic potentiality that could have done duty as a 'house-epic,' a means of glorification of the dynasty served by the poet. And yet almost from the initial consideration of the matter, which goes back to 1777,[9] it seems to have been doomed in Goethe's eyes. The fact that some work and effort were invested in the plan despite the unsuitability of the subject suggests some parallels with Tasso's discomfort between his sense of obligation towards the ducal family and his more universal obligations. A more naïve artist than Goethe might have strained with greater alacrity for the bait of the theme, the meteoric career of a mighty warrior. But if Bernhard was perhaps made of the stuff of Achilles, even the most strenuous invocations of the muse could not have turned his contemporaries into Ajaxes or Nestors. This becomes apparent from Goethe's observations on the project addressed to outsiders such as Merck and Lavater. They remind one a little of the ironic and semi-apologetic tone used for the descriptions of court entertainments. The references to the matter from the safe distance of thirty-nine years in *Tag- und Jahreshefte* (WA i xxxv 6) have even slightly farcical overtones and still seem to convey some feeling of relief that things had not gone worse. I am interested in the reactivation of the project during the Swiss journey, which I suspect was a quid pro quo for ducal resolutions of mature behaviour and true dynastic worthiness. Preliminary activity in the spirit of 'ordnen' is recorded shortly after the return to Weimar (20 January, possibly also 7 February). The acknowledgment of no fewer than fifteen volumes of Bernhard's papers on 28 February suggests that their dispatch had been arranged during the brief visit to Gotha in the same month. Even at this point Goethe keeps an eye on an escape hatch ('einem andern anvertrauen ...').

Epics and would-be epics were obviously on Goethe's mind during January (as were wreaths and crowns in March). In the first diary entry after the completion of the Swiss journey the mood of 'ordnen' is conspicuous; it is a *tour d'horizon* of a returning traveller and contains the following final section:

N.B. Jederman ist mit ♃ [i.e. Carl August] sehr zufrieden preist uns nun und die Reise ist ein Meisterstück! eine Epopee! Das Glück giebt die Titel die Dinge sind immer dieselben [17 January 1780 WA iii I 105]

This wry and somewhat sour remark is quite understandable to anyone who has ever returned home from a stimulating lengthy journey to the confines of continuing and accumulated business. But there is perhaps a firmer connection between this little outburst and the larger matter under consideration. One senses deep misgivings about the disproportionateness of the assessment of the enterprise by those who had remained at home, misgivings which seem qualitatively identical with those engendered by the expectation that the poet would grant epic rank to the career of an adventurous ancestor during the Thirty Years' War. Are not the satisfaction and praise recorded in the diary much like those accorded Antonio for his deed which, in Tasso's perspective, is subordinate to the point of pettiness? And Tasso's increasingly obsessive realization that his work is going to be appropriated and misused as a 'house-poem' seems to lurk behind this uneasiness. Here one is close to the main root of the claustrophobia of *Tasso*, and at this point the urge to take stock that seems to be the driving impulse behind the conception and completion of the play becomes, in turn, visible as the result of an acute sense of disproportion in Goethe's own situation. This notion is reportedly Goethe's own interpretive aid to the understanding of the play ('Disproportion des Talents mit dem Leben,' GES I 472).

If we gauge Goethe's situation in 1780 by the products of his pen (the only worthwhile gauge applicable to a poet), then we are bound to record a constriction and solidification capable of being experienced as a sense of disproportion. Goethe had been welcomed to Weimar, had welcomed the welcome, had been drawn by it, and had sunk towards it like the young fisherman of the ballad, for the self-same reason that had made him beloved of all the diverse and contending strata of the literary world – as the man who had plumbed the human heart to depths undreamed of before in

Werther, and who had discovered the human heart in the recesses of the past in *Götz*. The poet, in turn, had found in Weimar the measure of freedom which he felt to be acutely threatened in the last phase of his life in Frankfurt. With all its earthy fun and its courtly trappings and even with its sober exertions in council, the union with Weimar was an erotic one of which the Charlotte von Stein relationship is but the most personal manifestation. Goethe had responded to the lure without reservation. His unstinting contribution to the union was the fullness of his person and the genius of his mastery of the human heart. Weimar neither withheld the poet from the world nor did he withdraw from it, but in a love affair the world shrinks to the size of the Eden where it takes place and the Eden expands to fill the entire world. All proportions are right because none are left. But it is not inevitable that a poet would sooner or later step back and measure the yield of a period against his own projects and against the urgings of his own potentialities. Then he would discover the pattern of the only three larger works completed in the later seventies: *Triumph der Empfindsamkeit*, *Lila*, and *Iphigenie*. These works have been shown to depict in various ways the removal of afflictions of the soul, their close affinities with the courtly public for which they were intended have been traced, and it has been noted that, far from being imposed tasks, these were occasional works, commissioned, as it were, by the poet himself as his contribution to the integrity of the society which he had chosen and which had chosen him. Thus, at one time or other, perhaps in the mountain fastness of Switzerland, but surely not unpreceded by a gradual sensation of constriction, the realization must have grown in Goethe's mind that his mastery of the depths of the human heart had brought him, as a poet, to the position of heart specialist accredited to the court of Weimar, and that this therapeutic rôle, in which there was no sharp division between healer and afflicted since the solace was mutual, was threatening to mark his creative limits to the exclusion of the world beyond, the affairs of mankind past and present and the workings of nature as such, unrefracted by human sensibility.

Let it be reiterated that the constriction inherent in the rôle of therapeutist is not in the least felt or to be understood as exploitation of the artist by the powerful which would in any way diminish his human and artistic dignity. Nor should it be forgotten that the therapy administered in this relationship was the opposite of a facile cult of emotion and sentimentality. *Tasso* reveals with heartrending intensity the pain inflicted by the compulsion to abandon the security, warmth, and apparent wholeness of the courtly 'kleine Welt' in obedience to the call to discharge a higher responsibility, represented in Tasso's case by the assertion of the epic and messianic theme. The focus of this phase of the process is the princess because in her existence and relationship with the poet the therapeutic temptation with its yield of mutual solace is depicted in its purest and noblest form, as its failure is presented in the most drastic and almost scientifically analytic terms. A detailed examination of the concepts of sickness and health and the figures of physician and patient in *Tasso* would further reveal the complexities and ironies in the work. A more accessible illustration of the place of *Tasso* from this point of view is to observe the striking reversal of at least two crucial elements of *Iphigenie* in *Tasso*: the Elysian vision as the crucial therapeutic moment in the first play and its use as the moment of a stunning and decisive glimpse of the chasm between the poet's mission and social reality in the second. A second reversal occurs towards the end of the two plays. In *Iphigenie* the presence and accessibility of the divine brother and sister are finally achieved through the deciphering of the divine message. In *Tasso* the ruling brother and sister move away into distance and silence.

The point has now been reached where we may give at least passing attention to the question concerning the classification of *Tasso Torquato*. The taxonomical task could and should perhaps be skirted, but, on the other hand, the general purpose of this inquiry was served by tackling it in the case of *Iphigenie*, the dramatic neighbour of *Tasso*. In that instance I expressed misgivings about the usefulness of the 'official' designation of the play as 'Schauspiel,' arising from the belief that the term reflected perplexity instead of shedding light, and, once again, I utilize the map drawn by Northrop Frye for our bearings. There we find a region which is not usually given the measure of autonomy that would make it a fit habitation for a work of literary art. Irony is given this standing by Frye in different contexts as covering its own ground and linked with various phases of tragedy and comedy by relations of correspondence. It would be a misuse of this spacious, subtle, and immensely stimulating critical structure to try to prove the point by singling out from it descriptive fragments about irony and pointing out their applicability to *Tasso*, a work not referred to by the author. But one criterion which appears and reappears in the definitions of irony as a mode, as pre-generic mythos and in generic criticism proper can be singled out – the concealment of the poet's attitude, the effect of detachment and objectivity.[10] In the light of earlier considerations I suggest that a work of this nature with all its attendant elusiveness would readily (inevitably, by hindsight) spring from the condition of detachment and stocktaking, from the spirit of 'ordnen.' Also there appears to be an emergence of some instructive pattern of creativity if the triad of plays, *Iphigenie*, *Tasso*, and *Egmont* – all begun in Weimar and subjected to a process of clarification in Italy – are aligned on the spectrum of comedy, irony, and tragedy.

Turning to the final, irresistible question about *Tasso*, how it all comes out, one merely gazes in admiration at those who have ventured upon the open ocean of this problem, Rasch, Ryan, Wilkinson,[11] and not a few others. In the conclusion of the play the Virgilian-heroic element as such has simply dropped from sight; it is not explicitly rejected or discarded, it just disappears. This seems to be the final verdict on the viability of this poetic path and Goethe's silent diagnosis of the viability of corresponding efforts in his own time. With this disappearance the play inevitably and imperceptibly discards the specificity of historical reference. The historical setting has been shown to be a supporting element of the play, to have been used to unfold a dramatic conflict with subtle implications and fine shades of meaning. Yet in any work of art, as contrasted with a work of enlivened historiography, there is a point where the artist will find himself shedding the armour of historical commitment as more constrictive than supportive. In the case of this play, possibly in all works of the kind, this act corresponds to, reflects or transmits a sense of freedom to the proceedings. The curtain is now fully opened and the stage is revealed in its entire width.

It is not the least indication of the miraculous coherence and wholeness of the play that this final expansion is brought about by agencies and forces already present, rather than by some deus ex machina of spiritualization and universalization. It is the continued presence of Antonio that makes it possible for the curtain not to close upon a collapsed heap of humanity capable only of invective against itself and the world. As has been argued, Antonio is in this play about poets and poetry, the manifestation of the continued presence of the Ariostean element. His calm humanity in the face of a situation that exceeds all he has experienced and anticipated stands as a living confirmation of the sustaining and civilizing power of the

Once More into the Breach 213

poetry to which he has declared his allegiance. Could it be said that the devoted reader of the book about mad Roland is equipped to deal with mad despair? How does this capacity manifest itself in the final scene of *Tasso*? In a dozen lines and a wordless gesture, no more. But these few words have the efficacy of a series of aptly dosed electric shocks used to restore continuity of action to a faltering heart. They enable Tasso to do what corresponds to the impulse behind the writing of the play: to take stock, to sort out. Antonio says hardly more than that there is something left to be taken stock of and sorted out; that something is power and Tasso trusts Antonio knowing and now understanding the statesman's precarious position between power and powerlessness. The exploration in which Tasso engages now proceeds by stages, the first, ending in 'Und wenn der Mensch in seiner Qual...' (l 3432), is the rediscovery of the foundation of poetic existence, articulateness as such as a permanent proof of election. There is also a faint suggestion of the use of the gift as a weapon against those who would deny it, of Yeats' court poet who goes on a public fast to the death because he has been excluded from the king's council chamber,[12] of the Romantic poet's need to proclaim his agony and isolation. But this is not the whole of it. In the light of what is to come and of what we know of the range of meaning of 'Leiden' for a poet who was to describe colours as 'Taten und Leiden des Lichts' we cannot take this word as denoting only the effect of the whip applied to the flesh or the soul. And in the next and final phase of the survey Tasso comes to define suffering and weakness as part of the unity of contour and chaos, mould and material, challenge and response, seizing and yielding that forms the rhythm of artistic creation now capable of being defined by means of a metaphor of elemental nature.

The breach of the title of this chapter is the one described earlier in connection with 'Auf Miedings Tod' and 'Euphrosyne.' The most conspicuous biographic feature of the chasm was the period Goethe spent in Italy. The examination of *Tasso* has given a more detailed and accurate knowledge of the site. The ground leading up to the chasm cannot be bridged at the point of the great biographical caesura, but a more suitable spot is discovered some distance away where the poet conceived the work in which the cry 'to Rome' becomes a central expression of an artistic predicament. The chasm and bridge simile must be put aside in order not to nurture the illusion of systematic developments and plans when we are dealing with gradual shifts of orientation of which the degree of consciousness in Goethe's mind is not an important matter of conjecture. And yet, looking back on the sequence of occasional and courtly works after brooding over *Tasso*, it becomes possible to observe that the effects of the upsurge of stocktaking and sorting out prior to and in the spring of 1780 may lend themselves to a degree of verification. It will be recalled that Goethe supplied a series of court masques at the next opportunity, that is, for the next festive season of the court in January 1781. The socio-political reasons that help to account for their appearance and content at that time have been examined. But again, their formal traditionalism and conventionality is unprecedented in Goethe's work and in striking contrast to the 'therapeutic' contributions to the court prior to the spring of 1780. The court entertainments of 1782 and 1784 and the children's ballets continue the series. The mechanism that suggests itself in the light of *Tasso* is obvious. I have already referred to the relatively greater freedom at a court of a traditional court poet compared to the situation of Tasso in Ferrara. Goethe took a step in this direction out of the constriction of personal commitment.

But it is a small step in the whole of Goethe's work. The larger pattern may perhaps be glimpsed if we return to the final lines of *Tasso* about the shipwrecked sailor clinging to the rock of salvation. I am confident of not overstepping the bounds of interpretive decency to name this rock granite, 'die Felsen, deren Gegenwart meine Seele erhebt und sicher macht,'[13] and then to read the thoughts of that sailor and see his clinging as a loving embrace:

man gönne mir, der ich durch die Abwechselungen der menschlichen Gesinnungen, durch die schnellen Bewegungen derselben in mir selbst und in andern manches gelitten habe und leide, die erhabene Ruhe, die jene einsame stumme Nähe der grossen, leise sprechenden Natur gewährt...[13]

The prose hymn to granite of 1784 is thought to have been intended as part of a magnum opus 'Roman des Weltalls.' It was never written as such, but could it be that the reader of Goethe's occasional poetry has read a chapter of it?

Appendix A

Von dem Ursprung und Gebrauch der Hochzeitgedichten.
Bei Gelegenheit der am ersten November 1773 unter vielen
Seegenswünschen
glücklich vollzogenen Schlosser- und Goetheischen Vermälung
übergeben
von des Herrn Bräutigams Schwester und Schwager
Vign. (trumpeter)

Frankfurt am Main
mit Eichenbergischen Schriften

Ein Hochzeittag und kein Gedicht!
Das wär fürwahr ein feines Leben!
Nein, warlich, nein, das thu ich nicht,
Und solte alles widerstreben;
Und wenn die Musen alle neun
Mir wolten hier zuwider seyn;
Solt ich gereimte Prose schreiben:
So muss das Ding in Forma bleiben.

Der Dichter Privilegium
Soll nicht durch mich verdrungen werden.
Es schüzt sich mit dem Altertum,
Und wurde jung mit dieser Erden.
Dem Adam sange schon der Chor
Der Vögel, Hochzeitlieder vor.
Und, wo nicht Hochzeitlieder klingen,
Da kan kein Ehstand wohlgelingen.

Selbst Plato sahe dieses ein.
Sein Volk solt ohne Dichter leben;
Den Hochzeitdichtern ganz allein,
Versprach er seinen Schuz zu geben.

'Warum?' Wie, BRUDER, weist Du nicht
Warum der Weise, dem Gedicht
Das man vor Braut und Bräutgam singet,
Den Schuzbrief im Gesaez bedinget?

Hör zu: In eine Kuh verstekt,
Dem wachen Argus übergeben,
(Dem Aug an Aug den Kopf gedekt,
Wie Lokken die um unsern kleben.)
Sah von dem hohen Himmel her;
Die schöne Jo Jupiter,
Und seufzte: ach! was kan ich machen,
Wenn hundert Augen sie bewachen.

Dies hörte sein getreuer Sohn,
Der ihm, in den Galanterien
Mit schönen Mädchen, öfters schon
Nicht unnüz war durch sein Bemühen
Er flog hin, und sang Argus Ohr
Ein Liedchen von der Syrinx vor.
Kaum solt sie sich ins Wasser tauchen,
So schliefen schon die hundert Augen.

Das, sprach der Aerzten Gott, ist gut;
Der soll mir Hochzeitlieder singen,
Wenn Venus und ihr Sohn das Blut
In allzu starke Wallung bringen;
Dann soll dies Soporifikum,
Zu des Erfinders ewgem Ruhm,
Der Braut die süse Ruh gewähren
Die ihr der Bräutigan will stören

Und darum singen wir dies Lied.
Will DIR DEIN FREUND die Nachtruh stören,
Dann, SCHWESTER, lass von unserm Lied
IHN eine halbe Strophe hören.
Gleich bei der ersten Hälfte wird
Wie von dem Stab Merkurs berührt,
Der träge Mund gezwungen gähnen,
Und nach dem Schlaf das Aug sich sehnen.

Appendix A 217

Doch wisse, alle Arzenein
Sind, oft gebraucht, dem Menschen schädlich.
Bissweilen lass ihn munter seyn,
Ein steter Schlaf ist auch nicht rätlich.
Denk an die Nachwelt, LIEBE BRAUT
Im Schlaf wird sie nicht angebaut,
In Munterkeit, in Scherz und Lachen,
Muss man die Welt bevölkert machen.

Vign. (cradle)

(private print in the library of the Freie Deutsche Hochstift, Frankfurt)

Appendix B

Rochlitz' letter on *Maskenzug 1818* 14 April 1819

Ew. Excellenz

den gestrigen schönen Frühlingstag verlebte ich in meinem anmuthigen Connewitz, und da wollt' ich Ihr Gedicht geniessen. Ich habe es genossen: den ganzen Nachmittag, bis die Sonne hinunter war, hat es mich im Freyen, dann auf meinem Zimmer erfüllet, und die nun dazwischengetretene Nacht hat den süssen Nachgeschmack noch so wenig aufgelöset, dass ich jetzt, am Morgen, nicht eher etwas vornehmen kann, bis ich noch einmal meinen Dank, nun nicht mehr blos für das Geschenk, sondern für das Geschenkte ausgesprochen habe.

Was enthalten nicht alles diese wen'gen Bogen! Ist denn wol Eine Seite ohne, eng gedrängt, irgend eines der reinsten und schönsten Resultate eines hochbegabten, reichen, edlen, hellen, tiefen Lebens, in Liebe, Heiterkeit, lieblicher Klarheit, hehrer Einfalt, und mit allen Reizen der schönsten Form dargelegt?

Ich überdenke vorerst die Erfindung des Entwurfes, der so Vielfältiges und Verschiedenes, bey so vielfältigen und verschiedenen Interessen, zu Einem Blumenstrausse, locker und doch fest, bunt und hochharmonisch – wie auf Huysums oder van Osens Bildern – zusammenflicht.

Nun male ich mir das Aeussere der Erscheinungen, zuvörderst für's Auge aus, nach Charakter, Zeit, Costüme, Farbe pp. und es webelt um mich wie in reizendem Feenpalastn vollgedrängt, aber wohl geordnet, wunderlich gemischt, aber leicht übersehbar, immer munter, bedeutsam, einnehmend.

Jetzt aber betrachte ich näher – erst die Abgebildeten, dann das Abgebildete, und was jedem von jenen und diesem zu Theil worden. Wieland – ich darf sagen: ich kannte ihn; denn er achtete mich mehr als ich wol verdiene, und vertrauete mir mehr als ich je verdanken konnte – : nie ist das Lezte, Eigenste, Beste seines Wesens so rein und so schön ausgesprochen worden. – Herder, der von Mitlebenden nie ganz zufrieden zu stellen war, wäre es wahrlich, läse er, was hier, edel ergriffen und edel ergreifend, über ihn gesagt worden ist. – Schiller – ja wol.

Der Sinnende, der alles durchgeprobt, und der durch Proben, des Dichtens wie des Lebens, zuletzt in beyden so vollendet war, als solch eine Natur überhaupt auf Erden vollendet werden kann – : des Herrlichen Geist reicht Ihnen aus dem Himmel die Hand für das, womit Sie ihn hier, so treu und fest, so glanz-liebe-und freudenvoll, zur Verherrlichung aufrufen. – 'Und nun der Mann, der sich jetzt zur Einsamkeit bequemen muss' ... Soll ichs denn sagen? Hier flossen meine Thränen; und nie hab' ich erquickendere, gemischt von inniger Hinneigung, milder Rührung und überwältigender Freude vergossen. – – Von dem, was über einzelne Werke gesagt ist, will ich nur im Allgemeinen erwähnen, dass es unbeschreiblich wohltut, hier, eben von dem Führer der Zeit, in all diesen Angelegenheiten, eben jetzt, wo nichts mehr gelten soll, was bis hieher gegolten, mit solchem Anerkenntnis jeglichen Verdienstes in seiner Art, und in seinem Zusammenhange mit dem allgemeinen Verdienste der nächsten Vergangenheit – ja einer jeden – und dabey zugleich mit solcher Wärme, Anmuth und Freundlichkeit sprechen zu hören – noch unerwähnt die köstlichen Nummerperlen an sich, die dabey, in der schönen Verdeckung, den Kennern und Freunden, wie unter der Hand zugespielt werden.

Hab' ich nun alles das vor Augen und im Herzen, und die Gewalt dieser Sprache zugleich noch im Ohr: so darf ich mich auch verweilend und auskostend an noch anderen Einzelheiten weiden; wie z. B. an den herrlichen Sprüchen, die bald da bald dort wie Blitze hell und zündend, und, einmal erblickt, nie vergessen werden – –

Jetzt glaub' ich mich fähig, das Eine im Andern, und alles in Einem zu betrachten und zu geniessen; und jetzt ... Nun ja: jetzt nehme ich die Feder, und schreibe, so schnell sie fliegen will, was eben hier aufs Papier gekommen, weniger, um es Ihnen zu sagen, als um es los zu werden.

Und womit soll ich schliessen? Damit, dass ich Sie glücklich preise. Ja, Sie sind glücklich, Sie müssen glücklich seyn, im Bewusstseyn, glücklich zu machen. Was mich anlangt, so weiss Gott, dass ich Ihnen, wie mein schönstes, so mein dauerndstes Glück verdanke. Klingt das, wie der Ausruf eines Liebhabers: so übersehen Sie wenigstens nicht, dass dieser Liebhaber schon den einen Fuss aufhebt, um aus den vierzigen Jahren in das funfzigste zu schreiten.

Ew. Excellenz
froh und dankbar begrüssend
Rochlitz

Notes

CHAPTER ONE
Introduction: *Gelegenheitsdichtung*

1 Aside from widely scattered observations in biographies and monographs the following articles bear most directly on the subject: Carl Enders, 'Deutsche Gelegenheitsdichtung bis zu Goethe,' *Germanisch-Romanische Monatsschrift* I (1909) 292–307; Julius Petersen, 'Erlebnis und Gelegenheit in Goethes Dichtung,' *Goethe. Vierteljahresschrift der Goethe Gesellschaft* I (1936) 3–19; Ernst Robert Curtius, 'Goethe als Kritiker,' *Merkur* II (1948) 333–54 (esp. 348 et seq.); Horst Rüdiger, 'Göttin Gelegenheit. Gestaltwandel einer Allegorie,' *Arcadia* I (1966) 121–66. It will have been noted that periodicals seem to be inclined to wrestle with the question in the first flush of youth. Also see Wolfgang Schadewaldt in his 'Nachwort' to *Goethe und die Antike*, ed. E. Grumach (Berlin 1949) II 973–6.
2 Jacob and Wilhelm Grimm, *Deutsches Wörterbuch* (Leipzig 1897) IV i, ii, col. 2951
3 From 'Rettung des Horaz,' *Lessings Werke*, ed. J. Petersen and W. von Olshausen (Berlin, Leipzig, and Wien 1925–35) XIV 108
4 *Lucians von Samosata Sämtliche Werke, aus dem Griechischen übersetzt mit Anmerkungen und Erläuterungen versehen von C.M. Wieland* (Leipzig 1788) I 340
5 From 'Briefe zur Beförderung der Humanität,' no. 102, *Herders Sämmtliche Werke*, ed by B. Suphan (Berlin 1877–1913) XVIII 116
6 A fairly recent example is *R.M. Rilke, Gedichte 1906–1926: Sammlung der verstreuten und nachgelassenen Gedichte aus den mittleren und späteren Jahren*, ed. R. Sieber, Rilke and E. Zinn (Wiesbaden 1953).
7 *Briefwechsel zwischen Goethe und Zelter*, ed. F.W. Riemer (Berlin 1833) II 71
8 The temptation to draw one was considerable, e.g., by contrasting *Gelegenheit* with the more up-to-date concept of *Geworfenheit*. When an expansion of the scheme through the use of the prefix *ver* suggested itself, I thought it best to desist altogether.

9 Wolfgang Herwig, 'Eine Bibelstelle als Bildsymbol bei Goethe,' *Goethe* XXII (1960) 64–85. The citation is from *Bel and the Dragon*. (*The Apocrypha according to the Authorized Version*, introduction R.H. Pfeiffer [London and New York, nd] 211)
10 *Phaedrus Fab*. v viii. A German equivalent is 'Gelegenheit hat vornen Haar / Sonst ist sie hinten glatzig gar' (Henisch 1556). Quoted in *Deutsches Wörterbuch* IV i, ii, col. 2948

CHAPTER TWO
Frankfurt and Leipzig 1756–67

1 Fortunately, even Remak's intensive attack on the historicity of the Gretchen episode does not throw doubt on Goethe's activity as an occasional poet at that time. Henry H.H. Remak, 'Goethes Gretchenabenteuer und Manon Lescaut: Dichtung oder Wahrheit?' in *Formen der Selbstdarstellung* (Festgabe für Fritz Neubert), ed. G. Reichenkron and E. Haase (Berlin 1956) 379–95
2 Gräf VII 3
3 Quoted by Elisabeth Mentzel, *Wolfgang und Cornelia Goethes Lehrer* (Leipzig 1909) 371
4 'An Herrn Johann Andreas Cramer, bey seiner Verbindung,' *C.F. Gellert's Sämmtliche Schriften* (Berlin and Leipzig 1856) II 57
5 'Empfindungen der Dankbarkeit beim Nahmensfeste Ihro Excellenz der Frau Reichsgräfin von Hohenheim,' *Schillers Sämtliche Werke*, Säkular-Ausgabe, ed. E. von der Hellen (Stuttgart 1904–5) II 9
6 Cf. W.H. Bruford, *Die gesellschaftlichen Grundlagen der Goethezeit* (Weimar 1936) 248–50
7 Friedrich Gundolf, *Goethe* (Berlin 1930) 71
8 *C.F. Gellert's Sämmtliche Schriften* (Berlin and Leipzig 1856) II 60
9 In memory of August von Hoven, 'Eine Leichenphantasie,' *Schillers Sämtliche Werke*, Säkular-Ausgabe, ed. E. von der Hellen (Stuttgart 1904–5) II 27. In memory of Christian Weckherlin, 'Elegie auf den Tod eines Jünglings,' ibid. II 30
10 Johann Peter Uz, *Poetische Werke*, ed. C.F. Weisse (Wien 1805) II 88
11 Quoted in 'Bänkelgesang und Singspiel vor Goethe,' *Deutsche Literatur, Reihe Aufklärung*, ed. F. Brüggemann (Leipzig 1937) X 11
12 Georg Lukács, *Fortschritt und Reaktion in der deutschen Literatur* (Berlin 1947) 17. Another Marxist author who uses his chosen tools with great flexibility and stimulating results is Leo Balet, *Die Verbürgerlichung der deutschen Kunst, Literatur und Musik im 18. Jahrhundert* (Strasbourg 1937).

13 Adolf Strack, *Goethes Leipziger Liederbuch* (Giessen 1893) 96
14 Ibid. 97-8
15 *Goethe*, 59
16 Albert Fuchs, *Goethe: Un Homme face à la vie* (Paris 1946) I 73
17 Barker Fairley, *Goethe as Revealed in His Poetry* (Chicago 1932) 158-9

CHAPTER THREE
From Strassburg to Frankfurt 1770-5

1 Barker Fairley, *A Study of Goethe* (Oxford 1947), e.g., 29ff., 55ff.
2 On the jubilee and its repercussions throughout Europe see Martha W. England, *Garrick's Jubilee* (Columbus 1964). It cannot be doubted that the Shakespeare manifestoes by Goethe, Herder, and Lenz were inspired by the Stratford model. Cf. also DJG II 328.
3 Information on Darmstadt circle is derived from Valerian Tornius, *Die Empfindsamen in Darmstadt: Studien aus der Werther-Zeit* (Leipzig 1910) and Lilli Rahn-Bechmann, 'Der Darmstädter Freundeskreis' (diss. Erlangen 1934).
4 Fairley, *A Study of Goethe* 4ff., 25ff.
5 *Herders Briefwechsel mit Caroline Flachsland*, ed. H. Schauer. Schriften der Goethe-Gesellschaft 39, 41 (Weimar 1926-8) II 108
6 *Herders Sämmtliche Werke* XXIX 511
7 For an historical description of the marriage game see Carl Müller, 'Das Mariage-Spiel,' *Zeitschrift für den deutschen Unterricht* XX (1906) 515ff.
8 Fritz Moser, *Die Anfänge des Hof- und Gesellschaftstheaters in Deutschland* (diss. Berlin 1940) 168
9 Max Herrmann, *Das Jahrmarktsfest zu Plundersweilern* (Berlin 1900)
10 Cf. Rahn-Bechmann, *Der Darmstädter Freundeskreis* passim.
11 Heinrich Meyer, *Goethe: Das Leben im Werk* (Hamburg 1949) 115
12 Published in Wilhelm Hertz, *Bernhard Crespel: Goethes Jugendfreund* (München and Leipzig 1914)
13 Cf. Hans Moser, *Goethe und die Musik* (Leipzig 1949) 11ff.
14 Elisabeth Mentzel, *Wolfgang und Cornelia Goethes Lehrer* 371
15 K.R. Eissler, *Goethe: A Psychoanalytic Study, 1775-1786* (Detroit 1963). See especially the 'Cornelia' chapter, 32-121.
16 This poem was written, or perhaps only commissioned by Johann Martin Starck, brother-in-law of the bridegroom. He had married Maria Magdalena, sister of Johann Georg Schlosser, in 1770. For information and permission to use the poem I am indebted to Dr Josefine Rumpf, who is in charge of the library of *Freies Deutsches Hochstift*.

CHAPTER FOUR
Weimar 1775–80

1 The reader is also especially referred to the detailed and enlightening treatment of the situation in W.H. Bruford, *Culture and Society in Classical Weimar 1775–1806* (Cambridge 1962) chs 1 and 2.
2 Cf. Friedrich Sengle, *Wieland* (Stuttgart 1949) 269ff.
3 *Wielands Werke*, ed. G. Klee (Leipzig and Wien, nd) II 259, 301 resp.
4 Cf. Bernhard Seuffert, 'Wielands höfische Dichtungen,' *Euphorion* I (1894) 530.
5 Gräf VII 38. These conjectures were made by Urlich, von Loeper, and Kern respectively. Although the dates of origin of all three poems are uncertain, only 'Königlich Gebet' is likely to have been written during or before 1775.
6 Cf. Wilhelm Bode, *Der weimarische Musenhof* (Berlin 1917) and A. Diezmann, *Goethe und die lustige Zeit in Weimar* (Leipzig 1857).
7 Willy Andreas, *Carl August von Weimar: Ein Leben mit Goethe 1757–1783* (Stuttgart 1953)
8 Heinrich Düntzer, *Goethes Eintritt in Weimar* (Leipzig 1883) 59–60
9 Willy Andreas, 'Sturm und Drang im Spiegel der Weimarer Hofkreise,' *Goethe: Viermonatschrift der Goethe-Gesellschaft* VIII (1943) 129
10 Andreas, *Carl August* 311–12
11 *J.M.R. Lenz: Gesammelte Schriften*, ed. F. Blei (München and Leipzig 1909) I 175, 176, 177 resp.
12 Max Morris, 'Herzogin Luise v. Weimar in Goethes Dichtung,' *Goethe Studien* (Berlin 1907) II 1ff.
13 *Herders Sämmtliche Werke* XXIX 693–4
14 Published in *Goethe-Jahrbuch*, ed. Ludwig Geiger, VII (1886) 361ff.
15 It is gratifying to note that *Lila* has at last been granted the detailed attention it deserves – along with other 'minor' works – Gottfried Diener, *Goethes 'Lila'* (Frankfurt 1971). Diener's treatment does not necessitate, I believe, a revision of the functional observations offered here. Of course, I tend to scent more salt and less incense in the entire first Weimar period.
16 WA iv XXIX 299–301. Cf. also letter to F.L. Seidel of 3 February 1816 WA iv XXVI 248.
17 This and all chronological information about Weimar performances is derived from Carl August Hugo Burkhardt, 'Goethes Werke auf der Weimarer Bühne,' *Goethe-Jahrbuch* IV (1883) 107ff., and Gisela Sichardt, *Das Weimarer Liebhabertheater unter Goethes Leitung* (Beiträge zur deutschen Klassik 5) (Weimar 1957)
18 Bode, *Musenhof* 327–9

19 For the following cf. *ibid*. 325ff. and Andreas, *Carl August*, 342ff.
20 Ernst Feise, 'Quellen zu Goethes *Lila* und *Der Triumph der Empfindsamkeit*,' *Germanic Review* XIX (1944) 36–47
21 *Goethe Werke (Festausgabe)*, ed. R. Petsch (Leipzig 1926–7) VIII 17
22 Bruford, *Culture and Society* 127
23 Werner Vordtriede, "Das Problem des Dichters in Goethes 'Der Triumph der Empfindsamkeit,'" *Monatshefte für deutschen Unterricht* XL (1948) 149–56
24 Two such theories have been proposed; neither is convincing. Erich Schmidt regards the work as a response to a request by Gluck for a poem in memory of his niece ('Proserpina' in *Charakteristiken* II [Berlin 1901] 148–66). Edwin Redslob's conjectures are contained in his article 'Goethes Monodram Proserpina als Totenklage für seine Schwester' (*Goethe: Viermonatschrift der Goethe-Gesellschaft* VIII [1943] 252–69). The latter writer's evaluation of *Der Triumph der Empfindsamkeit* and *Proserpina* reveals the motivation which prompts such attempts at erecting a high dividing wall between them: '[Goethe, der] ... zunächst in den Niederungen der Posse sein Spiel trieb, bis dann dichterische Kraft, menschliches Erleben und entscheindende Natureindrücke in ihm so mächtig wurden, dass eines der grossen Werke seiner Dichtung wie ein edler Baum über das Gestrüpp der Gelegenheitspoesie emporwuchs' (p 257).
25 Cf. Robert Graves, *The Greek Myths* (Harmondsworth, Middlesex 1955) I 91.
26 Northrop Frye, *Anatomy of Criticism* (Princeton 1957) 282ff.
27 *Ibid*. 287, 290
28 WA I XVII 25. Cf. The article 'Aristophanes' in *Goethe Handbuch*, ed. Alfred Zastrau, 2nd ed. (Struttgart 1955–) I col. 371. For a corrective view on the nature of Aristophanes' influence in the early Weimar years and in later years, see Stuart Atkins, 'Goethe, Aristophanes and the Classical Walpurgisnight,' *Comparative Literature* VI (1954) 64ff.
29 Cf. Bruford, *Culture and Society* 127, and HA IV 597.
30 Cf. Julius Wahle, *Das Weimarer Hoftheater unter Goethes Leitung*, Schriften der Goethe-Gesellschaft, 6 (Weimar 1892) 6–18.
31 W. Andreas, *Carl August* 379–80
32 Wahle, *Das Weimarer Hoftheater* 16
33 W. Andreas, *Carl August* 391
34 H. Meyer, *Goethe* 319–20. There remains a question as to the occasion proper, if any. Franz Schultz in *Klassik und Romantik der Deutschen* (Stuttgart 1935) I 237, asserts: 'Bis dann ein äusserer Anlass, nämlich die Aufforderung, ein höfisches Festspiel zu schreiben für die Feier der am 3. Februar 1779 erfolgten Geburt einer Tochter des

Herrscherhauses, den Anstoss gab ... Wurde auch das Werk zu dem vorgesehenen Tage nicht fertig, so ward es doch rasch beendigt.' Schultz refers to Albert Köster (JA XII v) and Robert Petsch (*Festausgabe* VII 8ff.) for confirmation. Since neither authority offers proof that such a request was made of Goethe, it must be deemed conjectural. Requests of this kind seem to have been less common at that time than in the period between 1800 and 1820.

35 Cf. Grimm, *Wörterbuch* VIII col. 2375.
36 It is well to remember that Euripides' *Iphigenia in Tauris*, indeed much of that playwright's work, does not fit comfortably into established categories of Attic drama. Gilbert Murray calls *Iphigenia* 'not really a tragedy in our sense nor yet merely a romance' (*Euripides and His Age* [New York and London 1913] 143).
37 Ernst M. Manasse, 'Iphigenie und die Götter,' *Modern Language Quarterly* XIII (1952) 379–91. I feel free to appropriate this apt description even though my conclusions about the play vary greatly from those of my esteemed teacher.
38 Frye, *Anatomy* 286, and 'A Conspectus of Dramatic Genres,' *The Kenyon Review* XIII (1951) 543ff.
39 WA I II 86. The exact date of composition of this poem is not known, but there seems to be agreement in assigning it to the latter half of 1775, or the early part of 1776. Ewald Boucke (*Festausgabe* I 379) prefers the earlier dating, Morris (DJG (M) VI 515) is undecided but observes that the poem has 'eher Weimarischen Klang.'
40 Frye, *Anatomy* 286

CHAPTER FIVE
'Schule Geselliger Empfindung' 1780–3

1 Stolberg's letter to J.H. Voss of 2–3 June 1784, quoted by Gräf VII 85
2 Parallel passages from the Greek (Alcman and Sappho) which may or may not have to be regarded as sources of 'Wandrers Nachtlied II' are mentioned by James Boyd in *Notes to Goethe's Poems* (Oxford 1944) I 161–2. The epigrammatic nature of Goethe's poem is not, however, stressed by him. The matter of inscriptions in a different setting and in broad literary perspective is treated by Geoffrey H. Hartman, 'Wordsworth, Inscriptions and Romantic Nature Poetry' in *From Sensibility to Romanticism: Essays Presented to Frederick A. Pottle*, ed. F.W. Hilles and H. Bloom (New York 1965) 389–413.
3 Carl August to Merck, 5 August 1782, Gräf VII 80
4 *Herders Sämmtliche Werke* XV 205–21

5 Cf. Robert T. Clark, jr, *Herder* (Berkeley and Los Angeles 1955) 300 ff., and Alexander Gillies, 'Herder and Goethe,' *German Studies Presented to L.A. Willoughby* (Oxford 1952) 82–97.
6 Details from Bernhard Suphan's introduction to *Das Journal von Tiefurt* (JVT), ed. E. von der Hellen, Schriften der Goethe-Gesellschaft, 7 (Weimar 1892) i–xxxvi. 'Auf Miedings Tod' appears on pp 173–9.
7 Cf. Günther Müller, *Kleine Goethebiographie*, 3rd ed. (Bonn 1955) 93
8 Cf. Heinrich Düntzer, *Goethes Maskenzüge* (Leipzig 1886) 6. Hereafter cited as Düntzer
9 WA iv v 270–1. Düntzer 14. Gräf v 368
10 This is the version of these lines published in the anthology *Der Blumenkorb* (Altona 1784), WA i XVI 430. Cf. Düntzer 10
11 Letter to Hamann, quoted by Andreas, *Carl August* 545
12 WA i XVI 444–52. The concluding poem is 'Amor,' *ibid*. 198–9. Details re the name of the work, *ibid*. 444
13 Cf. Gräf v 371. Reports by Carl August to Knebel and by Luise von Göchhausen to Merck are involved.
14 Cf. Hans Kaiser, *Barocktheater in Darmstadt* (Darmstadt 1951) 136ff.
15 Quoted by Andreas, *Carl August* 599. The surmise that the formality of *Pantomimisches Ballett* was congenial to the duchess is strengthened by the detailed summary of the work and performance she sent to her sister Amalia von Baden. She refers to it as 'Comédie, mêlée de chants et de danses.' The transcript of this unpublished letter, dated 1 February, was made available to me by Professor Momme Mommsen.
16 Wilhelm Emrich, *Die Symbolik von Faust* II: *Sinn und Vorformen*, 2nd ed. (Bonn 1957) 188–90
17 Gundolf, *Goethe* 20. Gundolf employs the term to include' seine Singspiele und Maskenzüge, die er als Weimarischer Hofmann und *maître de plaisir* abzufassen hatte.'
18 Ben Jonson's treatment of the subject will serve as a representative example. 'The Golden Age Restored,' *The Works of Ben Jonson*, with a memoir by W. Gifford (London 1851) 598ff.
19 Emrich, *Die Symbolik von Faust* II 171
20 *Ibid*. 176

CHAPTER SIX
The Limits of Sociability

1 The *Teutsche Merkur* of 1785 yields two examples. In the June issue (p xcvii) there is an appeal for funds to endow an annual commemorative event for the benefit of the pupils of the garrison school of Frankfurt /

Oder. 'Er hat in den Seelen vieler Tausenden das seligste und wohltätigste aller Gefühle erweckt, das Gefühl von dem Werthe, der Liebenswürdigkeit und der Erhabenheit ächter Menschenliebe.' In the December issue (pp 267–74) there is a poem entitled 'Leopold' (by Karl Julius Fridrich?), a few excerpts of which at least deserve exhumation:

Hier war's wo es ein Fürstensohn empfand,
Dass er ein Mensch auch sey, mit uns aus gleichem Thone
Geformet von des Schöpfers Hand;
Dass Demanttropfen in der Herrscherkrone
(Ach! oft geraubt, erkauft mit eines Landes Glück!)
Nicht halb so mild und herrlich stralen,
Als Freudentropfen in der Menschheit Blick.

Die thatenlosen Gaffer sahn
Erschrocken es und schrie'n: Fürst! Schone dich!
Allein, entrüstet fragt er sie: Bin ich
Nicht auch ein Mensch, wie ihr? ...
So hat der seltne Fürst fürs Menschen Wohl gewacht,
Indesz, berauscht von Wollust oder Wein,
Der Weibische sich wiegt auf Flaumen ein!
Dank dir, dass du, beseelt vom Geist der Maurerey
...
...Dank, dir dass du den süssen Glauben
An *Menschentugend* neu in uns gestärkt, belebt.

2 Introduction to *Goethes Sämtliche Werke* II Cotta'sche Bibliothek der Weltliteratur (Stuttgart, nd) 13
3 Gräf II 282; Petsch, *Festausgabe* VIII 419; Kunz, HA V 511
4 *Sammlung von Reden und Glückwünschungs-Gedichten auf die Geburth des Erbprinzen Carl Friedrich* (Weimar 1783). There must have been some snickers about this collection. Wieland felt moved to publish a short conciliatory comment on it to the effect that, mixed bag though it may be, the rejoicing was universal and the intentions good ('Schreiben an einen Freund zu D**' in the August 1781 issue of the *Teutsche Merkur* 167–70). Villoison's Latin nativity ode with translation had appeared in the February issue and Wieland's own cantata in the March issue of the *Merkur*.
5 Eissler, *Goethe*. Section D ch. 5 II 752 et seq. The quotation is from page 789.
6 Pniower, JA IX 438. Andreas, *Carl August* 602
7 Goethe, *Gedenkausgabe der Werke, Briefe und Gespräche*, ed. E. Beutler (Zürich 1949) II 650

8 Cf. 'Zeugnisse geselliger Lebensfreude' in 'Die bürgerliche Gemeinschaftskultur der vierziger Jahre,' *Deutsche Literatur, Reihe Aufklärung*, ed. F. Brüggemann (Leipzig 1933) V 110–49.
9 'Bänkelsängerlied zum 26. Juli 1785, dem Geburtstage des Grafen Moritz Brühl,' WA I IV 223–6
10 WA I I 109–10, 121–3, 132–3, 144–5, 151 resp.
11 See 'Gesellige Lieder,' in Benedetto Croce, *Goethe*, tr. W. Ross (Düsseldorf 1949) 212ff.
12 *Schillers Briefe* VI 354
13 Johannes Urzidil, *Goethe in Böhmen* (Zürich and Stuttgart 1962). See esp. p. 181 et seq.

CHAPTER SEVEN
The Poet and His Public

1 Quoted in Julius Wahle, *Das Weimarer Hoftheater unter Goethes Leitung*, Schriften der Goethe-Gesellschaft 6 (Weimar 1892) 30
2 *Goethe in vertraulichen Briefen seiner Zeitgenossen, 1749–1803*, ed. W. Bode (Berlin 1918)
3 16 September 1786. *Tagebücher und Brief Goethes aus Italien an Frau von Stein und Herder*, ed. E. Schmidt, Schriften der Goethe-Gesellschaft 2 (Weimar 1886) 68
4 *Ibid.* 68–9
5 7 October 1786, *ibid.* 153
6 Cf. Wahle, *Das Weimarer Hoftheater* 35–6.
7 Karl Mantzius, *A History of Theatrical Art*, tr. L. von Cosel (London 1909) V 176
8 Cf. Carl August Hugo Burkhardt, *Das Repertoire des Weimarischen Theaters unter Goethes Leitung, 1791–1817*, Theatergeschichtliche Forschungen I (Hamburg and Leipzig 1891).
9 Cf. Bruno Theodor Satori-Neumann, *Die Frühzeit des Weimarischen Hoftheaters unter Goethes Leitung (1791 bis 1798)*, Schriften der Gesellschaft für Theatergeschichte 31 (Berlin 1922).
10 Emrich, *Symbolik*. See especially 152–5, 171–6.
11 Cf. Eduard Genast, *Aus dem Tagebuche eines alten Schauspielers* (Leipzig 1862–6). Quoted in BG I 180–1
12 Cf. Ernst Pasqué, *Goethe's Theaterleitung in Weimar* (Leipzig 1863) and Adolf Schöll, 'Goethe's Verhältniss zum Theater' in *Goethe in Hauptzügen seines Lebens und Wirkens* (Berlin 1882) 280–303
13 Satori-Neumann, *Die Frühzeit des Weimarischen Hoftheaters* 87n
14 The most comprehensive treatment of this subject and of earlier investigations (especially those of E.R. Curtius) is by Jörn Göres, 'Goethes

Verhältnis zur Topik,' *Goethe* XXVI (1964) 144–80.

15 Cf. Hans Pyritz, 'Humanität und Leidenschaft: Goethes gegenklassische Wandlung,' *Goethe Studien* (Köln and Graz 1962) 97 et seq., esp. p. 132.

16 Nor is the occasion external or social – a memorial service had been held in Goethe's absence. None other was ever discussed, but plans for a monument in the park were under way with Goethe's encouragement. Meyer had made a sketch for it. Cf. report in *Theater-Kalender auf das Jahr 1800*. Gotha as quoted in *Goethe im Almanach*, ed. A. Goldschmidt (Leipzig 1932) 210–12.

17 Viktor Hehn *Ueber Goethes Gedichte*, ed. E. von der Hellen (Stuttgart 1911); Max Kommerell, *Gedanken über Gedichte* (Frankfurt 1943) 173 et seq.

18 Friedrich Beissner, *Geschichte der deutschen Elegie* (Berlin 1941) 156

19 Lieselotte Blumenthal, 'Schillers und Goethes Anteil an Knebels Properz Uebertragung,' *Jahrbuch der deutschen Schiller Gesellschaft* III (1959) 71–93

20 Rudolf Bach, 'Begegnung im Zwischenreich: Die Elegie "Euphrosyne," *Leben mit Goethe* (Munich 1960) 74–101; August Koberstein, 'Ueber das neudeutsche Gelegenheitsgedicht, mit besonderer Beziehung auf Goethe's Elegie "Euphrosyne,"' *Vermischte Aufsätze zur Litteraturgeschichte und Aesthetik* (Leipzig 1858) 91–113; B. Litzmann, 'Goethes "Euphrosyne": Ein Erlebnis und seine Gestaltung,' *Deutsche Rundschau* CLXVI (1916) 414–38

21 Loeper in the Hempel edition cites instances by Garrick, Lessing, and Forster.

22 *Goethe und Seine Kritiker*, ed. O. Fambach (Düsseldorf 1953) 119

23 On the relationship of panegyrical ode, epitaph, and complaint, cf. Frye, *Anatomy* 296–7.

24 Henry Hatfield, *Winckelmann and His German Critics* (New York 1947) 116

25 Ernst Beutler, *Essays um Goethe* 5th ed. (Bremen 1957) 503

26 Kurt Karl Eberlein, 'Goethe und die bildende Kunst der Romantik,' *Jahrbuch der Goethe-Gesellschaft* XIV (1928) 94

27 The records are compiled in Momme Mommsen, *Die Entstehung von Goethes Werken* (Berlin 1958–) I 286–342.

28 Max Hecker, 'Sturm im Wasserglas,' *Jahrbuch der Sammlung Kippenberg* I (1921) 268–312

29 Thomas Mann, *Lotte in Weimar, Gesammelte Werke* (Berlin and Weimar 1965) VII 269. Incidentally, Robert Musil voiced a similar opinion on Goethe's occasional poetry. Cf. 'Rede zur Rilkefeier,'

Gesammelte Werke, ed. A. Frisé (Hamburg 1955) II 887.
30 Katharina Mommsen, 'Goethe und das Preisgedicht: Zum 'Rätsel' in den Gedichten 'An Personen,' *Jahrbuch der Deutschen Schillergesellschaft* XI (1967) 320–57

CHAPTER EIGHT
Weimar Skirmishes and Imperial Battles

1 Ernst Fischer, *The Necessity of Art*, tr. A. Bostock (Baltimore and Harmondsworth 1963) 49
2 Cf. Hermann Frhr. von Egloffstein, *Carl August auf dem Wiener Kongress*, Beiträge zur neueren Geschichte Thüringens III (Jena 1915).
3 Wolfgang Staroste, 'Symbolische Raumgestaltung in Goethes "Natürliche Tochter,"' *Jahrbuch der deutschen Schillergesellschaft* VII (1963) 251
4 *Ibid.* 240–1
5 Carl Frhr. von Beaulieu-Marconnay, 'Goethes Cour d'amour: Bericht einer Theilnehmerin,' *Goethe-Jahrbuch* VI (1885) 67–70
6 On the extent of his contribution to the prologue cf Wilhelm Fielitz, *Goethestudien*, Abhandlungen zu dem Programm des Wittenbergischen Gymnasiums (1881) 9; *Schillers Werke*, Ludwig Bellermann (Leipzig 1895–7) IV 358; L. Bellermann, *Schillers Dramen: Beiträge zu ihrem Verständniss* (Berlin 1897) II 149.
7 Quoted in *Goethe in vertraulichen Briefen...* 738–9
8 Cf. V.W. Robinson, 'Goethe's Allegorical Prologues and Those by His Predecessors and Contemporaries,' *Modern Language Forum* XXVI (1942) 193–9, and Iffland, *Fest-und Gelegenheitsspiele*, introd. A. Hauffen (Kürschner DNL 139) 207–8.
9 Cf. Katharina Mommsen, *Goethe und 1001 Nacht* (Berlin 1960) 78–84.
10 He reappears in the riddle of *Die romantische Poesie* of 1810. Cf. Wolfgang Kayser, 'Goethes Dichtungen in Stanzen,' *Kunst und Spiel: Fünf Goethe-Studien* (Göttingen 1961) 98n.
11 Croce, *Goethe* 206–10
12 Paul Hankammer, *Spiel der Mächte: Ein Kapitel aus Goethes Leben und Goethes Welt* (Tübingen 1943) 192. For a comprehensive investigation of the concept of 'Festspiel' see Gottfried Diener, *Pandora-Zu Goethes Metaphorik*, Frankfurter Beiträge zur Germanistik 5 (Bad Homburg v.d.H. 1968) esp. 60–93.
13 The following account is based chiefly on information taken from correspondence and notes in *Goethe und Oesterreich*, Schriften der Goethe-Gesellschaft 17–18 ed. A Sauer (Weimar 1902–4).

14 *Herders Sämmtliche Werke*, ed. B. Suphan, XXVIII, 247 et seq., Herder's reaction is recorded in Caroline von Herder's letter to Knebel, *Goethe in vertraulichen Briefen...* 671. See also Rudolf Haym, *Herder* (Darmstadt 1954) II 814.
15 *Herders Sämmtliche Werke* XXVIII 329 et seq.
16 WA i XI 333–4. For date of origin cf. *ibid.* 441; and F. Zarncke in *Goethe-Jahrbuch* IX (1888) 77–82.
17 *Herders Sämmtliche Werke* XVIII 377 et seq.
18 *Spiel der Mächte* 198
19 *Goethe-Zelter Briefwechsel* esp. I 323, 455
20 Hugo von Hofmannsthal, 'Einleitung zu einem Band von Goethes Werken, enthaltend die Singspiele und Opern,' *Gesammelte Werke: Prosa* IV (Frankfurt 1955) 177
21 Dr Reuter of the Goethe-und Schiller-Archiv, Weimar, kindly checked the WA text of this entry against the original.
22 In his letters of 31 March and 22 May – 1 June 1815, *Goethe-Zelter Briefwechsel* II 150–4, 187–9
23 In Hermann Frhr. von Egloffstein, *Carl August im niederländischen Feldzug 1814*, Schriften der Goethe-Gesellschaft 40 (Weimar 1927) 171
24 Cf. Friedrich von Müller, *Erinnerungen aus den Kriegszeiten von 1806–1813* (Braunschweig 1851)
25 W. Andreas, 'Preussen und Reich in Carl Augusts Geschichte,' *Kämpfe um Volk und Reich* (Stuttgart and Berlin 1934) 29
26 June 1814. *Goethes Briefwechsel mit C.G. Voigt*, ed. H. Tümmler, Schriften der Goethe-Gesellschaft 53–6 (Weimar 1949–52) IV 114
27 Riemer's diary, 9 June 1814. 'Fr. W. Riemers Tagebücher 1811–1816,' sel. and ed. A. Pollmer, *Jahrbuch d. Sammlung Kippenberg* III (1923) 66–7
28 Gersdorff to Voigt, 25 September 1815. Quoted in Egloffstein, *Carl August auf dem Wiener Kongress* 130–1
29 Andreas B. Wachsmuth, 'Der Briefwechsel Goethe-Voigt,' *Goethe* XXV (1963) 18
30 Wilhelm Mommsen, *Die Politischen Anschauungen Goethes* (Stuttgart 1948) 156–60
31 Riemer diary, 4 June 1814 (Fr. W. Riemers Tagebücher 1811–1816) 66
32 Emrich, *Symbolik* 198, 201–2, 330, 348
33 Luise Kraucher, 'Goethes Festspiel "Des Epimenides Erwachen" und die französischen Epimenides-Dramen,' *Chronik des Wiener Goethe Vereins* XXXVIII (1933) 24–6
34 Mommsen, *Die politischen Anschauungen Goethes* 156n; Konrad Burdach, 'Zum hundertjährigen Gedächtnis des West-Oestlichen Divans (1819–1919),' Vorspiel II, *Goethe und sein Zeitalter* (Halle 1926) 405

CHAPTER NINE
A Midwinter Night's Dream

1 *Zacharias Werner's Sämmtliche Werke*, Poetische Werke, (Grimma, nd) I 143, 144. Eleonore von Bojanowski, *Louise, Grossherzogin von Sachsen-Weimar und ihre Beziehungen zu den Zeitgenossen* (Stuttgart 1903) 308
2 Cf. Düntzer, *Goethes Maskenzüge* 61–3, and A. Hübner, 'Goethe und das deutsche Mittelalter,' *Goethe* I (1936) 83–99.
3 Arthur Hübner, *ibid*. 92
4 Quoted by H. von Maltzahn, *Gedenkausgabe* III 826
5 Rudolf Unger, 'Zur Deutung eines Goethischen Rätsels,' *Festschrift Th. Siebs*, Germanistische Abhandlungen 67. (Breslau 1933) 265–74. Werner quotation is from *Sämmtliche Werke* I 185
6 *Bei Allerhöchster Anwesenheit Ihro Majestät der Kaiserin Mutter Maria Feodorowna in Weimar Maskenzug*, WA I XVI 233–307. References to prose summary (originally 'Vorläufige Anzeige,' *ibid*. 235–43, are by page numbers; to the text proper, by line numbers.
7 *Alt-Weimars Abend: Briefe und Aufzeichnungen aus dem Nachlasse der Gräfinnen Egloffstein*, ed. H. Frh. von Egloffstein (Munich 1923) 137, and Düntzer 134
8 Cf. Emrich, *Symbolik* 37 et seq.
9 Cf. Frye, *Anatomy* 290; Emrich, *Symbolik* 302 et seq.
10 Cf. Karl Kerényi, *Die Religion der Griechen und Römer* (München-Zürich 1963) 65 et seq.

CHAPTER TEN
Once More into the Breach

1 Cf. Erich Heller, 'Die Reise der Kunst ins Innere,' *Merkur* XVIII (1964) 938–55, 1118–32; XIX (1965) 20–34.
2 Wolfdietrich Rasch, *Goethes Torquato Tasso: Die Tragödie des Dichters* (Stuttgart 1954) 39
3 Lawrence Ryan, 'Die Tragödie des Dichters in Goethes *Torquato Tasso*,' *Jahrbuch der Deutschen Schillergesellschaft* IX (1965) 283–322 passim
4 Cf. C.M. Bowra, *From Virgil to Milton* (London 1945).
5 Heinrich Düntzer, *Goethes Tasso*, Düntzers Erläuterungen zu Goethe 10 (Leipzig, nd) 70n3
6 Kuno Fischer has attempted the most complete reconstruction of the stages of composition of this work (K. Fischer, *Goethes Tasso* [Heidelberg 1890]). His and other attempts have failed to gain general acceptance.

7 The page references (G-L) for the Goethe-Lavater exchange are to *Goethe und Lavater: Briefe und Tagebücher*, ed. H. Funck, Schriften der Goethe-Gesellschaft 16 (Weimar 1901).
8 Friedrich Sengle, *Wieland* (Stuttgart 1949) and F. Sengle, 'Wieland und Goethe,' *Arbeiten zur deutschen Literatur 1750–1850* (Stuttgart 1965) 24–45.
9 The complete documentation of the project is Momme Mommsen, *Die Entstehung von Goethes Werken* (Berlin 1958–) I 214–22.
10 Frye, *Anatomy of Criticism*, e.g., 40–1, 223–4, 236–7, 297
11 Rasch and Ryan: see notes 2 and 3 above; Elizabeth Wilkinson, 'Goethe's *Torquato Tasso*: The Tragedy of the Poet,' in E. Wilkinson and L.A. Willoughby, *Goethe: Poet and Thinker* (London 1962) 75–94
12 W.B. Yeats, *The King's Threshold*, The collected Plays of W.B. Yeats (London 1952) 105–43. The complaints of the two poets are similar and the arguments used to soothe them are strikingly similar at times.
13 *Ueber den Granit* WA ii IX 176 and 173 resp.

Index

Recipients of letters and conversational partners are not listed, nor are authors cited only in the notes. Quotation marks are omitted for titles of poems and used for first lines only. This index was compiled with the assistance of Myrna McCormack.

Anakreontik 19, 23, 103
André, Joh. A. (1744–99) 37
Andreas, Willy *Carl August von Weimar* 45, 46, 62, 64, 99, 156
Ariosto, Lodovico (1474–1533)
  Orlando Furioso 199–201, 212
Aristophanes *Ecclesiazusae* 58
Austria 148ff, 152
– Joseph II (1741–90) 8, 43
– Francis I (1768–1835) 100, 135
– Ludovica (1787–1816) 100, 101

Bach, Rudolf 123, 126
Beaumarchais, Pierre-Augustin (1732–99) 31
Becker-Neumann, Christiane (1778–97) 108, 114–21, 126, 182; position in Weimar company 114; personality 119
Behrisch, Ernst Wolfg. (1738–1809) 14, 15, 17, 22
Beissner, Friedr. 122
Bellomo, Joseph 62, 188
Bertuch, Friedr. Justin (1747–1822) 140, 141, 163
Besser, Joh. von (1654–1729) 9, 32
Beutler, Ernst 129
Bielke, Friedr. Wilh., count 164

Blumenthal, Lieselotte 123
Bodmer, Joh. Jacob (1698–1783) 205, 206
Böttiger, Karl August (1760–1835) 108, 121, 140, 141
Brecht, Bertolt *Leben des Galilei* 137
Brühl, Carl Friedr., count (1777–1837) 50, 156
Brühl, Moritz, count (d1811) 99
Brühl, Christina (Tina), countess (b1756) 103
Brunswick, Leopold, duke (1752–85) 97
Burdach, Konrad 160

Canitz, Friedr. von (1654–99) 9, 41
Capodistrias, Joh. Anton, count (1776–1831) 167
Catullus LXI ('collis o heliconeici...') 23
Clodius, Christian Aug. (1737–84) 12, 13, 15, 21, 49
commedia dell' arte 84
congresses: Vienna 136, 157; Aix-la-Chapelle 167, 174; Karlsbad 168
conventions, literary; 'Bänkel-

sänger' song 19, 101;
'Bauernwirtschaft' 32, 84;
'Jahrmarktsfest' 32ff
Crébillon, Prosper (père)
  (1674–1762) 53
Crespel, Joh. Bernhard
  (1747–1813) 35
Croce, Benedetto 102, 147
Cronegk, Joh. Friedr. von
  (1731–58) 19
Cumberland, Richard (1731–1811)
  Der West-Indier 52

Die Entführung
  pantomime-ballet 85
Diede, Wilh. Christoph von
  (1732–1807) 77, 126
drama, forms of: comedy 56, 67,
  88, 142; Ideal Comedy 68–9;
  Festspiel 52, 147, 150, 151;
  Irony 211–12; Ideal
  Masque 171 (*see also* Goethe,
  Maskenzüge); comic opera 52,
  116; opera seria 51, 88, 152;
  pantomime-ballet 85, 88;
  Schauspiel 50, 65, 67, 211;
  Singspiel 46, 80, 110, 112;
  Zauberposse 88
Düntzer, Heinrich 45, 46, 82, 174,
  175, 186

Ebert, Joh. Arnold (1723–95) 101
Eberwein, Karl (1786–1868) 55
Eckermann, Joh. Peter
  (1792–1862) 1, 2, 15, 46, 47
Egloffstein, Henriette, countess
  (1773–1862) 138
Egloffstein, Julie, countess
  (1792–1869) 167
Einsiedel, Friedr. Hildebrand von
  (1750–1828) 110; 'Schreiben
  eines Politikers...' 46; *Die
  Brüder* (after Terence) 141
Ekhof, Hans Konrad D.
  (1720–78) 52, 145
Eissler, K.R. 38, 39, 99
Emrich, Wilh. 90, 91, 95, 96, 118,
  159
epigram 73ff
Euripides 70; *Ion* 141
Ewald, J.L. (1747–1822) 36

Fairley, Barker 24, 27, 29
Feise, Ernst 53
Fischer, Ernst 133
Flachsland (Herder), Caroline
  (1750–1809) 29, 30, 33
Fleming, Paul (1609–40) 9
France 135, 159, 167–8
– Marie Antoinette (1755–93) 25
– Louis XVI (1754–93) 135
– Napoleon I (1769–1821) 101,
  135, 148–9, 156–8, 162, 184
– Marie Louise (1791–1847) 100
Fuessli, Joh. Heinr.
  (1742–1825) 76
Friedrich, Caspar David
  (1774–1825) 76
Fritsch, Jacob Friedr. von
  (1731–1814) 45, 61, 163
Frye, Northrop 56, 57, 68–70, 211,
  212
Fuchs, Albert 22, 24

Garrick, David (1716–79) 28
Gatto, Elisabeth 113
Gellert, Christian, Fürchtegott
  (1715–69) 37; 'O Freund, welch
  angenehm...' 12; 'Auf Herrn
  Willens Tod' 16
Gentz, Friedr. (1764–1832) 167,
  169

Index 237

Gersdorff, Ernst Christian A. von (1781–1852) 157
Giannini, Wilhelmine Elis., countess 46
Goedeke, Karl 98
Gleim, Joh. Wilh. Ludw. (1719–1803) 19, 45, 101
Goethe, August (1789–1830) 128
Goethe, Cornelia (Schlosser) (1750–77) 10, 11, 38, 195
Goethe, Joh. Caspar (1710–82) 14, 38, 43
GOETHE, JOH. WOLFGANG (1749–1832)
  album verses 103
  birth as occasion 98–9, 166
  composers, relations with 110, 116, 152, 155
  courtliness and courtesy 130–1, 187–8
  death as occasion 13ff, 92, 94–7, 118ff, 125, 129
  encomiastic poetry 131ff, 170ff
  epigrams 73ff
  Gelegenheitsdichtung, claims for 1ff, 73, 96, 125
  journeys: Italy 107, 213; Switzerland (1779) 64, 207–8
  monuments 58ff, 73ff, 126ff; iconic 126–30
  masks, use of 84, 134
  masques *see* entries under GOETHE: PLAYS, MASQUES, PROLOGUES, EPILOGUES
  New Year as occasion 5, 18
  occasions: satirical and 'anti-occasional' response to 7–9, 13ff, 26, 34–5, 38; calendar as determinant 60; chosen 14, 28, 70, 89, 92; exigency and readiness, convergence of 96, 117, 158; divergence of 136, 142; decision on 153; festivity anticipated 136, 142, 190, 192; 'Poesie des Tages' 27ff
  professionalism, early 7, 24
  political communities, dimensions of 134, 157ff, 187–8; instability and revolution 116, 136, 137, 140; 'Grosse/kleine Welt' 25ff, 47, 187–8
  Romantics, and 2, 140, 162
  sociability, songs of 102, 130
  theatre:
    amateur 50, 60ff, 66; fiscal factors 62; stage resources 54; therapeutic function 50, 52, 60ff, 67, 209ff
    buildings: Lauchstädt 113, 139; Verona 111; Vicenza 111; Weimar 61ff, 139, 149
    professional: actors, training of 118, 134, 141; direction 108, 170, 178; public, education of 104, 109–12, 140
  themes, motifs, types: closed container 90, 91; clergy 159, 162, 178; Four Ages, 92ff; Mignon and Mignonesque figures 118; rejuvenation 88, 103, 179; seasonal cycle 92, 163
  visual elements, tableaux vivants 58ff, 123ff, 199. *See* monuments
  wedding as occasion 22, 35–9, 135, 166
GOETHE: PLAYS, MASQUES, PROLOGUES, EPILOGUES
  Aufzug der vier Weltalter 62, 85, 89, 92–5

Aufzug des Winters 81–5, 100, 165; addressed to court as institution 82; structure 82–4; use of masks 84
Claudine von Villa Bella 52
Clavigo 31, 35
Concerto dramatico 32
Das Neueste von Plunderweilern 85
Das Mädchen von Oberkirch 117
Der Bürgergeneral 116
Der Geist der Jugend see *Pantomimisches Ballett*
Der Grosskophta 116, 117, 135
Der Triumph der Empfindsamkeit (see also *Proserpina*) 32, 48, 51–60, 62, 64, 68, 87, 95, 105, 133, 143–4, 210; and *Lila* 54, 57; *Proserpina* as part of 54ff; as comedy of 'humour' 57
Der Zauberflöte, Zweiter Teil 90, 117, 153
Des Epimenides Erwachen 134, 153–60, 161, 162, 175; political background of decision to write 154–6; reflected in work 158–60
Die Aufgeregten 116
Die Geschwister 51, 52
Die Mitschuldigen 51
Die Mystifizierten see *Der Grosskophta*
Die natürliche Tochter 90, 117, 137, 138, 142, 151
Die Romantische Poesie 161–4, 231
Die ungleichen Hausgenossen 110
Die Vögel 89
Die weiblichen Tugenden 62, 85–7, 100

Egmont 60, 186, 189, 193, 212
Ein Zug Lappländer (30 January 1781) 81, 86, 100
Elpenor 98, 99
Epilog (11 June 1792) 114–15
Epilog (31 December 1791) 114–15
Epiphaniasfest 59, 80
Erwin und Elmire 51
Faust: Urfaust 138; *Faust* I 87, 117, 143, 179–80; *Faust* II 90–1, 95, 120, 127, 135, 136, 137, 159, 162, 169, 173, 181, 186
Götter, Helden und Wieland 42, 43, 48, 52
Götz von Berlichingen 25, 26, 35, 37, 44, 162, 175, 177, 178, 210; 1804 version 137
Hanswursts Hochzeit 33–5, 37, 43, 63, 64
Iphigenie auf Tauris 60, 64–71, 73, 86, 110, 123, 133, 180, 210, 211, 212; performers and audience 64–7; genre 67–71
Jahrmarktsfest zu Plundersweilern 32–3, 62
Lila 50ff, 60, 62, 64, 67, 87, 105, 143, 210; first festive Weimar play 50–1; and *Der Triumph der Empfindsamkeit* 56–7
Mahomet 175, 177, 178
Maskenzüge (general) 32, 61, 80, 87, 91, 96; 1781–2 groups 85, 214
Maskenzug ... 1818 2, 131, 159, 164–88; occasion, initial response 164; political background 166–7; relation to *Noten und Abhandlungen* 168–72; prologue 172–5; procession: Wieland, Herder,

Goethe sections 175–9;
  Schiller section 179–85
Maskenzug (30 January 1798),
  ('Der lang ersehnte...') 133
Maskenzug (30 January 1802,
  'Wenn von der...') 133, 143
Paläophron und Neoterpe 134,
  176, 177; and Herder 150
Pandora 90, 147–53, 155, 158,
  159, 186; occasion and
  site 147–9; Herder's Prometheus 150–1; abandonment
  151ff
Pantomimisches Ballett 62, 85,
  87–91, 92, 94, 95, 96, 100,
  227; political motivation, rejuvenation theme, and 'Ilmenau' 90; 'Amor' section 87
Planetentanz 81, 99, 100
Prolog (7 May 1791) 113
Prolog (1 October 1791) 113–14
Prolog (15 October 1793, *Der Krieg*) 115
Prolog (6 October 1794, *Alte und neue Zeit*) 119, 182
Prolog, Halle (6 August 1811) 139
Prolog, Berlin (26 May 1821) 139
Prometheus (fragment) 151
Proserpina 48, 52, 54–6, 58, 59,
  62, 64, 144. See also *Der Triumph der Empfindsamkeit*
Satyros 52
Scherz, List und Rache 110
Stella 35, 68
Torquato Tasso 60, 86,
  189–214; situation of court
  poet, questions of authority,
  timing, completion, ownership 190–3; nature, aims of
  T.'s poetry 193–8; presence
  of Ariosto through Antonio
198–201; G.'s situation
  and T. project 201–4; *Oberon*
  204–7; Bernhard biography
  208–9; genre 211; final scene
  212
Vorspiel, Hamburg 1827
  [sketch] 139
Vorspiel zu Eröffnung des Weimarischen Theaters 149
Was wir bringen 139–47, 163,
  187; motivation 140; Weimar
  controversies and education of
  public 143; description 146;
  Halle version 154

GOETHE: POEMS
Abschied an den Herzog... 100,
  104, 105
Achilleis 122
Adler mit einer Leier... 130
A Monsieur le Major General de
  Hoffmann 13, 14, 17, 26
Am siebenten November 130
An den Kuchenbäcker
  Händel 13, 14, 26, 35
An Hafis 173
An Personen 132
An Werther 103, 104
Auf Miedings Tod 54, 59, 60,
  79, 80, 91–2, 94–6, 105, 107,
  118, 120, 127, 137, 187, 213;
  occasion of elegy 92; ironic relation to masques 94; final
  tableau 94ff; and 'Euphrosyne' 121–3
B und K 141
Bänkelsängerlied zum 26. Juli
  1785... ('Ein munter
  Lied...') 99–101
Bei dem erfreulichen Anbruche
  des 1757. Jahres... 5
Beschildeter Arm... 130

Bey diesem neuen Jahres Wechsel... 6
Blinde Kuh 31
Brautnacht (Hochzeitslied an...) 22–4
'Briefgedicht' (6 November 1768, 'Mamsell...') 18
Bundeslied ('Den künftgen Tag...'/'In allen guten...') 35–8, 101
Das Göttliche 44
Dem Fürsten Blücher...('In Harren...') 129
Dem Passavant-und Schüblerischen Brautpaare... 37, 38, 79
Der Becher 79
Der Wandrer 29, 37
'Dich ergriff...' see Herzog Leopold
Die Lustigen von Weimar 102
Die Metamorphose der Pflanzen 124, 125
'Durchlauchtigster! Es nahet sich...' 45–7, 51, 104
'Ein munter Lied...' see Bänkelsängerlied
Elisium an Uranien 28
Elegie auf den Tod des Bruders... 14–7, 20
Elegie (Marienbad) 103, 104, 186
Epilog zu Schillers 'Glocke' 120, 127–9, 180
Er und sein Nahme 79
Ergo bibamus! 102
Erkanntes Glück 74, 77
Erklärung eines alten Holzschnitts... 58, 73, 74
Erschaffen und Beleben 102
Erwählter Fels 74
'Es ist nicht gut, die Formen...' 103

Euphrosyne 107, 108, 115, 118–28, 129, 130, 187, 213; motivation 121; traditional elements 122; as poem of vision 124; relation to other elegies 125
Feier der Geburtsstunde des Erbprinzen... 98, 99
'Felsen sollten nicht...' 74
Fels-Weihegesang an Psyche 28, 30, 32, 46
Geheimstes 101, 168
Gellerts Monument von Oeser 58, 126
Grenzen der Menschheit 44
Geweihter Platz 74
Herrn Staats-Minister von Voigt 129, 131
Hermann und Dorothea 117
Herzog Leopold von Braunschweig 97
Hochzeitlied an meinen Freund see Brautnacht
Ihro des Kaisers von Oesterreich Majestät 135
Ilmenau am 3. September 1783 46, 60, 89, 105, 134, 203, 207
'Im ernsten Beinhaus war's...' 127, 128
Im Namen der Bürgerschaft von Karlsbad 100, 104, 124, 129
Johanna Sebus 97
Ländliches Glück 74
Meine Göttin 203
'Meinen feyerlich Bewegten...' see Am siebenten November
Menschengefühl 69
'Mich ergreift, ich weiss nicht...' see Tischlied
Neue Lieder 20, 21, 24
'Neujahrsgedicht an den Gros-

Index

papa' [conjectural] 10
Neujahrslied ('Wer kommt...) 18–21, 23, 101
'O Schöne mit dem weissen Stabe...' 100, 102, 103
Phänomen 179
Philomele 74
Pilgers Morgenlied an Lila 28
Prometheus 48, 151
Römische Elegien 4, 102
Stiftungslied 102, 138
Stirbt der Fuchs... 31
Tischlied 102, 138
Trilogie 103, 124
Trauerloge 129
Um Mitternacht 183
Vanitas! vanitatum... 102
Vaudeville a. Mr Pfeil 14, 26
West-Oestlicher Divan 81, 101, 102, 130, 166, 168, 171
Wanderers Sturmlied 29
Wandrers Nachtlied II ('Ueber allen...') 74, 75, 77
'Warum seihst du Tina...' 103
'Was die gute (bedächtlich) Natur...' see Erkanntes Glück
'Was gehst du schöne Nachbarin...' see Stiftungslied
'Was ich leugnend...' 74
'Wie alle dich verehren müssen...' [authentic?] 48
Xenien 110, 122
Zueignung I ('Der Morgen kam...') 123, 143, 204
Zur Logenfeier des 3. Septembers 1825 130

GOETHE: PROJECTS
Bernhard von Weimar biography 14, 208, 209
Roman des Weltalls 214

GOETHE: PROSE WRITINGS
Addresses, novels, autobiographical, essays, reviews
addresses: Zum Schäkespears-Tag 28, 46; to Ilmenau 'Gewerkschaft' 109; Anna Amalia, memorial 120
Betrachtungen über ein dem Dichter Goethe ... zu errichtendes Denkmal 129
Das Luisenfest 62
Das Märchen 48
Denkmale 126
Deutsches Theater 145, 150
Dichtung und Wahrheit 3, 5, 7, 8, 12, 14, 15, 21, 25, 27, 31, 34, 35, 43, 145, 195
Die Leiden des jungen Werthers 25, 26, 39, 120, 189, 210
Die Wahlverwandtschaften 90, 126, 137, 140, 152, 161
Italienische Reise 112, 199
Lob-und Spottgedicht auf König Rudolf 171
Lyrische Gedichte von Johann Heinrich Voss 164
Kunst und Altertum 9
Noten und Abhandlungen zu besserem Verständniss des West-Oestlichen Divans 101, 166, 168–71, 174, 177
Philipp Hackert, Biographische Skizze 127
Proserpina 59
Regeln für Schauspieler 118
Tag-und Jahreshefte 54, 109, 138, 169, 208
Ueber den Dilettantismus 122
Ueber den Granit 214
Ueber die Entstehung des Festspiels zu Ifflands Andenken 110

Varnhagen von Enses Biographien 9
Weimarisches Hoftheater 118, 141, 144, 145
Wilhelm Meisters Lehrjahre 111, 118, 124; 'Mignons Exequien' 120
Wilhelm Meisters theatralische Sendung 66, 86, 195
Winckelmann und sein Jahrhundert 127
Zum Reformationsfest 167
Goethe, Katharina Elisabeth (1731–1808) 99
Goethe, Walther Wolfg. (1818–85) 166
Goldoni, Carlo (1707–93) *Der Krieg* 115
Görtz, Eustachius, count (1737–1821) 45, 46
groups, societies, etc.: *Cour d'amour* (Mittwochkränzchen) 137; Darmstadt circle 28 et seq. 79; *Deutsche Gesellschaft* (Strassburg) 28; *Hain* 28, 30; reading circle (1782) 78
Göschen, Georg J. (1752–1828) 110
Gottshed, Joh. Christoph (1700–66) 206
Gozzi, Carlo (1720–1806) 141
Gräf, Hans Gerh. 11, 82, 98, 201
Greek Anthology 77
Gundolf, Friedr. 16, 22, 91, 139
Günther, Joh. Christian (1695–1723) 21, 49; *In nuptias D.G. Nichisch* 23

Hagedorn, Friedr. (1708–54) 19
Haide, Friedr. (1770–1832) 149
Hankammer, Paul 148, 152
Hauptmann, Gerhart, *Festspiel...* (1913) 188

Hecker, Max 130
Hegel, Georg Wilh. Friedr. (1770–1831) 143
Hehn, Viktor 122
Hellen, Eduard von der 5
Heller, Erich 190
Herrmann, Max 33
Herder, Joh. Gottfried (1744–1803) 2, 29, 31, 46, 48, 61, 77, 86, 98, 110, 150, 151, 175–8; *Antwort auf die Felsweihe...* 30; Greek Anthology translations in *Zerstreute Blätter* 77, 78; *Aeon und Aeonis* 150, 151, 176, 177; *Adrastea* 150, 151; *Der Entfesselte Prometheus* 150, 151; *Voraussicht und Zurücksicht* 151; *Der Cid* 176
Hofmannsthal, Hugo von 153
Hübener, Arthur 163

Iffland, Aug. Wilh. (1759–1814) 118, 143–5, 150, 154–6; *Alte und neue Zeit* 119, 182
Ilmenau, mine 89, 109

Kafka, Franz 190; *Das Schloss* 188
Kalb, Joh. Aug. von (1747–1814) 64
Karlsbad 100–4, 135, 148, 167
Kayser, Philipp Christoph (1755–1823) 110
Kayser, Wolfg. 42
Kerényi, Karl 186
Kirms, Franz (1750–1826) 108, 154
Kleist, Heinrich von (1777–1811) 162
Klopstock, Friedr. Gottlieb (1724–1805) 30, 61, 79, 195, 206, 207; *Der Messias* 194, 207

Knebel, Carl Ludw. von
  (1744–1834) 66, 77, 78, 85, 93;
  Propertius translation 123
Koberstein, Aug. 123
Kommerell, Max 122
König, Joh. Ulrich von (1688–1744)
  August im Lager 14
Kotzebue, Aug. Friedr. von
  (1761–1819) 118, 119, 138, 140,
  143, 168; *Wirrwarr* 141
Krüdener, Barbara, Julie von
  (1764–1824) 175
Kunz, Josef 98, 152

Lavater, Joh. Caspar (1741–1801)
  75, 76, 80, 85, 205, 206, 208
Lenz, Joh. Michael Reinhold
  (1751–92) 31, 37, 47–9, 61; *Auf
  einem einsamen Spaziergang*
  48; *Als jüngst Amalia...* 48; *Auf
  die Musik zu Erwin und Elmiren*
  48, 49; *Aus einem Neujahrs-
  wunsch...* 48
Lessing, Gotthold Ephraim
  (1729–81) 1; *Nathan der Weise*
  141
Levetzow, Amalie Caroline von
  (1788–1868) 148
Levetzow, Ulrike von (1804–99)
  103
Litzmann, B. 123
Loewen, Joh. Friedr. (1729–71) 19
Lukács, György 21
Luden, Heinrich (1780–1847) 167,
  168
'Leopold' (by K.J. Fridrich
  [b1756]?) 228
Luisenfest 62, 63, 65

Maas, Wolff 'Ein schön Schir...'
  21
Manasse, Ernst M. 68

Mann, Thomas *Lotte in Weimar*
  131; *Der Zauberberg* 140
Marmontel, Jean-François
  (1723–99) 53
Mendelssohn, Moses (1729–86) 19
Merck, Joh. Heinr. (1741–91) 29,
  31, 63, 208
Metternich, Clemens W., prince
  (1793–1859) 167, 168
Meyer, Joh. Heinr. (1759–1832)
  135, 165
Meyer, Heinr. 34, 65, 67
Milton, John (1608–74) *Paradise
  Lost* 194
Mommsen, Katharina 131
Mommsen, Momme 227
Mommsen, Wilh. 158, 160
Morris, Max 5, 18, 23, 24, 35, 48
Möser, Justus (1720–94) 43
Moser, Fritz 32
Mozart, Wolfg. Amadeus
  (1756–91) 116–17; *The Magic
  Flute* 51
Müller, Aug. Eberhard
  (1767–1817) 155
Müller, Friedr. von (1779–1849)
  155–8, 165, 168
Musaeus, Joh. Carl Aug.
  (1735–87) 52
mythology, treatment of 12, 48–9

Novalis (Hardenberg, Friedr. von)
  (1772–1801) 126; *Die 'Christ-
  enheit' oder 'Europa'* 171

Oeser, Adam Friedr. (1717–99) 17;
  monument to Gellert 58, 126
Oken, Lorenz (1779–1851) 167
Ovid 92

Palladio, Andrea (1508–80) 111
parlour games 31–2
periodicals, almanachs, collections:

Der Teutsche Merkur 36, 43, 227–8; *Die Horen* 123; *Isis* 167; *Journal des Luxus und der Moden* 141; *Journal von Tiefurt* 78, 79, 92; *Musen Almanach für das Jahr 1799* (Schiller) 122; *Prometheus* 149, 153; *Schwäbisches Museum* 67; *Sammlung von Reden und Glückwunschungs-Gedichten auf die Geburth des Erbprinzen Carl Friedrich* 98
Petsch, Robert 54, 98
Phaedrus, *Fab. v, viii* 4
Pniower, Otto 99
Prévost, Antoine-François (1697–1763) *Manon Lescaut* 8, 222
Propertius 'Desine Paulle...' 122; 'Sunt aliquid Manes...' 123
Prussia, threat to Saxe-Weimar 64, 156ff
– Sophie Charlotte (1668–1705) 32
– Frederick II (1712–86) 42, 135
– Frederick William III (1770–1840) 148, 154

Ramler, Carl Wilh. (1725–98) 12, 18; 'An Hymen' 23
Rasch, Wolfdietrich 193, 212
Rauch, Christian Daniel (1777–1857) Schiller portrait 128
Raynal, G. Thomas François (1713–96) *Histoire philosophique ... des ... Indes* 78
Reichardt, Joh. Friedr. (1752–1814) 112, 116
Reuter, Christian (1665–c1712) 'Harlekins Hochzeit' 34

Reuter, Hans-Heinr. 232
Reimer, Fr. Wilh. (1774–1845) 46, 155, 157, 159, 165, 173
Rilke, Rainer Maria 188
Rochlitz, Joh. Friedr. (1769–1842) 131, 187, 218–19
Rumpf, Josefine 223
Russia 135–6, 158–9, 167–8, 184
– Michael (Mihail (1596–1645) 184
– Catherine II (1729–96) 42
– Paul (1754–1801) 135
– Maria Feodorowna (1759–1828) 164, 166, 168, 172, 185
– Alexander I (1777–1825) 148, 166–8, 175, 184
Ryan, Lawrence 194, 212

Sachs, Hans (1494–1576) 27, 33
Sartorius, Georg (1765–1828) 157
Sartre, Jean-Paul 190
Saxe-Gotha, August, prince (1747–1806) 88
Saxe-Weimar, duchy of 41–2, 44–5, 62, 75, 80, 88, 96, 135–6, 156, 167–8, 185–8, 210; two courts 41, 62, 79, 134
– Bernhard, duke (1604–39) 14, 208–9
– Anna Amalia, duchess (1739–1807) 41–2 (regency), 48, 49, 58, 61–3 (comp. music for *Jahrmarktsfest* 63), 79, 80, 108, 120, 134, 149, 185
– Carl August, duke (1757–1828) 41, 43, 52, 64, 65, 66, 71, 81, 104, 105, 108, 109, 130, 156, 157, 167, 193; early reign 45–7; and 'Ilmenau' 60–2; absences from Weimar 133, 134; and Congress of Vienna 136; after

Jena 148, 149; Swiss journey
203
- Luise, duchess (1757–1830) 41,
  45, 48, 50, 52, 60, 63, 65, 70,
  79–81, 86, 87, 89, 94, 98, 100,
  149, 161, 163
- Carl Friedrich, prince
  (1783–1853) 98, 135, 167
- Maria Paulowna, princess
  (1786–1859) 135, 136, 149, 164–6
- Constantin, prince (1758–93) 52,
  66, 82
- Caroline, princess (1786–1816)
  129, 161
- Carl Alexander, prince
  (1818–1901) 166, 185, 186
Schelling, Fr. Wilh. (1775–1854)
  143
Schadow, Joh. Gottfried
  (1764–1850) 129
Schiebeler, Daniel (1741–71) 19
Schiller, Joh. Christoph, Friedr.
  (1759–1805) 13, 16–17, 102,
  112, 121, 122, 127, 128, 139,
  144, 151, 175, 179–85; 'Eine
  Leichenphantasie' 16; 'Elegie
  auf den Tod eines Jünglings' 17;
  'Empfindungen der
  Dankbarkeit...' 13; *Die Braut
  von Messina* 180–2; *Die Huldigung der Künste* 136, 166;
  Wilhelm Tell 182–4;
  Wallenstein 182–3; *Wallenstein*
  prologue 139; *Turandot* 141,
  182; *Demetrius* 182, 184;
  Xenien 110, 112
Schlegel, Aug. Wilh. von
  (1767–1845) 140, 141, 143; *Ion*
  144
Schlegel, Friedr. von (1772–1829)
  124, 125, 141; *Alarcos* 144

Schmidt, Heinrich (1779–1857)
  149
Schönkopf, Anna Katharina
  (1746–1810) 21, 22
Schönemann, Anna Elisabeth (Lili)
  (1758–1817) 35, 36
Schreyvogel, Josef (1768–1832)
  149
Schröder, Friedr. Ludw.
  (1744–1818) 112, 113, 145
Schröter, Corona (1751–1802) 55,
  59, 63, 66, 80, 94, 134
Schwarzenberg, Carl Philipp,
  prince (1771–1820) 167
Seckendorff, Carl Siegm. von
  (1744–85) 46; *Minervens
  Geburt* 49, 79; 'Luisenfest' 62,
  63; 'Proserpina' music 55
Seckendorff, F.C. Leopold von
  (1775–1809) 149
Sengle, Friedr. 206
Seyler theatrical company 61
Shakespeare, William (1564–1616)
  28, *King John* 115, 118, 119;
  The Tempest 69
Staël-Holstein, Germaine de
  (1766–1817) *De l'Allemagne*
  188
Staiger, Emil 100, 139
Starck, Joh. Martin (1728–96) 223
Staupitz, Caroline von
  (1769–1838) 102
Sterne, Lawrence (1713–68) 30
Stein, Charlotte von (1742–1827)
  65, 70, 74, 79, 82, 193, 210
Stein, Friedr. von (1772–1844) 99
Stolberg, Fr. Leop. zu (1750–1819)
  74
Stoll, Joh. Ludwig (1778–1815)
  149
Stourdza memorandum 168

Strack, Adolf 22–3
Strauss, Richard 153
Sturm und Drang 25, 45;
  amateurism of 61

Tasso, Torquato (1544–95)
  Jerusalem Delivered 194–8;
  Jerusalem Conquered 198
Terence 141
Textor, Joh. Wolfgang
  (1693–1771) 5, 6, 10
Textor, Joh. Jost (1739–92) 21
Textor, Maria Magd. (Möller)
  (1750–98) 21
Tieck, Ludwig (1773–1853) 3, 141
Tiefurt, villa and park 79ff
Trunz, Erich 46, 120

Unger, Rudolf 163
Urzidil, Johannes 102
Uz, Joh. Peter (1720–96) 101;
  'Neujahrswunsch des
  Nachtwächters...' 19

Viëtor, Karl 139
Villoison, Jean-Bapt. d'Ansse
  (1750–1805) 77
Vischer, Friedr. Theod. 145
Voigt, Joh. Karl Wilh.
  (1752–1821) 131, 157, 167
Voltaire, François Marie d'Arouet
  (1694–1778) 42
Vordtriede, Werner 55
Voss, Joh. Heinr. (1751–1826) 164

Wachsmuth, Andreas B. 157
Wahle, Julius 109
Wartburg 161; 'Wartburgfest'
  (October 1817) 167
Weber, Bernh. Anselm
  (1766–1821) 155
Weimar *see* Saxe-Weimar
Werner, Zacharias (1768–1823)
  161, 163; 'Der Mönch und die
  Nonne' 161; Nibelungen
  parody 163
Werthern-Beichlingen, Jacob,
  count (1739–1806) 93
Wieland, Christoph Martin
  (1733–1813) 1, 42–4, 49, 61, 80,
  98, 110, 175–6, 178, 204;
  Alceste 42; *Die Wahl des
  Hercules* 42–3, 175; 'Das Urteil
  des Paris' 49; Lucian translation
  1, 49; *Musarion* 175–6;
  Oberon 176, 204–6
Wilkinson, Elizabeth 212
Wolf, Friedr. Aug. (1759–1824)
  143
Württemberg, Katharina, queen of
  (d1819) 166

Yeats, William Butler *The King's
  Threshold* 213

Zachariae, Fr. Wilh. (1726–77) 17
Zelter, Karl Friedr. (1758–1832)
  127, 153, 156
Ziegler, Luise von (1750–1814) 30,
  33

This book
was designed by
WILLIAM RUETER
under the direction of
ALLAN FLEMING
and was printed by
University of
Toronto
Press

www.ingramcontent.com/pod-product-compliance
Lightning Source LLC
Chambersburg PA
CBHW071154070526
44584CB00019B/2783